Higher Education Re-formed

Higher Education Re-formed discusses the challenges faced by universities and colleges in the turbulent environment of the new millennium – challenges to their institutional integrity and intellectual authority. Despite its remarkable persistence over the centuries, from the Middle Ages to modern times, the university may struggle to survive in this new environment.

This book contains specially commissioned chapters by some of the most respected academics currently working in the field of higher education. The contributors outline the situation as it is now and look forward to the developments of the coming years.

The challenges are examined from historical, managerial, organizational and epistemological perspectives. The broad conclusion is that, despite the scale of these challenges, the university is likely not only to survive but to thrive in the new millennium – but that, to do so, it must undergo a sea change.

Contributors: Jonathan Adams, Ronald Barnett, Denis Blight, Dorothy Davis, Geraldine Kenney-Wallace, Diana Laurillard, Alan Olsen, John Randall, David Robertson, Sheldon Rothblatt, Peter Scott, Roger Waterhouse and Alan Wilson.

Peter Scott is Vice-Chancellor of Kingston University. Previously he was Professor of Education, then Pro-Vice-Chancellor of the University of Leeds. He was also Editor of *The Times Higher Education Supplement* for 16 years.

This book is one of the New Millennium Series which aims to make accessible, both for the lay reader and the professional, the complexities of education at all levels.

New Millennium Series

How Shall We School Our Children?
Edited by Colin Richards and Philip H. Taylor

Early Education Transformed
Edited by Lesley Abbott and Helen Moylett

Special Education Re-formed
Beyond Rhetoric?
Edited by Harry Daniels

Higher Education Re-formed
Edited by Peter Scott

Further Education Re-formed
Edited by Alan Smithers and Pamela Robinson

Higher Education Re-formed

Edited by Peter Scott

London and New York

First published 2000
by Falmer Press
11 New Fetter Lane, London EC4P 4EE

Simultaneously published in the USA and Canada
by Falmer Press
Garland Inc., 19 Union Square West, New York, NY 10003

Falmer Press is an imprint of the Taylor & Francis Group

Typeset in Garamond by Taylor & Francis Books Ltd
Printed and bound in Great Britain by TJ International Ltd, Padstow

British Library Cataloguing in Publication Data
A catalogue record for this book is available from the British Library

Library of Congress Cataloging in Publication Data
Higher Education Re-formed/edited by Peter Scott
(New Millennium Series)
Includes bibliographical references and index
1. Education, Higher – Great Britain – Evaluation.
2. Education, Higher – Great Britain – Forecasting.
I. Scott, Peter.
II Series.
LA637.H66 2000
378.41–dc21 99-36825 CIP

ISBN 0–750–70978–2 (hbk)
ISBN 0–750–70977–4 (pbk)

Contents

Contents

Illustrations

Figures

Table

Introduction

This book is an attempt to describe how higher education will be reformed, or re-formed, in the new millennium – literally formed again not simply developed, adapted or improved. The starting point, therefore, is that higher education faces radical, even disruptive, change. The university of tomorrow will not simply be an extension of the university of today, still recognizable as the institution forged in the successful scientific, industrial and democratic revolutions of the past two centuries. Instead the university will be a transgressive institution penetrating, and penetrated by, other knowledge organizations in a new kind of society. Nor will higher education in the twenty-first century be the culmination of the system-building, state-sponsored, public-education projects of the recent past – sadly perhaps. Systems as they exist today are likely to be progressively eroded by new patterns of management, novel approaches to policy-making and the impact of new technologies. The future will be a foreign country.

But the book begins with the past. Sheldon Rothblatt recalls the modern university's *longue durée* and, peering into an uncertain future, discusses whether it has a role – organizationally and normatively distinct – to play in the new millennium. The rest of the book is divided into two parts. The first focuses on systems, institutions and students. Alan Wilson considers how universities can respond strategically and managerially to these new challenges; Roger Waterhouse describes his own university's experiment in 'distributing' itself around its host community; Geraldine Kenney-Wallace discusses the dynamic future of corporate universities; David Robertson argues that new funding regimes can both empower students as individuals, as consumers/customers, and also enable broader social and political goals to be pursued; Denis Blight, Dorothy Davis and Alan Olsen describe the globalization of higher education; and, finally, in a chapter that links to the second part of the book – on learning and teaching, research and knowledge in its broadest sense – Ronald Barnett argues that the university must be reconfigured in both sociological and intellectual terms.

In the second part Diana Laurillard considers the impact of new communication and information technologies on student learning and the university curriculum; John Randall discusses the tensions between professional autonomy and public accountability; Jonathan Adams anticipates the emergence of new patterns of research; and finally I argue that a new kind of university is likely to emerge which is both dynamic, volatile and transgressive but is also a force of stabilization in the 'white-water' society of the new millennium.

Peter Scott, June 1999

1 A Connecticut Yankee?

An Unlikely Historical Scenario

Sheldon Rothblatt

The purpose of this chapter is to review the history of the 'modern' university, concentrating on a few salient characteristics in order to provide a working baseline for changes now underway and likely to continue, with the inevitable ambiguities and surprises. The past is not an irrefutable guide to the future, but it always provides a starting point or measure. A perspective is needed because present rates of change are breathtaking (and contradictory) compared to the adjustments and innovations of the nineteenth century, when the university – and higher education systems – as we understand them took shape. The totalitarian dictatorships of the twentieth century demonstrated the speed with which central governments could transform, indeed destroy, institutions built up slowly over the centuries, although Napoleon at the end of the eighteenth century was the first to demonstrate this aspect of tyranny.

The process of rebuilding eastern European institutions has gone slowly, handicapped, as in Poland, by the absence of resources and experience, as well as the survival of mentalities unsuited to a dynamic age (Olesky and Wasser, 1999: 97, 102). But even there new structures, ideas and experiments are emerging, if as yet under shaky auspices. How quickly established foundations – or new institutions following healthy precedent – can adjust under what might be termed normal conditions is a subject of some moment. By any measure, the rates of structural change in western Europe and the United States, and more so in the former than in the latter, are dizzying. Planners and policy-makers, whether within government or in universities and think tanks, find themselves overtaken by events, nearly desperate (or so it appears) for sensible and workable alternatives. Instability in general takes many forms, but in all countries it is challenging the financial and administrative capacity of the differing systems. In Europe the distribution of authority between central ministries and their representatives in universities, councils and lay boards, faculty deans, rectors and vice-chancellors equipped with greater discretionary resources, and the teaching and research staffs is undergoing daily change. A greater variety of external publics, as well as perceived and real pressures from industries and agencies with special agenda, adds a dimension of negotiation and compromise not typical of university systems in many countries.

The resulting intellectual and educational effects have yet to be assessed, but the rapidity of change within the knowledge base itself is also a factor, and the combination appears to be causing work overloads, endless committee meetings and occupational strain. In this regard the academic world *circa* 2000 bears little similarity to its predecessors. A century ago student numbers were small. Even in the United States, where market discipline had been present since the eighteenth century, there were only some 250,000 undergraduates in the nation or about 1–2 per cent of the available cohort, a figure including students who would not be counted in higher education in Europe. The percentages were therefore about the same as abroad. Only 400 doctorates were awarded in the United States in the last decade of the nineteenth century (Burke, 1982: 215, 217). The strategic importance of higher education, its central relevance to critical national aims and objectives, including military and foreign policy initiatives, was not fully apparent outside Germany until about 1900.

The old university world was a world of relative leisure, of time to work out difficulties, less subject to the mentality of productivity, not quite so universally or intensely concerned with reputation, apart from the handful seeking national and international distinction (the Nobel Prize had just been established with the opening of the new century). Academic lives were largely centred on the institutions themselves. A university was a home in which a lifetime was spent. Outside, social or community status was probably more important than professional distinction. Academics enjoyed being part of a socially privileged stratum, from which in most countries they came. Travel and communications, although vastly improved over earlier centuries, still lacked the frenetic quality of the present, with overnight flights and over-committed academics, and, to borrow another bit of contemporary jargon, multi-tasking. It is also possible that energy levels were lower since the typical academic lifestyle did not involve efforts at diet or exercise, and low-cost servants were available. But this is pure conjecture, and it would be a mistake to overlook the accounts of neurasthenic disorders with apparent career origins that are noted in the Victorian biographies of professors recording their inadequacies and failings.

None of these distinctions is meant to glamorize the past at the expense of the present. In every country – more so in some than in others, and with qualitative differences between countries – class, religious, gender and ethnic bias was evident. Women, Jews, members of the working classes and ethnic minorities faced begrudging acceptance and condescension, exclusionary policies respecting admissions and appointments, and other slights. The absence of universal access to the upper levels of secondary education exacerbated the situation for outsiders. Academic communities were not models of toleration; and towards the end of the nineteenth century some academics succumbed to vicious theories of racial inferiority that forever shames them and mars the histories of their countries. In this respect, despite the affirmative action debates so prevalent in the United States today, or their equivalent in parts of Europe, universities and colleges have vastly improved; so much is this the case, that higher education is virtually expected to set an example of open-mindedness for society and even (this was not true of the nineteenth century) to avoid national partisanship and chauvinism. Hence the university at the end of the twentieth century is preeminently global in its orientation, much like the emerging world economy itself, in which the national ownership of economic resources is no longer always obvious, and yet at the same time – one of many current para-doxes – subject to the fickle policies of governments designed to enlist or coerce higher education in what are defined, broadly or narrowly, as national objectives.

Several caveats are in order. In an era in which the 'European university' is to be found in every country in the world, and in which new institutions appear almost instantly, referencing all of them and their infinite variety is impossible. At a time when a typical history of universities project consists of multiple volumes with numerous contributing specialists, a sketch can be no more than that, a quick briefing on more or less newsworthy highlights. Furthermore, the historical record is always more problematical than even a detailed account could possibly illustrate. It is invariably ironical, and irony is the great enemy of all future-minded studies. While a degree of simplifi-cation, even over-simplification, may be necessary in order to make the big points, cautionary remarks will from time to time haunt the narrative. One such remark needs to be made at the outset lest it be assumed that there is particular significance to either the notion of a *fin de siècle* or millennial beginning. Historians generally have difficulty fitting the events and circumstances of the past into the matrix of any such conception of decline or rebirth. Institutional change is always uneven; and the more complex the organization, the less likely are we to find uniform transformations. Older values and attitudes, as well as governance and administrative structures, do not disappear but carry over into different phases. Some fields of scholarship retain their customary methods; others are either new or transformed.

Interior changes cannot always be connected to social, political or economic changes, even broadly. For example, no one denies that one of the great transformations of history was the industrial revolution, yet the scien-tific and technical knowledge that we would like to associate with that revolution, as well as the commercial utility of other subjects, did not become a major part of the university until the second half of the nineteenth century. In many countries, including the United States, an applied mission had first to be developed within new institutions unencumbered by the value systems obtaining in the old – civic universities in England, technical universities in Germany and Austria, land grant state universities in

America, and various technical colleges and institutes. The multiversity concept, the idea that a single university could embody a variety of different missions and purposes, sorting out through internal argument and the play of vested interests the required priorities and resource allocations, was resisted. To remain true to its inheritance, a university must, so it was said, be worthy of that name and direct its energy to pure or higher cultural and intellectual tasks. Other institutions might adopt utilitarian functions, but they must be called by a designation other than 'university' and denied the capacity to award a form of certification called the 'degree'. The fact that the historical legacy of universities was mixed or confusing, that no university had ever avoided some form of applied knowledge – indeed, professional education was a central concern from the start – was ignored or played down.

The 'idea' of a university has had both positive and negative implications for the history of the modern university: positive in maintaining a standard of intellectual achievement, negative in delaying the onset of broader considerations of public responsibility. While the title 'university' is still protected in some countries, such as Sweden, and 'mission creep' discouraged in others (various state systems in America), efforts at maintaining distinct institutional boundaries associated with funding and other privileges seem rapidly to be failing. If there is any single trend that is truly revolutionary in the history of the modern university, it is the erosion of traditional conceptions of institutional integrity. Professional identity, once more closely aligned with a particular university, has leaped the fence (to borrow an image from the history of the English garden) into meadows of wider affiliation. And in those countries where professional academic identity was intimately connected to civil service status, it is now more closely referenced to the world of high tech business.

Definition of the 'Modern University'

If the attraction of fixing the stages of university history at the beginning of a new century is of limited use in understanding the changes that have occurred in university history, is it absolutely the case that useful chronological divisions cannot be made? In fact they can, and one way to understand the twentieth century is to put a significant break at the post-World War II decades. The last forty years show signs of major departures from the type of 'modern' university understood earlier; and to comprehend these, as well as to understand the ways in which the departures represent an intensification of trends noticed earlier, it is necessary to provide a composite portrait of the modern university along with several of its variants. For the purposes of the discussion that follows, the 'modern university' will be discussed in relation to the following characteristics. First is the adoption of a research mission. Second, already alluded to, is differentiation by function and mission. Third is the development of instruments for measuring or maintaining quality; and the fourth feature is control over higher education by central (or regional) governments. Each of these features is also a heading under which many other critical, related developments may be grouped.

Research

The adoption of a research mission challenged the supremacy of the historic teaching mission and eventually profoundly transformed the interior culture of universities, the nature of knowledge production and dissemination, the criteria for measuring academic success, models of organization and governance, funding and physical appearance. Begging the question of the different definitions of research (discovery, new knowledge, new methods and conceptions, the 'higher criticism'), let it be said that no other feature of the modern university is so pronounced or even so universal. In most countries institutions that do not have a recognized research function aspire to the privileges associated with it, producing rivalries and conflicts.

Research in the meaning of an ethic of discovery, entailing an acceptance of the possibility that prevailing or received modes of inquiry, assumptions and conclusions are likely to be surpassed, is inherent in all intellectual activity. Creative thinking will always produce results that may be unfamiliar or startling. The central point is, therefore, whether research is raised to the level of a conscious mission, requiring institutional resources and influencing academic appointments, and whether the pursuit of originality is compatible with normative undergraduate teaching. For centuries the main body of academics resisted incorporating certain kinds of intellectual activities and shifts into the structure of teaching precisely on the grounds that it was upsetting to undergraduates, threatened to undermine the financing of traditional subjects or represented an alarming challenge to normative values. Experimental science, engineering, modern languages, new professional subjects often had to find alternative homes, or enter traditional institutions as poor relations relegated to the margins. Boundary protection was an established art.

A research ethic took hold in the nineteenth century; and while it did not overwhelm all parts of the university at once, in the long run original work became the touchstone for determining the highest form of academic success. We cannot in the beginning exactly correlate this immense change in the culture of universities with any external demand for research. 'Research' does not automatically suggest what is commonly thought of as 'applied research'. Indeed, the kind of research carried out arranged itself in a hierarchy of investigation, so that research that was 'fundamental' or 'basic' or 'pure', undertaken with no other goal than extending the frontiers of knowledge, was deemed to be the highest. That ethic has not departed, but there are many signs that the classic distinction between basic and applied investigation is no longer uncontested or even valid (Gibbons et al., 1994). In Germany the origins of discovery or critical inquiry lay in the conditions of the late Enlightenment and were extended with the reforms of the Von Humboldt brothers in the early part of the nineteenth century, largely as part of the rebuilding of the German states following conquest by the French.

Research is closely associated with highly advanced postgraduate instruction and the diversion of resources to doctoral programmes. This too is a nineteenth-century higher education development, with Germany as the model for the kinds of academic apprenticeship and discipleship systems that characterize advanced degree work. The main exception was Britain, whose record in this respect belongs more to the twentieth century and particularly to its second half (Simpson, 1983). American universities began to grant the doctorate for academic work in the 1860s, when Yale University offered a PhD in comparative literature; but general acceptance of the idea of a research-based degree was slow and painful. The great innovation in the United States was the establishment towards the end of the nineteenth century, carrying over into the next, of administratively separate divisions or graduate schools within universities, with separate admissions policies. The graduate school was an innovation that cannot be easily correlated with demand. It appears to have been a creation of the professoriate for its own purposes and could not really become significant until the second half of the twentieth century (Storr, 1953).

The graduate school stimulated the elevation of standards, since in comparison to Europe the American undergraduate curriculum was of lower quality, more like school. It allowed generations of better-prepared academics, 10,000 of whom had studied in Germany during the century, to teach to their specialities, thus strengthening the importance of the module as the basic mode of delivering instruction (Jarausch, 1995: 195). For much, perhaps most, of the nineteenth century, American professors and lecturers were handicapped by the absence of elite secondary schools, the spread of which in Europe is one of the most notable educational features of the nineteenth century. Institutional differentiation by student achievement was therefore not only a policy but unavoidable in the American context.

With few exceptions, the teaching staff of the graduate school was drawn from the undergraduate programmes, which were themselves slowly becoming 'departments' of specialities. The history of the department ('institute' elsewhere) has yet to be written, despite the fact that it is now ubiquitous, has spread to other countries and is still the primary source of teaching in universities and colleges. Departments were not common in Europe, where, outside Oxford and Cambridge, the medieval 'faculty' organization was preeminent, and chairholders presiding over institutes, seminars and laboratories were a law unto themselves. The switchover to departments in the United States began late in the century and was accompanied by a new conception of the academic career as a series of well-defined stages of advancement from lower to higher ranks of the professoriate, whereas promotion to senior rank on the continent or Britain generally entailed applying for vacancies competitively as they occurred, most often in another institution. Graduate degree instruction was in the hands of the chaired professors, who directly admitted students to higher degree work. A system of discipleship was created, with strong personal bonds (even if formal) between teacher and student, to be distinguished from the developing American system where the department determined the career paths of students as well as the curriculum for specialized studies. Thus was formed what sociologists call the 'bottom-up' university, in which all critical decisions affecting teaching, staff and student recruitment and academic career are made or initiated at the lower administrative levels of the university structure. The loosening of established authority and the tendency to challenge seniority were generally typical of American culture, with its weak inheritance of social and professional elites, although the decline of the seniority and adoption of collegial forms of decision-making was delayed until such time as the university became a more central institution in American history.

Criticism today of the departmental structure exists in all countries. The department is viewed by detractors as a vested interest standing in the way of broader forms of undergraduate teaching. New universities often attempt to establish teaching units that are field- rather than discipline-based. The accuracy of the criticism is open to question, especially since contemporary scholarship and science draw heavily from adjacent disciplines, and the variety of departmental structures and their capacity to encourage interdisciplinary teaching remain too great for adequate generalization.

Differentiation

The second feature, already alluded to, was differentiation by function and mission, a mix of institutes, research centres, colleges, universities and professional schools that in the twentieth century would be discussed as parts of a national system of higher education. Relating the parts to one another has been a particular concern of American policy-makers and accounts for several other cardinal features of the American system. It is not yet a major concern in Europe, where diversification within the higher education system remains prevalent, but relating the parts is resisted for reasons of quality control and funding. Differentiation by function in the United States meant wide variation in admissions and degree standards, the purpose of which was to provide different educational experiences and life chances for different populations. Differentiation by mission also inevitably produced a ranking system or pecking order of institutions, contending in the marketplace for brand name recognition. A historian might conclude that such an outcome was deliberate and virtually designed.

Institutional differentiation exploded in the United States, and here we can in fact link certain characteristics of the higher education system to broad external factors. The heterogeneity of the American population, its religious and ethnic divisions, the importance of local and regional factors, the absence of inherited social class and aristocratic institutions, and the development of a private sector of higher education led rapidly in the nineteenth century (and even before) to a multiplicity of colleges and universities geared to niche marketing (Trow, 1993). Private education was given an enormous boost by the Supreme Court's decision of 1819 in the Dartmouth College case, which rejected the claims of the state of New Hampshire to authority over the former colonial foundation and recognized the legality of corporations and original charters (Herbst, 1982: 237–243). The American constitution assigned responsibility for education at all levels to the constituent states; and beginning with the University of North Carolina at the end of the eighteenth century, they created public universities throughout the following two centuries. The federal government assisted with the land grant act of the 1860s (and a sea grant much later), allowing for the creation of another wave of state-supported universities combining the missions of polytechnics and universities. Single-sex colleges, church-related colleges and universities, colleges for African-Americans (who, with the notable initial exception of Antioch College in Ohio in the middle decades of the nineteenth century, were excluded by prejudice or income from other institutions) burgeoned.

Germany and Austria had technical universities for high-level engineering science, with a corresponding preparatory sector of secondary schools. The French network of *grandes écoles* dating from the 1790s, provided Europe and America with the idea of elite training institutions for government or industry without a research mission (some modification of that restriction is occurring today). French examples inspired the origins of the London School of Economics and Political Science (Dahrendorf, 1995: 5). In England, Wales and Ireland non-residential universities proliferated to attract student populations without the resources or social connections of those attending Oxford and Cambridge; and this expansion of higher education was substantially influenced in organization and teaching by the Scottish universities, whose impact on the origins of the first London University was remarkable. In addition to institutions of this newer type, there were conservatories or academies for music, normal schools (ie. teacher training institutions), schools for the performing and plastic arts, for industrial design and forms of engineering preparation closer to entry level labour market requirements than could be expected of universities.

Quality Control

Whereas differentiation by mission and population was typical of the provision for higher education in all societies, it was only in the United States that status was largely determined by competition in the market, and the differing segments were eventually interlinked through a system of student transfer. A reputation for excellence or quality could therefore be earned only through relative insulation from the market or by restricting transfer to high-achieving students. For less privileged institutions, the graduate school led the way in upward academic drift.

In Europe the general response to differentiation was to create external examining systems appropriate to the different categories of higher education. They provided an independent check on the quality of individual institutions. A distinction needs to be made, however, between admissions to universities and the receipt of degrees upon successful completion of a course of study. It was the latter rather than the former that external examining was designed to protect; but as the degree itself rose in perceived value, social and occupational, the admissions process became more meritocratic, with all the qualifications of class and opportunity that lie behind conceptions such as achievement by merit.

In the German system (with corresponding versions in other countries), the *Staatsexamen*, the government-administered degree (or degree equivalent) examination was the ultimate test. Universities were therefore primarily teaching (or teaching and research) but not examining institutions. This permitted the rise or continuation of the legendary German *Wandervogel* student who, in the medieval university tradition, sought out the leading scholars of the day irrespective of university. In Britain diversification led to an intensification of the practice of using external examiners (at Oxford and Cambridge the examiners belonged to the universities but were 'external' to the colleges), the creation of unprecedented examining universities such as London or the later Victoria University (which were not really universities but examining centres). Ultimately the precedent led to the establishment in the second half of the twentieth century of the Council for National Academic Awards (CNAA), the external examining authority for the polytechnic system created by government legislation in the 1960s. From thence, the principle well established, it was a simple mental jump to the various other quality control bodies created or discussed in the 1980s and 1990s (Rothblatt, 1997: Ch. 5).

Differentiation by function, and the growth of new institutions in the nineteenth century, obviously meant that the higher education system was enlarging in numbers and serving larger sections of the population, generally middle-income groups. But the university had been an imperialistic corporation from the outset of its history in the medieval period, expanding with surprising rapidity all over Europe and into the empires created by European exploration and pillage. Nevertheless, individual universities were still formed with an elite staffing ratio, so that the actual numbers of students in the relevant age cohorts going on to higher education were small. It is not until the twentieth century, and especially since 1945, that we can begin to think in terms of mass access. Consequently, as mass education arrived in Europe in the final decades of the twentieth century, the subject of how to maintain standards of student achievement, or how to assess quality teaching occupied the attention of most nations. No continental polity has concerned itself with the issues as much as the British government, whether under Conservative or Labour domination, although Dutch interest is high, probably because no other country has so rapidly unravelled important components of its inherited elite system. The problem is acute in certain sectors where funding difficulties have led institutions into transnational and even overseas commercial activity, where dubious financial schemes have occurred.

At the core lies an historical problem not easily resolved, bequeathed to the twentieth century by the nineteenth and to the twenty-first century by the twentieth, which is how to make relatively cheap mass access higher education compatible with high quality conceptions of a university education. One way out is to accept American definitions of multiple standards, but this is not an intellectually satisfying solution for countries accustomed to different traditions of assessing worth. It is redolent of the utilitarian philosopher Jeremy Bentham's deliberately provocative remark that the game of push-pin was as intellectually valuable as poetry.

Overall quality assurance in the United States, from a European perspective, was presented with another challenge by a series of connected innovations that certainly made any attempt at an external measure of student achievement virtually impossible. They included the division of the degree programme into a body of distinct modules consisting of requirements and elective choices (assigned credit-unit value in the twentieth century) and the union of teaching and examining in the person of a single instructor without the 'protection' of blind marking adopted elsewhere. The attractions of what has been mocked as a supermarket, bazaar or *smörgåsbord* curriculum were (and are) continuous assessment, a high element of student choice, and virtual control over the classroom curriculum by the instructor, subject only to general peer approval.

This distinctive American development has occasioned surprisingly little criticism in the United States, despite its invitation to students to bargain. American modular or credit-unit arrangements – however we wish to designate a system that has no familiar name – effectively inhibited the possibility of standardized evaluation and assessment. Each course rose or fell on its own merits. In order to provide some sort of measure of overall achievement, an arithmetical system of averaging was created at some point in the first third of the twentieth century. That history has not yet been adequately told.

A modular curriculum and variable standard were combined with, and made possible, yet another unique American creation (with doubtful Scottish origins), a system of student transfer, especially outside the older elite sector. Ladders of opportunity were provided for ambitious students to move from less to more competitive institutions. Certain colleges or universities would *ipso facto* attract highly motivated students. Certain programmes and departments of study within those institutions would attract better prepared and more intellectually minded students than others, so that differentiation took place within as well as between institutions. Put in other terms, the American university, whether private and public, has needed to provide diverse opportunities in order to maintain its social contract with actual and potential patrons. However, one type of institution 'protected' another, so that access to the 'system' rather than to a particular institution was the legitimate marker of a democratic conception of higher education. The greatly publicized ideological debates over minority entrance to undergraduate, graduate and professional schools in the 1970s, 1980s and 1990s, the shifting mood of state electorates with respect to ethnic set-asides and *de facto* quotas, suggest a very uncertain future for a traditional understanding that mass access guaranteed through the system itself provides the legitimacy for competitive entry to any part of it.

Government

A fourth feature of the modern university concerns patronage, or again to employ current terminology, the 'buyers' of educational services. In the United States the patrons were a mix composed of fee-paying students, philanthropists and local or state governments, depending upon whether institutions were private or public. To ease the burden of dependency, some institutions, to include public ones, were able to make use of endowments and gifts. (This source of income, prevalent in the medieval university, had to be rediscovered in the Europe of our day.) In Europe of the nineteenth century fee-paying was prevalent; in England the colleges of Oxford and Cambridge were able to meet some operating expenses from endowments – a number of colleges were very much richer than others – and while instances of philanthropy are recorded, the trend in all continental countries was towards becoming virtual wards of central governments (in Germany the princely states and later the *Länder* were significant), Scotland, accustomed to crown patronage, leading the way in Britain (Withrington, 1999). For Britain generally, the story mainly belongs to the twentieth century, consisting of a series of parliamentary and local government grants in the 1890s and Edwardian period, followed by the regularization of government support by the formation of the University Grants Committee (Shattock, 1994). For the European university, accustomed in some way to the support of royal government and established churches, monopoly control of the financing of higher education was accepted as natural and preferable. The alternative, greater reliance on the 'bourgeoisie', possibly the business interests emerging as powerful in countries like Germany and England, seemed more threatening, too challenging to an aristocratic culture with which academics had long been associated (Vom Bruch, 1997: 6; Rothblatt, 1981). Identification with the state, the guardian of standards and culture in the German system, and in those northern European countries adopting the German system, provided the necessary status assurance.

The power of government was feared in the United States even if it was needed, is still needed and will always be needed; but republican values, the absence of a landed aristocracy, professions that were market-driven rather than state or guild protected, a plural religious heritage, and the absence of a well-defined constitutional role in education for Washington obviated the possibility of clear alignments. Hence it was in the interests of American colleges and universities to diversify their sources of income and to use their lay governing boards – a colonial inheritance rooted in the English law of charities and corporations – to provide the necessary outreach connections (Trow, 1993). Government has never been an indifferent feature of the history of American colleges and universities, and virtually every state university has had to contend with the views and laws of governors and legislators intent on imposing their own notions of a suitable education on universities. The University of California at Berkeley, founded in 1868, nearly collapsed in the constitutional crisis of the late 1870s (Van Houten, 1996). Church-related colleges and universities have their own versions of this story, the standards of an increasingly secular world contesting for supremacy with particular religious traditions (Marsden and Longfield, 1992; Gleason, 1995). This history of conflict over institutional autonomy has led historians such as Richard Hofstadter to talk about anti-intellectualism and questions of academic freedom as central American features, although they are just as central elsewhere, if not always perceived as such (Hofstadter, 1996). One measure of the stature of a university or college president has been the ability to steer among competing interests; but it must also be acknowledged that those skills would be less effective in a modern parliamentary system controlled by a majority party than in a political system of checks and balances.

Post-war Developments

The later twentieth century has been a true watershed in the history of universities. In western Europe, recovery from war and the spread of social democracy produced decisions of the utmost importance for the history of universities. Perhaps foremost amongst them were policies designed to stimulate higher levels of participation in higher education by encouraging demand, especially the demand for education from working-class populations, historically 'soft'. Income redistribution measures, changes in school-leaving examinations, even the virtual destruction of the meritocratic state-supported grammar schools of England in the 1960s and 1970s and their replacement by supposedly more egalitarian or comprehensive high schools were characteristic introductions. Almost everywhere the traditional selective *gymnasium* lost ground. The result over some decades was indeed a great rise in the numbers of students who qualified for university admission, with a corresponding investment by government in new universities and the upgrading of older institutions. In many respects the states of Europe have been far more successful in reversing the attendance patterns typical of preceding centuries than perhaps at first anticipated.

As the twenty-first century begins, demand is high, but the numbers cannot always be accommodated. In France one unhappy result has been heavy overcrowding in many universities, with corresponding demonstrations and protests from students. Government attempts in France to limit enrolment in certain university departments have been unsuccessful. The situation in Italy is described as even more alarming, with new universities like Sapienza, the largest in Europe, admitting numbers that are staggering and cannot possibly, given Italian staffing ratios, be satisfactorily taught. Scandals are often reported, notably in teaching appointments where nepotism is practised and in the perfunctory conduct of examinations. In Britain there have even been recent efforts to dampen demand through budgetary cutbacks and the introduction of student fees. Such policies, non-existent until recently, have predictably stimulated criticism and controversy. A middle policy of simultaneously charging and capping fees is emerging, and the funding situation remains volatile and indeterminate. In the meantime, student indebtedness mounts, especially in professional education such as medicine. (A similar situation has emerged within the University of California federal system. The campuses would like to use higher fees to offset shortfalls in state government appropriations, but the public and legislature are opposed.)

Working-class participation throughout Europe has remained dismayingly limited, however, but partly because the middle-income ranks of society have proportionately increased, owing to the return of economic prosperity to Europe. The middle ranks of society have always supplied universities with their main client base, however, irrespective of country, and every expansion in the provision for higher education usually involves another segment in the middle. The problem of how to stimulate a demand for education in families where such priorities have been low, or feared for their negative effects on class loyalty, remains largely unsolved for most countries. The totalitarian governments of eastern Europe had their own versions of mass access. Quotas favouring peasant or worker populations and universities emphasizing applied subjects (justified in Marxist thought as somehow more suitable for a workers' democracy) never succeeded in attracting significant representation.

No western European country except Germany, carrying the burden of the former German Democratic Republic, is facing the formidable task of converting universities demoralized by communist policies into self-reliant, dynamic institutions open to proven talent and offering stimulating teaching, especially where academic time-servers inherited from the age of the commissars are still in evidence. It would, however, be remiss not to recognize pockets of successful activity, younger talent influenced by western practice and the academic freedom of university systems to the west, especially in an era of travel and innumerable international conferences. Today the German system is in flux, a mixture of pre-1930s ideas about the supremacy of the chaired professor and centres of innovation or at least concern for new ideas and structures. As in France, however, the removal of the research function from universities and their siting in about 60 separate Max Planck Institutes has raised questions about the quality of university teaching when it is institutionally separated from activities that provide a higher intellectual stimulus.

One inescapable result of the extraordinary expansion of opportunities and numbers, stimulated by etatist policies and post-war recovery, is the inevitable cost of maintaining mass higher education systems and funding research at the levels required by contemporary society. This issue is especially critical wherever, as in Britain, a 'binary line' dividing institutions by mission has been abolished and the title 'university', with its expensive implications, freely distributed. No country is able to escape the formidable economic realities unless the accumulation of family income can increase at levels that allow for even higher rates of taxation or greater levels of disposable income. Even in currently prosperous America, with its booming stock markets, low unemployment (but high job turnover) and negligible inflation, the costs of higher education have outpaced inflation – a situation that provokes criticism but does not take fixed costs into account – and in Europe the volatility of the economy is continuous despite overall wealth improvement. In countries such as Spain, Germany and Sweden unemployment is substantial; and while European states are either adopting policies significantly reducing government expenditures, or contemplating so doing, public demand for traditional safety net services understandably remains high. So higher education is not the only burden that governments must bear and will continue to bear as the familiar social problems of ageing, housing, income maintenance, health, schooling – there are so many – demand attention. (It is always surprising for visitors to California to learn that maintaining the penal system is as expensive to the state as funding its three higher education systems.)

The Search for Revenue

These are commonplace facts for observers of the current higher education scene. Equally commonplace is the conclusion that, as the costs of maintaining some combination of elite and mass education are now seen to be beyond the resources available to states, the search for alternatives is inevitable. Here again we encounter aspects of the near future that were already present in the final decade of the twentieth century – indeed, were apparent for several decades, leading to a number of interlocked and logically connected developments. First is the tendency for central governments to offload some of their financial responsibility for higher education on to the constituent institutions, forcing them to scramble for income through a number of expedients. These include the introduction of student fees as noted in the case of Britain, but resisted by countries such as Sweden; the search for donors and philanthropists and heavier representation of business interests in university affairs (today half of the 38 chancellors of Australian universities are from industry, according to the *Times Higher Education Supplement* (1999: 10)). The creation of science parks in the vicinity of universities like Oxford and Lund is typical, and universities are also attempting to increase their outreach and service in the hope that financial rewards and research grants will enhance their visibility and income flows. The results, as expected, greatly vary, some notable successes mixed with disappointment. Of all the controversial issues of the 1990s, none gives more cause for academic anxiety than the selling of academic products in the open market, the concomitant franchising of the university's reputation and willingness to advertise the names of donors. But there are recorded gains, as Australian researchers have recently reported. University research in Australia that is funded by industry has led to greater academic productivity, a strong record of service to the institution itself and enhanced commitment to the supervision of research students (Harman, G., 1999; Harman, K., 1998).

Research with industrial application, if not in scale but in principle, may not be absolutely novel in university history given the history of the technical universities of Germany and Austria, or the applied research of London and the civic universities a century and more ago, or the general experience of many American state universities undertaking economic tasks for their masters. Wars provide an immense stimulus to university-based technology, especially the total wars of the twentieth century, involving virtually all university specialities. Within the social sciences the 'applied' tradition certainly goes back in time; but of course it was possible to 'apply' one's subject, as did the urban researchers at the University of Chicago or the London School of Economics or in the famous polytechnics of the continent, and not necessarily be rewarded with extra income, released time or other material gains. University administrators generally did not expect their researchers to bring in large grants to support laboratories and generate overheads. During the Cold War American academics in receipt of largess from the federal government in Washington often maintained, with justification, that as no immediate practical results were expected from their investigations, to all intents and purposes they were able to do pure or basic science. Consequently academics generally flattered themselves by maintaining that their interest in research and scholarship was fundamentally disinterested or, to use a vexed word, 'Humboldtian', and needed no other incentive or reward than the opportunity to pursue their specialities.

Yet the necessity to acquire outside income as the expected sources dwindle is, if not absolutely unprecedented in some cases, assuredly new in scale, scope and circumstance and far greater in its implications for university independence than before. Greater attention is being given to such matters as 'intellectual property' (its ownership), 'technology transfer', patent laws, the proper use of academic time and teaching 'loads', the problem of the maintenance of traditions of institutional collegiality in the face of material temptations, and the internal maldistribution of academic income between academic ranks and teaching and administration. If present trends continue, Europe will become increasingly concerned about a problem that has long haunted the multiversity of the United States, which is whether the services required by patrons in highly competitive industries are likely to compromise the norms of value-free enquiry, or what John Ziman calls 'public knowledge' (Ziman, 1968). Open access to university-created discovery is a cardinal principle of academic freedom. The right to pursue knowledge implies the right for others to share it. One of the great conundrums for universities that undertake research on military and strategic problems has been the secrecy entailed by such commitments as much as the question of whether universities should, in the absence of a national emergency, participate in defence-related projects.

Offloading universities from the government to society and the economy requires new internal forms of university governance and management, new efforts at coordination and agenda determination unknown in the faculty structure of decision-making with its medieval, corporate roots. The shifting of some responsibilities from the middle or faculty levels of the European university upwards towards the administrative top (or towards the deans of faculties) has produced consternation in universities without traditions of market response. In a more optimistic mood, Burton Clark has recently described the new forms of internal governance and management that are occasioning greater institutional freedom and can, by eroding inherited bottlenecks, attitudes and dependencies, lead to vigorous shared governance between central administration, faculties and departments, lay councils and boards (unprecedented in some countries) – one result of government withdrawal. In his analysis, the heavy hand of the state has historically constrained the imagination and innovatory capacity of European universities. His examples are drawn essentially from new institutions (Warwick and Strathclyde in Britain, Twente in The Netherlands, Chalmers in Sweden and

Joensuu in Finland), which (until they too become set in their ways) have a freedom to act unencumbered by the great inheritances of the nineteenth century (Clark, 1998).

A Connecticut Yankee?

Amongst the short list of astonishing alterations in the historic fabric of higher education in Europe has been a widespread interest in American institutional practices and traditions. Since the nineteenth century the custom for European observers of American higher education developments was to deplore most of what they found, although no one was greater in his contempt for the commercialization, boosterism and intellectual deficiencies of the American university (with Britain running second) than the outraged Abraham Flexner (Flexner, 1994). Earlier in the century that *enfant terrible* and former Stanford University lecturer, Thorsten Veblen, excoriated the wealthy benefactors of American colleges and universities for their parvenu obsessions, pretentious campuses and philistine interests. Foremost among European criticism was the American commitment to mass education, entailing remediation, commercialism and tolerance for low quality institutions. By and large observers from abroad, whose universities were protected (or seen to be protected) by bureaucracies drawn from the same social class that produced academics, failed to understand the social contract basis of American higher education, its vulnerability to democratic and populist sentiment, and its survival strategies. The process by which access guaranteed through entry into the system and mobility through student transfer protected elite functions was poorly appreciated.

Whether these processes special to United States history and culture are now understood in Europe is problematic, despite more open and accessible discussions of the issues. Nevertheless, features of the American university that developed in the nineteenth century are now showing up throughout the European higher education structure, although rarely in any pure form of borrowing. Credit-unit arrangements, modular courses (although not necessarily dispensing with external examining), the introduction of the American professorial system with more certain advancement upwards from junior status, an emphasis on disciplinary departments, separate graduate schools in Belgium, The Netherlands, France and Germany, with distinct and well demarcated undergraduate bachelor degree programmes are now familiar features. There is a tiny but growing interest in Germany and The Netherlands in American collegiate forms of liberal education, an extraordinarily vexed historical subject. Liberal education has had multiple objectives, partisan and ideological differences, and inspires long perspectives and short tempers (Rothblatt, 1993; Liedman, 1993; Nussbaum, 1997; Kimball, 1995; Grant and Riesman, 1978). The University of Utrecht now includes a residential American-style liberal arts college, and others are appearing. Such interest as does exist in Europe arises from the emerging realities of mass education at secondary levels. The numbers of students eligible for some level of higher education having increased exponentially since the 1950s, doubts have arisen about whether quality has kept pace and whether students are entering universities with the requisite skills and subject preparation. Furthermore, the mobility of populations, with 'guest workers' from the Middle East or eastern Europe remaining longer than expected (or wanted), has led to a reconsideration of the teaching necessary to promote ethnic toleration, a knowledge of western political traditions and preparation for higher education. Thus in some respects the conditions that made American liberal arts education a nagging concern from 1776 are now present in today's Europe.

Decentralization or privatization is a trend, if, like so many others, an uncertain one. More and more choices over salary, curricula and advancement opportunities are being made by institutions themselves, whereas in the past government policy established uniform admissions policies, salary and other levels of compensation and approved appointments to chairs. This is another aspect of the separation of academic life from civil service norms. The simulation of features common to the United States has by no means systematically replaced time-honoured arrangements, but their very presence is a major historic departure.

With just a few exceptions, however, the critical heart of the American opportunity structure is resisted. The process of student transfer has not been widely adopted. In Britain generally, the three-year degree (the dominant form) militates against transfer. Elsewhere the transfer process appears unworkable in systems without credit-units where terminal examinations are the rule. Furthermore, the loss of institutional control over degree quality wherever large numbers of students receive half their education in some other institution is an appalling notion. Some alteration in traditional attitudes and structures, however, was inevitable once the European Union (and its predecessors) created student mobility possibilities such as SOCRATES and ERASMUS. The ramifications of these programmes are still being worked out, as well as the implications of the European Union for the structure and values of higher education itself. Given language and system differences, the crossing of national university boundaries is hardly a matter of marching, and the energy and resources needed to shape and implement policies across the Union is yet another form of workload increase outside the classroom (Teichler et al., 1998). The association between universities and nation-state aims has been strong ever since the nineteenth century, and the movement to a supra-national conception of educational policy is at the moment daunting as well as confounding.

It is a nice historical question whether the changes in Europe are direct borrowings from the United States or represent logical, nearly determined system responses to transformations in European society and politics.

Borrowed ideas and structures invariably get reinterpreted, as in the case of the American adoption of German conceptions of self-development or *Bildung* and efforts to make it part of a liberal education. Like organ transplants, borrowings will not 'take' in an unreceptive environment. The political policies of the post-war period stimulated demand for secondary and higher education, and the democratization of society has created more publicly responsive governments. Global economic changes and the spread of a high technology sector dependent upon university education has produced a search for the optimum conditions favouring such relationships. The result is unaccustomed discussion of the market as a determinant of economic success, and privatization policies, no two of which are exactly alike but all of which imply a relaxed grip of government over the economy and higher education. That process is still mercurial and uncertain, however. Governments give and take back, but broadly speaking, in such circumstances, more nearly resembling the conditions that produced the American system of higher education, certain policy decisions appear inevitable.

Higher Education: Reactive and Proactive

How many of the changes in Europe following the post-war period could have been foreseen, or were foreseen, especially those that have been occurring within the last two decades? The 'Americanization' of European higher education, even as a metaphor, is a surprise. Policy-makers of the 1960s generally thought in terms of expanding the provision for higher education on elite models, and their arguments were largely focused on defining the size of the elite. In France, where the favoured sector of higher education was not the university but the specialized higher 'schools', the consequences of increasing the numbers of students passing the baccalaureate examination and qualifying for higher education were not regarded as alarming. In Sweden a social democratic government led by Olof Palme had aims of its own, derived from Swedish history and political traditions, and one consequence, later reversed, was the integration of non-research colleges with research universities, the very opposite of the concept of differentiation by mission and function that would later find a more receptive audience. Although it is always possible to find traces of some innovations in unlikely places and decades, it remains the case that the transformations in values, attitudes and policies, the introduction of new structures and systems of evaluation, constitute a historic turnaround in Europe.

The role of the state, however, remains unclarified. As indicated, a loosening of ties has occurred. Institutions have been given greater latitude in determining the essential parameters of their private lives. Chalmers Institute of Technology in Gothenburg, Sweden, has been released from government control and will one day be expected to live of its own. In Finland universities such as Uusimaa are the beneficiaries of government decentralization of the higher education system. The University of Leiden in The Netherlands has been asking for similar autonomy (while retaining some government support) and has symbolically dropped the word 'state' (*rijk*) from its title of *Rijksuniversiteit Leiden*. The university has also opened a lobbyist's office in The Hague (*Times Higher Education Supplement*, January 8, 1999: 11). In France a few universities, or a few departments within them, have even acquired a research mission. But the hand of government is still visible. It is by far the dominant and – for all intents and purposes, irrespective of private income – the overwhelming patron of higher education. Government policies with regard to higher education are contradictory and unpredictable, with powers delegated and powers retracted occurring with confusing rapidity, so that the freedom for individual institutions to make decisions is at the same time restricted by a variety of constraints affecting enrolments, work loads, revenue allocation and academic career opportunities. The combination of constraints vary widely by nation.

What can be said of the United States itself, whose higher education system has undergone enormous expansion but according to a pattern already evident a century ago? Are there dramatic transformations? Certainly not in comparison to Europe, and there is no American interest in borrowing structures or systems from Europe, although American literary and historical scholarship has been profoundly affected by European philosophical and linguistic studies, especially French and German. Questions about quality throughout the system sometimes lead to an interest in external examining (the six accrediting regions of the United States are more concerned with quality as a minimal rather than an optimal measure), but the American course structure and autonomy of the classroom teacher limit that interest. A typical American demand of its higher education system is that there be more of it, more readily available to minorities and women as students and professors, less expensive, friendlier to the part-time student (a criticism of the elite institutions) – in sum, that it toss out most of the conceptions of a university inherited from the great European traditions of the nineteenth century. The prestigious institutions are often attacked as elitist, a word that has several connotations but in this context means unwarranted privilege. Questioning about the commitment of universities to liberal education is, as mentioned, a continual criticism but one that can only lead to introductions at the margins.

One legacy of the nineteenth century is the view that universities exist to criticize society and to hold its failings up to the light of reason and scientific inquiry. The radical student generations of the 1960s, buoyed up by their success in drawing national attention to racist attitudes, laws and restrictions, took the intellectual position one step further and attacked America's involvement in the Vietnam War. That attack broadened into anger against virtually every established American institution or value. Thus the American university was drawn into a role for which it was ill-prepared;

for there was a major difference between science as the benefactor of mankind and the university itself as an instrument for the remaking of society on an ideological basis. The inheritance of the 1960s was internalized, so to speak, in subsequent generations. Its major manifestation at the present lies in what are sometimes called 'politically correct' regulations that often intrude upon notions of academic freedom, or the 'culture wars' and the 'science wars', profound disagreements over what should be taught in universities, how they should be taught and whether the methods for the acquisition of knowledge are indeed relatively 'value-free' or always involve ideological and gender commitments (*Daedalus* 1997). The first belief implies the possibility of objective analysis, the second opens the door to political advocacy. At stake is the soul of the university. Such battles are evident in Britain as well, and occasionally on the continent, but nowhere are they as much in evidence as in the American university, which is consequently subject to public, media or political scrutiny in ways that continually challenge the judgment of campus leaders.

The change in internal culture, the decline of a certain kind of collegiate consensus about the purposes of scholarship and the purposes of higher education is one of several major changes in the American university that could not quite be foreseen in the euphoric days of post-war expansion and system building. The decline of internal cohesion, sometimes expressed as loyalty to the institution, is an intensification of the American practice of competitive hiring, so little known in Europe before the present. It also represents an increase in the internal differentiation of academic rewards, as well as questions about the equity basis of those awards. Wealth generation for society, income generation for the institution itself, govern many decisions regarding appointments and emphases, and in this respect Europe is becoming one with the United States.

The Profession versus Institution

The growth of an international academic culture on a scale conceivably unknown even in the high period of the medieval university, at least in numbers, with jet air travel and computer technology making communications rapid and continuous, has strengthened professional disciplinary networks but weakened internal cohesion. A.H. Halsey speaks of the 'decline of donnish dominion' to describe this phenomenon (Halsey, 1992). The physical boundaries of the university are less significant for academic culture than once evident, as 'invisible colleges' provide more of the career satisfactions bestowed by the actual institutions. One may well wonder whether the great monuments and symbols of American higher education, as represented by the long and unique tradition of campus planning and campus beautification, have any significant meaning for the future. And in an era where a 'new production of knowledge' can dominate research, so that useful distinctions between pure and applied knowledge can no longer be drawn, it almost does not matter where one works or whether personal relationships are transient or lasting.

More historical changes, involving greater resources and populations, have been compressed into the last 40 or 50 years than in any comparable period of university history. The record is breathtaking. It also appears to be the case that the university form, being protean, contains every kind of enquiry that can be imagined, and at every level of sophistication. Universities are studied and probed as never before, so that the literature on higher education today is unprecedented in volume and description, to the degree that it is quite indigestible. In so many ways, the university has never been stronger or more important to more interests, nor has it been more influential. Yet curiously enough, its integration with society, the economy and government is so pronounced that it is almost fading into an undifferentiated landscape where different kinds of institutions simulate one another. The transition of industry from rust belt to high technology has made mini-universities of certain industries, and the threat, already present, of vastly commercialized 'virtual universities' raises even further questions about the value of expensive forms of undergraduate instruction or how talent is to be identified, recruited and educated or trained. Fear of the competition of for-profit interactive teaching technologies is widespread, raising questions of quality maintenance, audience, the fate of non-vocational education and the academic profession as a 'protected' community. A special concern is whether the new technologies themselves, so brilliantly compelling, may detract from teaching as a relationship between teacher and student, wherein the relationship itself is as important as the communication of knowledge. But many different forms of educational technology are now in use, from videoconferencing to computer-mediated communication. Not all of them carry the same implications for the future of the profession, and many either reach audiences otherwise neglected or supplement conventional teaching in creative fashion. Distance learning is already well established as a major part of any nation's higher education provision (Guri-Rosenblit, 1999). One of the great achievements of the nineteenth-century university was its ability to draw boundaries around itself, actually and philosophically. In that process it acquired a certain magic or mystique as a unique place with a distinct 'idea' (Rothblatt 1997: Ch. 1). That very uniqueness in time gave rise to both affection and envy. At the start of a new century, and a new millennium, neither sentiment appears relevant.

References

Burke, Colin B. (1982) *American Collegiate Populations: A Test of the Traditional View*, New York and London: New York University Press.

Callahan, Daniel, Caplan, Arthur L. and Jennings, Bruce (1985) *Applying the Humanities*, New York and London: Plenum Press.

Clark, Burton R. (1998) *Creating Entrepreneurial Universities: Organizational Pathways of Transformation*, Oxford and New York: Pergamon Press for the International Association of Universities.

Dahrendorf, Ralf (1995) *A History of the London School of Economics and Political Science, 1895–1995*, Oxford: Oxford University Press.

Flexner, Abraham (1994) *Universities: American, English, German*, New Brunswick, NJ, and London: Transaction Publishers (originally published 1930).

Gibbons, M., Limoges, C., Nowotny, H., Schwartzman, S., Scott, P. and Trow, M. (1994) *The New Production of Knowledge: Science and Research in Contemporary Societies*, London: Sage.

Gleason, Philip (1995) *Contending with Modernity: Catholic Higher Education in the Twentieth Century*, New York: Oxford University Press.

Goodheart, Eugene (1997) 'Reflections on the culture wars', *Daedalus* (Fall), 153–176.

Grant, Gerald and Riesman, David (1978) *The Perpetual Dream: Reform and Experiment in the American College*, Chicago and London: Chicago University Press.

Guri-Rosenblit, Sarah (1999) *Distance and Campus Universities: Tensions and Interactions, a Comparative Study of Five Countries*, Oxford: Pergamon Press.

Halsey, A.H. (1992) *Decline of Donnish Dominion: The British Academic Professions in the Twentieth Century*, Oxford: Clarendon Press.

Harman, Grant (1999) 'Science and technology academics: University-industry research links and Australian universities', forthcoming in *Higher Education*.

Harman, Kay (1998) 'Industry-driven research centres and managing transformed research boundaries in Australian universities', unpublished conference paper, Consortium of Higher Education Researchers, Kassel, Germany, 3–5 September.

Herbst, Jurgen (1982) *From Crisis to Crisis: American College Government 1636–1819*, Cambridge, MA: Harvard University Press.

Hofstadter, Richard (1996) *Academic Freedom in the Age of the College*, New Brunswick and London: Transaction Publishers (originally published in 1955).

Jarausch, Konrad H. (1995) 'American students in Germany, 1815–1914: The structure of German and U.S. matriculants at Göttingen University', in *German Influences on Education in the United States to 1917*, eds Henry Geitz, Jürgen Heideking and Jurgen Herbst, Cambridge: Cambridge University Press, 195–212.

Kimball, Bruce A. (1995) *Orators and Philosophers: A History of the Idea of Liberal Education*, New York: College Entrance Examination Board.

Klingenstein, Susanne (1991) *Jews in the American Academy, 1900–1940: The Dynamics of Intellectual Assimilation*, New Haven and London: Yale University Press.

Labinger, Jay A. (1997) 'The science wars and the future of the American academic profession', *Daedalus* (Fall), 201–220.

Liedman, Sven-Eric (1993) 'In search of Isis: General education in Germany and Sweden', in *The European and American University since 1800: Historical and Sociological Essays*, ed. Sheldon Rothblatt and Björn Wittrock, Cambridge: Cambridge University Press, 73–106.

Marsden, George M. and Longfield, Bradley J. (1992) *The Secularization of the Academy*, New York and Oxford: Oxford University Press.

Nussbaum, Martha C. (1997) *Cultivating Humanity: A Classical Defense of Reform in Liberal Education*, Cambridge, MA, and London: Harvard University Press.

Olesky, Wieslaw and Wasser, Henry (1999) 'Transformation of higher education in Poland after 1989: Case study of the University of Lodz', in *Higher Education in the Post-Communist World*, ed. Paula Sabloff, New York: Garland Press, 97–135.

Rothblatt, Sheldon (1981) *The Revolution of the Dons: Cambridge and Society in the Nineteenth Century*, Cambridge: Cambridge University Press (first published by Faber and Faber in 1968).

——(1993) 'The limbs of Osiris', in *The European and American University since 1800: Historical and Sociological Essays*, ed. Sheldon Rothblatt and Björn Wittrock, Cambridge: Cambridge University Press, 19–73.

——(1997)*The Modern University and Its Discontents: The Fate of Newman's Legacy in Britain and America*, Cambridge: Cambridge University Press.

Shattock, Michael L. (1994) *The UGC and the Management of British Universities*, Buckingham: Open University Press.

Simpson, Renate (1983) *How the PhD Came to Britain: A Century of Struggle for Postgraduate Education*, Guildford, Surrey: Society for Research into Higher Education.

Storr, Richard J. (1953) *The Beginnings of Graduate Education in America*, Chicago: University of Chicago Press.

The Times Higher Education Supplement, 8 January 1999.

Teichler, Ulrich, Barblan, Andris, Kehm, Barbara M. and Reichert, Sybille (eds) (1998) *Emerging European Policy Profiles of Higher Education Institutions*, Kassel: Wissenschaftliches Zentrum für Berufs- und Hochschulforschung der Universität Gesamthochschule Kassel.

Trow, Martin (1993) 'Comparative perspectives on British and American higher education', in *The European and American University since 1800: Historical and Sociological Essays*, ed. Sheldon Rothblatt and Björn Wittrock, Cambridge: Cambridge University Press, 280–299.

Van Houten, Peter (1996) 'The university and the constitutional convention of 1878', in *The University in the 1870s*, ed. Carroll Brentano and Sheldon Rothblatt, Berkeley, CA: Center for Studies in Higher Education and Institute of Governmental Studies.

Vom Bruch, Rüdiger (1997) 'A slow farewell to Humboldt? Stages in the history of German universities, 1810–1945', in *German Universities Past and Future: Crisis or Renewal?*, ed. Mitchell G. Ash, Providence, RI, and Oxford: Berghahn Books, 3–27.

Withrington, Donald J. (1999) 'Ideas and ideals in university reform in early 19th-Century Britain: A Scottish perspective', in *The European Legacy*, 4 (December), Cambridge, MA: MIT Press.

Ziman, John (1968) *Public Knowledge: The Social Dimension of Science*, Cambridge: Cambridge University Press.

——(1996) 'Is Science Losing its Objectivity?', *Nature*, 282 (29 August), 751–754.

Part I

Systems, Institutions and Students

2 Strategy and Management for University Development

Alan Wilson

Introduction

How can we think about strategy and management for universities in the Millennium – for time horizons like 2020 or 2050? Forecasting can be either normative or predictive: what ought to be, or what will be. Predictive forecasting is feasible for the short run – but, for complex systems, more or less impossible for the long run. A normative approach at least allows speculation and exploration, and this will be the one adopted here. However, to make sense of this, it is still necessary to make some predictions about the environment of universities, and in this case we can start from the here and now, because the elements which are likely to be important for universities in the future are already visible.

We begin, therefore, in the following section of this chapter, with an analysis of the environment of universities. It is then argued that any speculation about the future of universities must be rooted in an analysis of academic structure. This provides a platform for the analysis of strategy and management in turn. The threads of the argument are drawn together in a concluding section. Inevitably, much of the argument will be rather assertive, and the reader's indulgence is requested at the outset. The conjecture is that detailed supporting arguments could be supplied given appropriate levels of space and skill!

The chapter is written from the perspective of a university with two prime kinds of activity: research, and teaching and learning in an atmosphere of research. This level of specification, however, still begs all the questions: what kinds of research and teaching? For whom? And then: how to encompass the inevitably partial answers to these questions into a strategy for development? Finally: what are the management priorities? For each of these questions, we can explore the likely (or possible) differences between present and future.

Alan Wilson

The Environment of Universities

An easily agreed starting point is to argue that universities are concerned with the conservation, communication and creation of knowledge. The first of these roles is not directly associated with research or teaching, but is a necessary precondition in some instances. (An issue for an electronically-networked future is the extent to which archival and 'library' resources can be more cheaply and effectively provided from some 'central' source.) It is much less easy to agree what constitutes 'knowledge' in this context. This opens up a number of value questions – indeed, philosophical questions. For example, is there some objective set of knowledge foundations which universities have a responsibility to maintain and extend? A positive answer to these questions will identify roles for universities that complement more instrumental and vocational ones. It is probably then relatively easy to argue that both kinds of knowledge are appropriate in a university setting; the more difficult question is to judge the balance of resource allocated between the core and the professional (or vocational).

These prior issues are important considerations in characterizing the environment. Universities have always been concerned both with the professions and with core knowledge that might be characterized as scholarship. In an elite university system, the vocational role could be defined in terms of the 'higher' professions; in a mass system, as participation rates have grown, a much larger percentage of the workforce is being university educated and inevitably, the vocational emphasis has shifted towards utility and employability.

These broad questions are concerned with the role of universities in society, and the answers will be determined through social processes – for example, the extent to which there are social obligations (in the area earlier defined as scholarship) over and above roles in the economy. These social processes will include the sometimes conflicting demands of different kinds of stakeholders – students, parents, employers, research funders, and so on. The issues of what constitutes core and professional knowledge cannot be divorced from questions of interest and importance, which are inevitably subjective. If we take the adjective 'academic' to define what is important and interesting for universities, then in the next section, I will argue that universities should be concerned with – at the core – the big systems: physical, biological and human (economic, geographical and social). In the professions, this knowledge can be applied in the key sectors of the economy: industry, education, health, transport, financial, legal, and so on. These interests combine in the big issues of the day: globalization and the associated political agenda, the environment, urban and regional development, social exclusion, the organization of business, the role of the arts and the future of work. We must also speculate on not just the knowledge base of the future – which will be research driven – but also on how that can be communicated: universities will be changed by technology as much as other institutions.

These contexts define the environment of universities. The rapid rate of change in contemporary societies means that this kind of agenda – and the associated demands of different kinds of stakeholders – changes ever faster, and this hugely complicates the tasks of defining appropriate strategies and management systems for the universities of the future. Can we identify, on the basis of the analysis so far, a set of issues to be confronted?

The knowledge-based sector of the economy will be the fastest growing and most important; and universities will play an ever-increasing role in its development. The work patterns in this economy will demand certain skill sets in graduates.

To the extent that universities do not meet the demands of a knowledge-based economy, others will; the development of professional trainers and corporate universities illustrate the possibilities. In the long run, however, the number of jobs may fall, and universities may have more emphasis placed on another role: maintaining 'civilized' or 'educated' values – again, begging many questions.

The funders of universities will make their judgments on what is needed and what can be afforded. They will be partly accountable to the variety of stakeholders who have interests in university development. A division of labour will evolve between the university sector and what can be considered either as competition or as partners – depending on the perspective to be adopted. Will corporate universities become 'real' universities, awarding their own degrees – in effect deregulating universities' degree awarding powers?

Academic Structure

Decisions about directions of change in the strategy of universities, and their management structures, should be made in the context of a position on academic development in the sense defined above: how should the knowledge system be structured in research universities, and what are the developmental priorities?

It is not too difficult to articulate an approach to the basic disciplines of universities from first principles, building on the above argument about major systems of interest, the professions and the big issues. There is one preliminary issue: it can be argued that there are key enabling disciplines which are obviously interesting in their own right but which also facilitate the development of other disciplines. The most obvious examples are mathematics and computer science, though philosophy also provides another example; the language disciplines in part play this role, but mainly, in universities, as a bridge to the study of a variety of cultures.

The major systems are the physical, biological and social sciences, and the humanities, each of which can be subdivided (and then further subdivided) in a variety of ways. For example, the physical sciences obviously include physics and chemistry; and chemistry further subdivides into, say, physical, inorganic and organic, the last of these showing the beginnings of an overlap into the biological sciences. The humanities provide a special case. A discipline involving literature, for example, involves a very different methodological approach to a corresponding social science discipline that relates to essentially the same subject matter – a particular society. There are more specialist disciplines which often combine the skills and concepts of a number of core disciplines through a particular focus: archaeology is a good example. We can then add the professional disciplines: engineering, medicine, education and law are good examples, and each of these has its own structure. There is, of course, an intimate connection between core and professional disciplines. An appropriate set of core disciplines, in each case, provides the science foundation for the professional discipline. In universities at the present time, there is often an emphasis in professional disciplines on providing their own science base. The classification of disciplines through definitions of major systems is not, of course, exact. There are disciplines such as geography or psychology that straddle the major groups.

It is also important to recognize that, while disciplines can partly be defined in a relatively objective way through systems' concepts, they should also be recognized as socially defined coalitions and are maintained as such (see Becher, 1989, on academic 'tribes'). He quotes one of his interviewees: 'When under attack, chemists draw their wagons into a circle, and then start firing into the middle'. We can also note (from a broader context), Bailey (1977):

> Each tribe has a name and a territory, settles its own affairs, goes to war with the others, has a distinct language or at least a distinct dialect and a variety of other ways of demonstrating its apartness from others.

In some cases, closely related disciplines have such different perspectives that it is a difficult task fully to reconcile them: economics and accountancy provide an example. New discoveries can create new systems' foci and new coalitions: biochemistry and molecular biology are obvious examples. At any one time, some new problems can be tackled only through combinations of skills from current disciplines, and these are the interdisciplinary areas of the time. Some of these new areas – biochemistry again – become established as new disciplines.

It is against this kind of framework that it is necessary to make judgments about new academic developments. This is particularly difficult in the context of the knowledge explosion: building appropriate structures for universities, choosing research priorities and deciding what to teach. We consider each of these issues in turn.

Future development will in part be determined by how effectively research priorities are established. Each academic unit will have a substantial number of research groups (which may be individual researchers in some cases), and it is the relative investment in these groups that represents priorities. In universities, the possibility of making these judgments is an important element of academic freedom. The knowledge explosion and the pace of change create particular problems in determining teaching priorities. It is no longer possible to teach 'everything' in a discipline, and so it is necessary to establish core concepts and to provide a framework within which students can progress to lifelong learning – supported by the appropriate technology.

Strategy

Academic Development

We begin by building on the analysis of academic structure to work out a strategy for academic development. It is a safe bet that the core disciplines associated with the major systems have a long-term future. However, this probably becomes an even safer bet if the structure can be engineered in such a way that the units are relatively large: this facilitates interaction between sub-disciplines and allows for the reallocation of resources within the larger units as priorities change. It also seems to be a safe bet that what will often be recognized as the most important problems at any one time will be interdisciplinary. This is partly because the core disciplines need each other – biologists need physicists and chemists, for example. And it is partly because what were described as the big issues in the environment, such as the study of cities, are so large and complex that they can only be effectively tackled using the skills of many disciplines. We will consider the appropriate management structures in the next section.

So far so good – but how are things going to look different in 2020 or 2050? I would still expect to find core academic units in faculties or schools of physical sciences, biological sciences, social sciences and the humanities. I would still expect to find disciplines such as physics and chemistry and history and English within these areas. However, I would expect to see the fruits of more interaction between disciplines which share the same subject matter. Could history and the social sciences ever merge? Is history the social science of particular periods? Whither cultural studies? To some extent, these questions can be addressed relatively objectively. We can see the validity of different perspectives – of method, place and time, for instance – but we can see from the present situation that narrowly defined disciplines must represent a sub-optimum approach to understanding. This arises, at least in part, from the argument that disciplines are social coalitions; historians, for example, while having a legitimate focus on past periods, restrict their range of methods unnecessarily.

There would still be specialist disciplines, and a structure that supported a large number of interdisciplinary enterprises. An advantage of larger schools is that this kind of work would be facilitated, though there will always be areas which can function only across faculty boundaries. I would expect to find more and larger interdisciplinary centres focused on the big issues of the day. Some of these are obvious, but no less important for that – such fields as environmental or communications or urban studies. Others are less obvious, combining the experience of particular research areas with the skills of key enabling disciplines: the study of complex systems and the further development of mathematical modelling are examples.

I would hope to find major differences in the ways in which professional education was conducted. All professions need a knowledge base, and this can be subdivided between what can be called the 'science' foundations (meaning something slightly broader than the conventional) and the practice base. We can then learn a lot from what is done now in various areas and speculate on how it can be done better. In each case, there is an element of apprenticeship: some learning must be through practice in the profession's environment. It is interesting to observe the current differences between professions in this respect and to try to disentangle the extent to which there are good reasons for the differences, or whether they represent out-of-date practices reinforced by social coalitions. (And, of course, the social coalitions are often institutionalized, as with the medical Royal Colleges or the engineering institutions.) The situations are complex and here it is only possible to give what may amount to caricatures.

In medical education, there is a clear division between the pre-clinical and clinical training – say two years of the former and three years of the latter. Pre-clinical learning will typically be the responsibility of biologists; clinical, of practising doctors in a teaching hospital. And yet, within a school of medicine, there will be a considerable science base, accelerating in the shift towards genetic medicine. For the students, there is a smooth progression to on-the-job specialist training after graduation. A similar argument can be put for professions associated with medicine. The argument is further complicated by the need to connect medical practice with teaching and research on how that practice is best delivered – the field of health services research. In engineering, undergraduate education is usually more science-based, with less industrial practice built into the course. Specialisms are usually built into the degree course, based around the agenda of the engineering Institutions – mechanical, electronic and electrical, civil, and so on. Education is something of a special case. Schoolteachers at an advanced level have to 'know' a subject and it can be argued that a degree in that subject followed by a postgraduate teaching qualification is the best basis; though an alternative is clearly an undergraduate course which combines the subject and educational skills. That might be particularly appropriate for primary education. Similar analyses can be carried out in relation to professions like architecture, social work, law and the church. Business is also a special case. Business schools are partly concerned with the education of managers for industry, and partly with research on business – very different kinds of activity. There is an analogy with education: the courses can be either undergraduate, or postgraduate – in this case following almost any other degree, partly because such a wide range of skills are appropriate as a background in various roles in different kinds of industry.

Before drawing conclusions, two general comments are useful. It can be argued that the kinds of thinking skills that are appropriate to professional practice are fundamentally different from the traditional analytical skills of academe. They typically involve the synthesis of very different elements of knowledge, and some kind of problem-solving, as in medical diagnosis or engineering design. Medical students learn these skills by working with practitioners as part of their course. Engineering students usually only begin to learn these skills in employment.

There is also an argument to be put about systems and systemic thinking. Systems' concepts have been used in the argument above to define, for example, the major disciplines. It can also be argued that there is a more fundamental issue to be confronted: that academic knowledge has mainly been built from reductionist perspectives and that too little work – research or teaching – involves a systemic view. Of course, the reductionist approach has been remarkably successful, for example in molecular biology and elementary particle physics. But it can now be argued that some of the big questions for the future are essentially systemic: the brain, computers, economies, cities, and engineering and medical practice, for instance. Not only do these represent relatively neglected fields for analysis in academe, but it can be argued that, because students are not trained to adopt a systemic viewpoint (which need not be exclusive!), there is a loss of effectiveness in professional practice.

Can we anticipate or plan for, on the basis of this analysis, any major changes in academic structure, reflecting academic development priorities, in the new millennium? I would argue that radical changes are desirable; it is more difficult to judge whether they will be achieved. In a number of areas, it may be possible to strengthen the knowledge base through integration, and the professional base through separation, and the recognition that a different kind of thinking is involved. Would it be sensible to have a school of biological and medical sciences (integration), for instance, with the school of medicine focusing on clinical practice (separation)? There are obvious advantages of scale on the science side, but it would also be necessary to facilitate science-practice links in joint research teams because, of course, there are critical elements of medical research which depend on access to patients. There must also be an argument for further development of systems' thinking in clinical practice: the tendency to increasing specialization is almost certainly making aspects of medical diagnosis more difficult.

In engineering, there are signs on the industry side of an explicit demand for systems engineers. The major companies are working on very large systems – for example aircraft. This need at present is being largely met by training within industry, though in such areas as civil engineering, it is reflected in universities through an increasing emphasis on areas such as construction management and project management. There must be an argument for breaking down some of the divisions between the traditional engineering departments and possibly refocusing engineering departments more on systems and practice; and developing engineering science separately – possibly, if the medical analogue holds, in conjunction, with physical sciences. (Though in the context of biotechnology, this should include biological sciences as well.)

These arguments can be replicated for other areas: the social sciences in relation to the big social problems for example; arts departments in relation to the arts' 'industries'. In some areas, the focus of change would be on greater working together (systems again) and on enhancing links with practice outside universities. This may be particularly important for business schools. In effect, if there was more focus on professional practice, then the 'teaching hospitals' model' may be more widely applicable.

Research

The first step in the argument is to remind ourselves that the discussion above about academic structure – disciplines, specialisms, interdisciplinarity, the big issues – provides the platform for a discussion of research strategy, since research is concerned with new knowledge within this framework. We should also note that the argument about disciplines as, to some extent, social coalitions also applies here: research priorities are in part determined by the ecology and history of research groups. Ultimate success is determined in the markets of the global economy of knowledge, and in general these are efficient mechanisms for making the judgments about importance and interest. However, there are areas – the development of a rather abstract and arid branch of mathematical economics for instance – which seem to have been maintained by an inward looking coalition. It is also worth recognizing in the British situation that the research assessment exercise has a downside in relation to the evolution of appropriate structures to facilitate research: it is strongly focused on existing disciplines and implicitly discourages ambition and adventure in the development of interdisciplinary groups.

The second preliminary step in the argument is to review kinds of research, say on a basic ('blue-skies')–strategic–applied spectrum. Traditionally, university research has been more concerned with basic; industry more with applied. Fundamental research should remain a key university role. The freedom to choose will depend on the maintenance of the dual funding system in the UK, since research council programmes are likely to be increasingly thematic and prioritized. The themes are likely to be connected to what I have called the big issues and will drive university groups increasingly towards interdisciplinarity. However, given the continually increasing pace of change, the difference between the basic and the applied ends of the spectrum will be less marked. Also, research universities are interested in developing their own IPR, and so will in any case add more 'applied' to the 'basic'. And there are more universities in the research market, some of whom are more attracted to applied research. Finally, industry is increasingly seeing research outsourcing as a possibility.

The third step in the argument is to pose the question: what kinds of research are universities best at? There is clearly an argument for maintaining a framework within which some universities are funded to do 'blue-skies' basic research on a 'free' basis. History shows this mode to have been very productive, though it is not easy to see why particular major discoveries are made in particular places at particular times. But a research base must be maintained to ensure that these possibilities remain. It is also the case that a base of scholarship must be maintained in research universities. This can be seen as a corollary of this argument; or simply as the need to maintain a certain style of teaching in at least some universities. However, there are problems in some instances – for example where very expensive equipment or very large teams are needed. Then, universities may not be the best place – though even in that case, university groups may be able to work with other players, whether through organizations like CERN or in partnership with, say, the pharmaceutical industry.

This argument, combined with that of the preceding section, provides a clear basis for some elements of strategy for a research university. First, the basic core must be maintained and enhanced. We should recall the earlier discussion that implies a need to switch resources from the reductionist to the systemic. Second, there should be more opportunity for the development of interdisciplinary research on major problems. The scale of effort (and equipment in many cases) needed for this research will demand more work in partnerships – or much of the most interesting research will be conducted outside universities. Third, effective means must be found for bolting on applied research teams, again usually in partnerships with organizations outside universities.

Teaching and Learning

We have already noted that the knowledge explosion has consequences for teaching and learning: not 'everything' can be taught within a discipline. It is necessary to focus on key concepts and examples that develop knowledge power in each student. We need a measure of progression that recognizes the ability of each student to cope with 'difficulty', for depth of understanding to be increased, for minds to be stretched. But this has to be done in such a way as to provide capability and flexibility of mind for the future. It has become fashionable to build 'transferable skills' into degree courses – concerned, for example, with writing ability, numeracy, languages perhaps, and communication. This argument is often put in relation to 'employability', but fortunately, these skills also enhance academic capability. The argument can be extended, however: knowledge power could be enhanced in many cases by freeing a significant percentage of time in programmes to add the bones of key ideas, particularly of enabling disciplines combined with systemic perspectives from other disciplines. This would provide a platform for interdisciplinary thinking in some future graduates.

Teaching and associated learning environments are already being considerably enhanced through technology: for example, multimedia interactive software extends the concept of the 'book'. The notion of the 'library' will broaden enormously. Teaching will be more widely available on a global basis, and this leads to the idea of lecturers as learning managers, perhaps more actively in collaboration with new kinds of librarian. Since this kind of delivery is via a PC workstation, the student is no longer tied to the university campus, and perhaps the most dramatic change in the university environment will be the percentage of students who are off-campus for most of the time. I would still expect the 18-plus cohorts to be on campus for three years, but there should be an enormous expansion in off-campus continuing education to meet future needs. Much of the continuing education will be in partnership with external organizations and will meet their needs as well as those of individuals.

Again, the key elements of strategy follow from this preliminary analysis. First, there will be a continuing need for revisions of, and paring down of, disciplinary curricula, with additions to increase the knowledge power of the graduating student. Second, there will be considerable investment in the IT basis of teaching and learning, with new kinds of electronic libraries, access to teaching resources on a global scale. Lecturers will continue to be scholars and researchers, but might have less of a teaching role and more of a learning-management role. Of course, many will contribute to the multimedia world as they now write books. What is not known is the extent of direct student–teacher contact that is necessary to achieve full understanding; a reasonable conjecture is that this will remain important, certainly in the 'difficult' disciplines like mathematics, but that this contact is more likely to be through tutorial teaching rather than conventional lecturing. Third, it is necessary to plan for a major expansion in the facilities for continuing education and the associated student constituencies. It will perhaps be particularly in this third area that research universities will be able to make a major contribution to widening access to higher education – though, in collaboration with schools and FE colleges, there will be change in the 18-plus core as well.

Technology: The Networked University

We have already seen, in the context of teaching and learning, that some of the biggest changes for universities will stem from further advances in IT. In that case, two key trends come together: a capacity for interactive networking which will connect any university to a global audience and the development of multimedia material. Interactive collaboration at a distance will also be important in research. Such collaborations already exist, and the relevant systems have been well tested. A key element of strategy will be the investment in the infrastructure that facilitates these developments.

Management

What kinds of management structures and systems are needed to implement these strategies? We can start from where we are now. A university needs a strong internal structure that includes a capability to interact with appropriate elements of its external environment. The central management of the university has a number of key roles: ranging from defining systems and 'rules', through accounting and resource allocation, to the developmental. However, the key internal elements will be the faculties, schools or departments – with the terminology indicating decreasing size. Since universities are typically large and complex, management responsibility for teaching and research (and most key functions) will be devolved to these kinds of units – as this kind of structure is both the most effective as well as the most efficient. In universities at present, different judgments are made about the size of the devolved units. If devolution is to faculties, then this may imply a further management layer – to schools or departments. For simplicity, assume that it is possible to achieve devolution to a single layer, and that this should be made up of schools. Some schools may have subsidiary departments to represent disciplines. However such a structure is created, some interdisciplinary work will involve crossing boundaries, and this is usually achieved through the development of centres or institutes. It may still be helpful to have faculties for specific purposes, such as teaching quality control (which should be at a level broader than the school), and to encourage interdisciplinary development.

In the case of Leeds University, the devolution is to 27 schools. The history of the evolution to this point is probably not untypical. In the mid-1980s, there were 96 departments, each with considerable autonomy, though within a centrally-planned system. When the devolved system was introduced around 1990, the number of 'resource centres' – schools or departments – was around 55. This was reduced to 27 schools at the start of the 1997–98 academic year. This structure is supported by highly professional management in both the central administration and schools – managements which are still nonetheless accountable to the wider academic community and the university's governing body through Senate and Council and the associated (relatively streamlined) committee structure.

Will this kind of structure still be found in 2020 or 2050? Devolved structures are almost certainly here to stay: they represent the strongest structures for large and complex organizations. There will also always be a tension between the core schools and interdisciplinary centres and institutes. This follows from the analysis of academic structure – that there is no way of defining a relatively small number of schools or departments in such a way that there are no longer any 'inter'-disciplinary issues. So I would guess that a large research university will have around 30 schools and 50 or more inter-disciplinary centres. I would also guess that similar structures of accountability will be in place. Mintzberg (1983) shows that for what he calls professional bureaucracies, such as hospitals or universities, the profes-sionals will always want to have a say in the management. However, this argument does not imply that everything will be the same, and so we should now focus on the differences.

It was argued in the section 'Academic Development' that the core academic structures could change, particularly with a new division of labour between science and professional disciplines. This is likely to happen in some institutions. Whether it does or not in a formal sense, there is a need for much greater collaboration – for example between engineering science and practice, between biological and medical sciences. And there are new development needs – for more systemic approaches in various disciplines, for instance – engineering and medicine again providing good examples. Whether change is to come about through new structures or, as is perhaps more likely, through new collaborations and interdisciplinary enterprises, achieving the potential is a major management challenge.

A part of this challenge is for management to be sufficiently fleet of foot to be able to respond quickly as the need arises. The present signs are not good in this respect – not because the management systems are themselves slow, but because very tight funding in universities does not provide an adequate investment margin. For example, how many universities have responded fully to the consequences of the converging technologies in telecommunications, media and IT? The challenge, therefore, is to recognize these needs and – through partnerships or otherwise – to identify the invest-ment which will support the new development. So, through these processes, the universities of the future will certainly be very different. We can all speculate, as I did in the section above on 'Academic Development', on what these directions of development might be. What needs hard thought now is how to develop our management structures to provide our universities with the capability to be in the right place in the future.

We can perhaps summarize what is needed in broad terms as follows:

- academic excellence
- speed of response
- collaboration through partnerships
- investment in appropriate infrastructure
- the highest quality staff (a need which has been implicit throughout the argument).

Universities have always had their share of the brightest talents, and if this can be maintained, then academic excellence will be maintained. I will return to this issue below. We should add to this, however, that the pace of academic change will continue to accelerate and the academics of the future will need to develop their own responses to this challenge. This will be facilitated by collaboration, both to extend the intellectual range and depth of a particular university and to focus and integrate investment through partnerships. What can this mean in terms of the management challenge? Investment in infrastructure will be a precondition. We can already see that the power of the Internet will be extended (as in Leeds) through concepts such as virtual science parks and virtual knowledge parks. This needs to be matched by investment in new kinds of partnership building. In Leeds, for example, we have established an Institute for Corporate Learning, which is within the Business School but which has university-wide responsibilities to enhance external connectivity. University companies provide other means of linkage. In the university of the future, I would expect to find many more of these kinds of institutions – some quite large – bolted on to the conventional academic structure. Some of these partnership-building activities, and the associated units, will need new kinds of staff and part of the ongoing management task will be to identify and to recruit these people and to attract them from their more conventional career paths. Some partnerships will additionally involve collaboration between universities – as in the White Rose Consortium of Leeds, Sheffield and York. Academics will also increasingly play direct roles in all of these kinds of activity. It has recently been argued that a major cultural change is needed (CVCP-Gatsby, 1999) and that American universities have already shown the way – fuelled by a tradition of one-day-per-week of consulting or external profession activity and, frequently, nine-month salaries. All this means that career management for academics will be an increasingly important issue.

Can all this be achieved? Staff recruitment and retention are the critical issues. This cannot be divorced from the issue of academic salaries. It can be argued that the higher education system in the UK is at a bifurcation point – possibly with three branches. First, if academic salaries continue to decline relatively, then universities will be critically weakened and, even by 2020, they will be second- or third-best organizations with excellent teaching and research being conducted elsewhere – either in other countries or bolted on to industry. A second alternative is that universities will do slightly better than this with a small number of stars paid relatively well, but average salaries still too low. The third and desirable option is for the salaries' issue to be solved. If, as is likely, this cannot be achieved through public funding, then this will have to be solved within the universities themselves. The development of major partnerships, with staff in alliances being treated on an equal footing, could be a major contribution to a solution.

Conclusion

In this chapter, I have tried to offer a first-principles review of the strategic and management challenges facing research universities in the new millennium. I will now summarize the argument through the eyes of two other authors, the Swedish economist Åke Andersson and the American academic, Burton Clarke.

Andersson (1993) argued that the successful societies of the future would be C-societies with substantial communications, cognitive and creative capacities. Although a decade or more old, this argument still holds. Universities will play a major role in these societies. They clearly have the cognitive capabilities, and indeed for this reason alone, they should be treasured and supported by governments! They have substantial creative capacities and, again, it is a reasonable conjecture that enhancement of these capacities would be for the public good. They have good communications capacities in relation to their student constituencies and their current research funders. But it has been argued here that only a major expansion of their communications capacities through partnership building will enable them to be strong in the future. Andersson was writing about successful regions rather than universities, but he certainly saw higher education institutions as being critical components of these – and, of course, from the universities' point of view, this is one of the most important alliances to build. This is so, notwithstanding the argument that research universities are international first, national second and regional third: it is success on the broader geographical scales in the global economy of knowledge that makes a regional contribution potentially formidable. And, of course, universities can be more successful if surrounded by the thriving organizations of a vibrant region – Silicon Valley being perhaps the most striking example, with world-class universities such as Stanford having a symbiotic relationship with Palo Alto region.

Clark (1998) begins with an analysis of the current environment. He notes the existence of much more competition for universities and goes on to argue that universities face an overload of demands (essentially because resources cannot be made available in relation to the demands of the knowledge explosion), an under-supply of response capabilities and a limited financial base. He emphasizes his points by quoting Charles Vest, the President of MIT, as saying that universities are overextended, under-focused, over-stressed and under-funded. Clarke then argues for a strength-ened steering core, an expanded developmental periphery, a diversified funding base, a stimulated academic heartland and an integrated entrepreneurial culture – all in a devolved collegiate system. (However, he does argue that there is a need to 'unhook' collegialism from a defence of the status quo to a bias in favour of adaptiveness and change.)

This resonates very strongly with the argument of this chapter and can be taken as a valuable summary in different language. And I take it as support, because his argument is worked out from different evidence – from a survey of a number of universities in Europe and North America that he takes to be entrepreneurial – rather than experience in one research university. I have put a reassessment of academic development priorities at the top of the agenda, and I take this as consistent with his argument for a stimulated academic heartland. The rest of his bullet points are consistent with the strategic and management priorities I have argued for earlier in this chapter. If there is a downside to Clarke's argument, it is that he sees the change as a 10–15 year programme – 'though the outcome is priceless' – but not good for those of us who are more impatient.

So what will the university of 2020 (or 2050?) look like? It will have:

- a devolved collegiate structure
- an academic core with a recognizable 'ecological' trace back to the present
- a substantial number of interdisciplinary centres and institutes
- large schools, centres and institutes will mostly be better connected to wider constituencies than at present
- fundamental research will continue to expand in research universities, complemented by a large expansion of partnership-based applied research, and there will be symbiotic relationships between the two sectors
- there will be a growth in units such as institutes for corporate learning and university companies which are even more directly connected to partner organizations
- the on-campus students will be exceeded numerically by those who are mainly off-campus, connected by high-bandwidth networks and powerful interactive workstations
- the enterprise will be supported by excellent, well-paid staff with skills ranging from the core academic to the academic entrepreneur.

Can it be done? Some of this possible future can be seen now – the likely elements are all visible somewhere at least in embryonic form. The founda-tions are being laid; there will be a variety of ways forward. Only the arrival of 2020 or beyond will show us whether we have been successful.

Alan Wilson

References

Andersson, Å. E. (1993) 'Economic structure of the 21st century', in Å.E. Andersson, D. F. Batten, K. Kobayashi and K. Yoshikawa (eds) *The Cosmo-Creative Society: Logistical Networks in a Creative Economy*, Berlin: Springer-Verlag.

Bailey, F. G. (1977) *Morality and Expediency*, Oxford: Blackwell.

Becher, T. (1989) *Academic Tribes and Territories: Intellectual Enquiry and the Culture of Disciplines*, Milton Keynes: Open University Press.

Clark, B. (1998) *Creating Entrepreneurial Universities: Organizational Pathways of Transformation*, Oxford: Pergamon.

Committee of Vice-Chancellors and Principals–Gatsby Charitable Foundation (1999) *Technology Transfer: The US Experience*, London: CVCP.

Mintzberg, H. (1983) *Structure in Fives: Designing Effective Organisations*, Englewood Cliffs (NJ): Prentice-Hall.

3 The Distributed University

Roger Waterhouse

This is not an everyday story of farming folk. Nor is it really a story of rural deprivation in one of the most beautiful parts of England. Rather it is about a modern university attempting to respond to social and economic need, and in the process calling into question our inherited model of what a university should be like. Like many of the modern universities in the United Kingdom, the University of Derby had its roots deep in the local community. It was formed over a period of 150 years by the progressive amalgamation of specialist colleges. By the early 1990s it was a comprehensive institution offering a broad spectrum of undergraduate and postgraduate courses in most of the major fields of knowledge. It was, however, still proud of its origins, and determined to retain its commitment to serving the locality. About a quarter of its students came from Derbyshire, and another 25 per cent from elsewhere in the East Midlands. It had a large number of part-time students, and all courses were available to be studied on a part-time as well as a full-time basis. The majority of its students were over 21 on entry, and it was proactive in encouraging adult learners to return to study.

This orientation was reflected in both the content and the structure of its curriculum, and in its internal organization. Most programmes of study were broadly vocational in nature, and covered the full spectrum of professions from engineers to nurses by way of teachers, accountants, geologists and designers. In response to the needs of these professions the university had retained and extended its range of 'sub-degree' qualifications. It had also developed a thoroughgoing credit accumulation system which actually did enable students to accumulate credits over a period of time towards diploma and degree awards. It ensured particularly that those mature and part-time students for whom the intensive three-year full-time course was not a practical possibility could nevertheless gain qualifications and continue learning.

The whole of the curriculum was modular in structure. Students were able to opt for programmes which were highly flexible and could be reoriented as their own learning process or career aspirations evolved. We early adopted a 'learning outcomes' approach to all modules. In each case there was a specification of the knowledge and skills which the successful student could expect to attain, and our internal validation mechanisms ensured that both modes of delivery and forms of assessment were appropriate to the intended outcomes. This inevitably challenged some long-established academic practices, but we saw it as particularly important in fulfilling our side of the learning contract. It has stood us in good stead in moving towards a culture where all students are more conscious that they are purchasing our services, and are becoming more aware of their rights as consumers. Credit accumulation systems, whose objective is to deliver bespoke programmes to suit the individual clients' needs, require sophisticated and transparent administrative systems. At Derby we invested heavily in these. Compared with many UK universities we would be regarded as a centralized university. Decisions are taken collectively in accordance with the overall mission, and the schools of the university all have the common framework of policies and procedures within which they must work.

Many of our students are first-generation graduates. They come from families where the parents had not the opportunity nor, in some cases, the inclination to aspire to the social elite. In many cases the careers chosen by the students would not have been graduate professions a generation ago. There is, therefore, a backlog of underdeveloped talent in the communities which we serve, and older members of families are frequently stimulated to return to study by the success of the younger ones. We have, therefore, for a long time provided structures which enabled older or disadvantaged students to access higher education. Some of these we provide in-house by way of 'access' or foundation courses. But essential to our way of working has been the development of a network of partnerships across our region. We have a series of compact agreements with schools and colleges designed particularly to facilitate the progression into higher education of able but disadvantaged individuals. Whilst the primary targets of these agreements are young school students, the secondary and increasingly important targets are the parents, particularly where the domestic or cultural environment is not encouraging – for example, Asian women.

Integrating Further and Higher Education

More important in terms of accessing the 700,000 adults we estimate live within our heartland is the Derbyshire Regional Network – a network which includes all the further education colleges in Derbyshire except the north-eastern corner (and beyond the county, including east Staffordshire). Throughout the early 1990s the University of Derby worked with partner colleges on a variety of collaborative schemes to enable students to access higher levels of study. These were typically delivered on college premises distributed across the region, and included preparatory courses for higher education (access courses), foundation courses, franchised parts (typically the first year) of degree or higher diploma programmes, or complete higher diploma programmes delivered jointly by the university and college. In the mid-1990s this plethora of bilateral projects crystallized into the more formal structure of the Derbyshire Regional Network.

The network was founded on the collective resolve to develop and implement a comprehensive credit accumulation framework, spanning the full range of work in both the colleges and the university. The ideal was a single integrated system through which the student could progress. At the lowest level it would start with basic literacy and numeracy. At the highest it would reach the lofty heights of the PhD. As with the university's existing credit framework, the objective was to produce bespoke programmes to suit the needs of an individual or indeed an employer. We already knew that some college students were enrolling at the university to take one or two higher level courses, whilst university postgraduates were enrolling at colleges on basic skills courses which had not been included in their first degree. The objective was to offer the individual a menu of units which could encompass that diverse range of needs within a single system. As far as employers were concerned, we could offer to satisfy all their training needs from a single source.

First, the credit framework itself was designed and developed in some degree of detail. The next step was to articulate the content, and this is where the great benefit emerged for the further education providers. Unlike universities, further education colleges are not awarding bodies in their own right. They prepare students for a wide variety of qualifications variously assessed by a whole host of recognized awarding bodies. In an area such as business studies, for example, a college might be offering courses leading to the awards of City and Guilds, Royal Society of Arts, BTEC/EdExcel and several of the A level awarding boards. Different students want different awards. There are large degrees of syllabus overlap but ultimately discrete examinations. The credit accumulation framework, with learning outcomes as an intrinsic part of it, enables these different curricula to be split into small units each of which is credit-bearing. A common unit can be commonly taught, and the college can strike a judicious balance between increasing the efficiency of the teaching operation on the one hand, and broadening the range of opportunities to the student on the other. Only those parts of the curriculum which are specific to a particular awarding body need be taught separately in (perhaps uneconomic) small groups. The credit framework, therefore, produces three benefits – increased efficiency for the college, increased range of choice for the student, and certificated accreditation of successful learning even where this is not accumulated into a national award. By participating in the unitization of the FE curriculum, the university has ensured that a very broad range of activities already going on in the colleges is effectively made into access routes into higher education. Which brings me to the next part of the story.

A Comprehensive University

In the summer of 1998, the university and one of the colleges in the network took the concept of the single comprehensive system to its next logical step and merged into a single organization. The college was High Peak College just outside Buxton. The college draws students from all over Derbyshire and indeed beyond, but particularly serves the northern districts of the High Peak and the Derbyshire Dales. Which is where the farming folk come in. For those who do not know Derbyshire well, it sits at the southern end of the Pennine mountain range, at the point where highland northern Britain meets lowland southern Britain. It encompasses some very beautiful and very varied scenery. It falls roughly into three regions – the Dark Peak characterized by high moorland and rocky outcrops in the north, the White Peak consisting of limestone uplands with gorges, caverns and hill farms, and the Lowlands south and west of Derby which are altogether more lush. Much of the north lies in the Peak National Park – the first such park to be established in the United Kingdom. It is the most visited National Park in the world (after Mount Fuji), with 22 million visitors per year. The vast majority of visitors come from the surrounding conurbations of south and west Yorkshire, Manchester, Stoke, Nottingham and Derby. Whilst the stated aim of both institutions was to serve the people of Derbyshire, the catchment areas of the university and the college were largely complementary. Most Derbyshire students attending the university have their homes in the south or the centre of the county. Most Derbyshire students attending the college have their homes in the centre and the north. An objective in developing a comprehensive education system for the hundreds of thousands of adults in this region was to distribute the opportunities for both further and higher education more evenly throughout the rural areas.

The 1992 legislation which brought both the Further and the Higher Education Funding Councils into existence charged the former – the FEFC – with ensuring an 'adequacy and sufficiency' of further education throughout the country. No such responsibility was placed upon the Higher Education Funding Council – it obviously not occurring to the then government that access to higher education was a right which should be widely available across the country. Effectively, in its mission to serve the adult population of its region the merged University of Derby was taking upon itself the responsibility to provide for the 'adequacy and sufficiency' of both further and higher education on its patch – which presents a major challenge.

The Economic Base

Historically three main industries have dominated the economy of the High Peak and the Derbyshire Dales – agriculture, mining and quarrying, and manufacturing. All three industries are in long-term decline, which has had drastic effects on the rural economy, on communities and not least on employment opportunities. Much of the area is officially designated by the European Union as one of severe rural deprivation. Hill farmers, often using marginal land, already had their problems before being severely hit by the BSE crisis and more recently a collapse in the market for lamb. Forthcoming reforms in the Common Agricultural Policy are more likely to exacerbate than alleviate their situation.

Derbyshire lead mining, a major industry from time immemorial, ceased earlier this century, whilst coal in the east collapsed within very recent memory. Mineral extraction, processing and quarrying continues (often to the detriment of the natural environment) but is largely conducted by national and multinational firms employing very few quarrymen and putting little back into the local economy. Textile manufacturing, on which the prosperity of the industrial towns of north-west Derbyshire was based, is almost at an end. The last mill in New Mills is closing as I write. Other forms of manufacturing, where they survive, employ less workers but demand higher and higher skills. The potential for economic development to offset this decline in the traditional areas, is limited. It is focused upon service industries, light manufacturing which can be IT based, and tourism. In all these cases the skill base of the workforce needs considerable and continuous enhancement.

In an area known for its natural beauty, the development of tourism presents a particular challenge. The Peak District may be the most visited National Park in the United Kingdom, but the 22 million visitors per year on average spend only 62p each. The vast majority of them are day trippers. They come to walk, to cycle, to climb rocks, to go canoeing or simply to enjoy the scenery. They do not come to eat a dinner or a lunch; they do not require a bed for the night; they do not go shopping – in short, they do not come to spend. Currently they bring relatively little benefit to the local economy, and 95 per cent of them come in cars. This presents a major traffic problem, particularly in the summer months, when private motorists add to the problems caused by quarry wagons and tractors. The watchword is 'sustainable tourism', and if anywhere needs an integrated transport strategy it is the Peak District of Derbyshire. The challenge for the tourist industry is essentially how to attract people from farther afield. Unlike the Lake District, which attracts nearly 20 per cent of its visitors from London and the south east, Derbyshire attracts hardly any from outside its immediate hinterland.

The Learning Revolution

The University of Derby has developed the organization and infrastructure to begin to address the long-term needs of the communities which it aims to serve. But just as those other industries in our area have been transformed by technological and economic change, we believe that our own industry is in the early stages of a similar change process. If we are to build a robust provision for the twenty-first century we must think clearly about the direction in which our industry is heading. The first major factor impinging upon us is technology. It is widely recognized that computers and all they entail are vastly increasing our access to information. The problem is not now too little information but too much – not how to find the information, but how to search it, select it, analyse it and present it – in short, how to use it. Instant access to information is in process of transforming the increasing number of knowledge-based industries, and changing the skills needed by workers in those industries. If the popular concept of knowledge is 'knowing the facts', it has never been less important. Skills of interpretation and understanding – popularly part of what counts as wisdom – have never been more so.

Universities which work closely with employers will be aware of their changing needs. Recently the political rhetoric has emphasized 'employability' at all levels of education with its stress on skills and social interaction. Any course of further or of higher education which takes employability seriously must examine, as we have done, the actual learning outcomes achieved and change its delivery and assessment mechanisms accordingly. And although so far the pedagogic practice of university lecturers has hardly been dented by the new technology, only ostriches could suppose that it will not be transformed over the coming years. Education and learning are essentially about communication. Someone said recently that for the first time in history the young have a greater understanding of the means of communication than their elders. The technology is changing the way they learn. The average teenage computer buff or net surfer knows an enormous amount, is highly skilled, and keeps up to date in a field that moves with unprecedented speed. But he or she has not learnt much of this from any adult, has not read the manual, and has not been extrinsically motivated by the aim of getting a qualification or earning more money. He or she has done it for fun, by playing (ie. experimenting), and by talking incessantly – usually electronically – with his/her peers. He or she belongs to a virtual, self-instructing community where the most important printed word is this month's glossy, electronically published, magazine.

At the University of Derby, in the autumn of 1997, we opened a huge new Learning Centre packed with computers, and we simultaneously wired all our Halls of Residence to give access to the Internet and thereby the worldwide web. From the day the centre opened we have had student complaints that it is inadequate to their needs. At a stroke we had quadrupled the availability of electronic learning support. The students expectations were far more than quadrupled. The Learning Centre is much more than just a huge computer laboratory/library. It was designed to facilitate group work both round screens and in break-out rooms. These tutorless groups do form without any guidance from their instructors. The group rooms are fully used throughout the week. Whether we like it or not, a transformation is taking place in the way in which students learn. What they are learning and the way in which they are learning it are giving them the skills they need for the new world of employment and beyond. Our problem as the providers in this service industry is how to overcome our conservatism and our caution and respond quickly enough to the need.

While the higher education wing of the University of Derby was responding to the technological expectations of the new youth, the further education wing through High Peak College was using technology to address a complementary problem. Hill farming was in crisis. An obvious response of those who wanted to stay in business was to diversify. The development of farm tourism was one of the few options available. But the whole of the tourist industry in Derbyshire is characterized by small and medium-sized enterprises (SMEs) – usually very small enterprises – operating on low margins. What was needed was collective action and some pump priming. This is where the college came in as a facilitator and trainer with the ability to access European funds. Working initially with 30 farms and then with a much larger group the college provided the support in business training, customer care, marketing and promotion. Key to the project's success was the creation of a website and electronic bookings system which enabled the farmers to access that part of the tourist market otherwise in very short supply in Derbyshire – the ones from further away who want to stay overnight.

Derbyshire Dales Farm Holidays, and Peak and Moorlands Farm Holidays have both become commercially successful, Internet-based, marketing organizations. Success has bred success, with small domestic units originally engaged solely in primary production transforming themselves into service industry sites. An allied development has been in farm products, with SMEs developing speciality foodstuffs or craft products marketed collaboratively via the Net. In all these developments the college has provided not only the technological skills, but also the increasingly sophisticated business training needs. In our model of the comprehensive university it is at the lower levels of knowledge and expertise that both the volume and the urgency of market need exists. The signs are that we are growing this on to higher levels as these service industries develop. There are, however, powerful countervailing forces at work at a national level.

Conservatism – the Higher Education Disease

Even a university like Derby, which takes pride in its responsiveness to local communities, was not unaffected by the strong pressures towards conformity which followed the ending of the binary line in higher education in 1992. Wealth attracts wealth, and the rewards go to those with the high research profile in accordance with a long-established national pecking order. We have prided ourselves on becoming ever more efficient by increasing productivity whilst simultaneously enhancing the quality of the students' learning experience. In spite of the liberal use of market rhetoric, particularly by the previous government but also by the present one, these commercial virtues are not rewarded by our system of public funding – indeed the very reverse. We have been forced to reduce higher education student numbers, thereby increasing our inefficiency and reducing student access, in order to avoid public embarrassment of our less efficient colleagues elsewhere. We do measure client satisfaction, and regard this as a much more important indicator of quality than the opinions of the teams of inspectors we get from the quality industry. (You may remember from your school days that even very young children are excellent judges of the quality of their teachers.) But what we have never done in any serious way is market research.

Supplier-driven Higher Education

As with the rest of higher education, we have always operated in a market totally dominated by the suppliers. The government, by the very definition of academic freedom, was not allowed to call the tune. The students, by the very definition of academic standards, were not allowed to either. For the most part students were young and inexperienced, grateful to have been admitted in the first place, delighted to survive, and privileged to get a degree. They were not even picking up the bill. Most importantly, higher education is a service industry in which the volume of the supply has been strictly limited by government to a level below that of qualified demand. We are not market-driven because for the bulk of our trading there is no market. The exceptional parts are, of course, part-time students, full fee payers and overseas students. For all but a few institutions, these categories are financially marginal to the main business of universities. We have, of course, thought about the demand for our courses. But with the exception of those few areas which over time have become unfashionable, we could always assume that, unless we got it very wrong, we would be able to fill the course. Course design, and to a large extent course content, was really no business of the student applicants. If they did not like it when they got here, they could flunk out or go elsewhere. That was not our fault. They were either too thick, too lazy, or schools were at fault in steering them towards the wrong choice.

Market-led Further Education

Further education had quite a different culture. It really was close to the market, and its funding regime in recent years has made it even more market-led. Not only did those in further education have to attract students in competition with schools and training providers, but they had to retain them and indeed achieve outcomes in order to get reasonable levels of funding. High Peak College did conduct market research. Admittedly it accessed European funding to do so, but it went out into the communities of the Peak and the Derbyshire Dales and worked with them to assess their education and training needs. Out of this came some specific projects. So called 'training clubs' were established in the Hope Valley, in Bakewell and in Ashbourne, again with the help of European money. These clubs, in modest physical premises, provided electronic learning support on an outreach basis right at the heart of the communities concerned. They were linked into the centre in Buxton, and video conferencing facilities meant that students at the remote sites could have face-to-face discussions with their tutors at the centre of the hub. The outcentres were staffed by learning facilitators whose job it was to help, but not in any conventional sense teach, the students. More recently two new, smaller outposts have been opened, one in a village pub, at Brassington, and the other in a village shop, at Ipstones. Essentially these provide only the electronic link without facilitators or other support workers on site. We know that we are serving the need, and are using the technology to do so. In the process we are challenging the model of how we should facilitate learning at any level.

Cyber-solutions

In addition to these elements of a distributed system, the university and the college together opened a 'cyber cafe' at a high street location in the centre of Matlock – a town of nearly 20,000 people. We called this 'The Dial' – Derbyshire Internet and Access to Learning. The facility is open from 8 until late, 7 days a week, and has in addition to a suite of computers, access to the worldwide web, the home site at the University of Derby, as well as an electronically supported seminar room and facilities for individual discussions with students. It is a well-used facility with regular as well as casual clients. Identified needs have tended to focus upon IT and basic business skills. Out of these and other initiatives has come the project we have called the 'University of Derby Online'. This is our version of the virtual university where a student can access not simply learning support materials of all sorts but the full range of services – tutorial, guidance, administrative, etc., which are provided for real in Derby and Buxton. We have been working on this project for the past two years, and parts of it are now going live. The concept is based very much on our situation and our mission to serve a particular region for its further and higher education needs. It is clearly not the traditional university offering, but nor is it a fully fledged distance learning university. Our ideal is to be able to offer to the individual student or employer a tailor-made solution to suit his or her individual circumstances. The essential goal is that the students should learn successfully. We will support that learning by a wide variety of means which yield a spectrum of opportunity. To the student willing and able to attend full time on a conventional basis, that option is available. However, for the student who cannot attend except at specific times, whose needs change, who can only afford the money or the time for short episodes of study, we aim to support that learning also. Through our credit accumulation system such learning episodes, however brief, can potentially be accumulated into a publicly recognized certification of achievement. So the support we offer may be in the flesh, print-based, online, CD-Rom, e-mail, interactive links and so on.

The limitation upon our ability to deliver to this format is primarily one of content. Academic staff are used to producing hand-outs, bibliographies, etc. in hard-copy form and of various qualities of production. We have been slowly encouraging them to produce comparable materials in electronic form. One barrier to overcome has been the assumption that any video of a lecture or presentation must be of broadcastable quality. The measure is fitness for purpose. Hard-copy hand-outs are usually fit-for-purpose but are not normally of textbook design quality. Another and more intransigent problem is the 'not-invented-here' syndrome. In spite of a wealth of good-quality learning support materials, on many subjects, there is often a reluctance by the teachers to make use of them. The learners have no such hangups. At its worst the disparity between the two attitudes can ultimately come down to one of supply-side control – 'I set the exam paper and mark it so you'd better learn it my way'. However, if we start with the near market position and attempt to serve the real needs of people, often in employment and often with scant resources to support their learning, we can approach the servicing of that need in a different way. We can use a variety of materials, we can use learning facilitators, tutorless groups, video conferencing, to maximize the value – that is to maximize the return on the investment which the individual learner is making.

The further challenge which the University of Derby Online is posing for us lies in the production of quite sophisticated, often interactive, learning materials. Academics, even experienced and seasoned teachers, do not innately have the skills of technical authorship. We have found it necessary to employ an increasingly large team of people who do have those skills. They work with the academics advising, guiding, writing and helping rewrite the materials. Mostly what we produce to date is in CD-Rom format although in principle it can all be available online. Ten years ago, we had virtually no such people as these technical authors, the learning support technicians in the Learning Centre, the learning facilitators and other support staff in the outcentres. Indeed we provided little of the structured and work-related Guidance Service which we now regard as central to our mission. The balance of our workforce is changing. New roles are emerging and adjustments are having to be made in old ones. There are those at Derby advocating a clearer delineation between the teams producing learning support materials and those involved in face-to-face learner support. Others find this deeply threatening. In any event, new career structures will have to emerge if we are to retain and develop the highly skilled practitioners of the new technology.

These technological developments centrally inform our thinking about distributed delivery. The High Peak and Derbyshire Dales area has many small village communities, and a few towns. There are also a lot of isolated farms. The problems of travel should not be underestimated. Bus services are poor and unreliable, and there is no through rail link from the north to the south of the county. It is a part of the world where official European reports regard personal transport as essential for access to basic services. However, even remote farms have telephones and TVs, and computers are daily becoming more essential to running even a farm business. We work on the assumption that most people will not travel more than about four miles to get education or training, and some people are not able to travel at all. If we are to service the need then we must take the product into the communities, and in some cases into people's homes. In our model for the learning Net in north Derbyshire we have differentiated four levels. At its centre is the hub based in Buxton. That is linked to a number of major outcentres which are learning centres in their own right (these will be discussed in the following section). The hub is also linked to what we describe as outposts. These are small facilities, typically only one or two computers with little or no staff support. They are situated in places used by the community for other purposes – the pub, the village shop, the community centre, etc. And then at the final level (as yet to become active except in our residences) is the direct link into people's homes.

A Learning Community

The above description may sound like a wiring diagram, but behind it is a pedagogic strategy. Individual learners will position themselves at different points on the spectrum offered by the University of Derby Online. The farmer's wife in the remote hill farm will do most of her studying at home, be it paper-based or electronically supported. If she has an electronic link she will have little need for visiting an outpost except possibly to use a video conferencing facility. The outpost will be used in small communities including by those people who do not have access, or adequate access, to the technology in the home. The 'learning centre' is altogether a different concept. It is intended to be an environment which supports a 'learning community'. The facilities there include not only the electronic links but also group study rooms and spaces for one-on-one discussions with tutors or advisors. Ideally there is something going on there every day, or certainly every evening. Some of these will be directly related to the university's programmes of learning, attract credits and lead to qualifications. Other activities are rather more recreational, be they clubs, drama groups or whatever. In these learning centres the citizen students find their mutual learning support. They also find resident learning facilitators and itinerant specialist tutors and other workers. Every sizeable community has such a centre. They are magnets for other learners whose main study time is at home or at an outpost. These centres are intended to be at the heart of the communities and will normally be located in facilities which already exist – village halls, schools, etc. Our intention is to work closely with the local education authority in order to create the right learning ambience for adults, even where facilities are also used by children.

At the centre of this distributed network in the High Peak and the Derbyshire Dales is High Peak College in Buxton. It will have an electronic Learning Centre comparable to (though smaller than) the one which already exists in Derby. This will be used by the full-time students based at the university in Buxton, by the other learners in Buxton, and by any student from the extensive outreach network. These citizen students from the smaller communities will find, in Buxton, a vibrant college providing both further and higher education which has revitalized the town. A centrepiece of the new college will be the International School of Tourism and Hospitality Management. This builds on the long-established excellence which High Peak College has had in the area of catering and hospitality management, and is synergic with north Derbyshire's major developing industry. The extensive network of international connections already available through the university is thus being put at the service of local economic regeneration.

One final loop remains to be closed in this vision of the people's university of the electronic age; this has to do with knowledge production. The tourist industry in Derbyshire already, in a minor way, offers learning experiences. The Peak District Park offers formal three-day or week-long courses in the archaeology or ecology of the Peak. Private providers offer craft courses in such skills as wood-turning. Small galleries have art exhibitions. The Buxton Festival spawns quasi-educational events, whilst museums have permanent displays of local (Derbyshire mining) or national (tramways at Crich) significance. The development of the tourist industry in the direction of longer-term and international visitors will enhance the demand for these quasi-educational services. The more sophisticated and better educated tourist of the future will expect more help in interpreting the many layers of meaning in the beautiful landscape.

Derbyshire abounds in societies and clubs founded in particular interest groups. Be they railway enthusiasts, rock climbers, mushroom gatherers, amateur geologists or industrial archaeologists, local networks are active in informal systems of knowledge production. Many of these networks will meet in the community learning centres. For the moment their knowledge is shared with a small circle, and either not reproduced at all or reproduced in print of indifferent quality and archived inaccessibly. The new technology could transform all that. The same electronic systems which can deliver the producer-driven, formalized learning support materials, can also create the virtual networks of self-learners doing their own things without reference to the official institutional structures. If that happens – when that happens – the learning revolution which the new technology can facilitate will have taken place, and we will have a genuine learning society.

4   Plato.com

The Role and Impact of Corporate Universities in the Third Millennium

Geraldine Kenney-Wallace

Competitiveness and the Academy

Plato's Academy, founded in the early fourth century BC, was arguably the first permanent western institution to merit the claim as Europe's first university. In shaping the early principles of advanced education, linking a balance of the theoretical and practical, linking philosophical research and teaching, and introducing the notion of a core set of disciplines through which to study and best educate the mind, Plato also opened a debate and a Pandora's box whose issues still resonate today.

To what extent is the ultimate objective of learning knowledge for knowledge's sake alone? Or is there also an immediate practical and professional application for knowledge and the results of research towards competitiveness, for which the university, its students, faculty and leaders have an intellectual, economic and societal responsibility? Indeed, are universities solely responsible for developing the advanced reasoning ability of individuals, researching into the nature of our physical and humanistic world, of generating and communicating such knowledge, and thus preparing society on the way forward? If the competitiveness of an enterprise is rooted in education as part of life-long learning, what are the linkages between intellectual enquiry, innovation and competitiveness in a company and in a society? Where do we draw the line between private and public benefit? Who pays for what?

Reflecting on the role of higher education and research on the eve of the third millennium, one is also conscious of the abundance of multicultural and scholarly thought and dissertations on such issues over the past several decades. It appears to me that over the centuries there have been discontinuities or technical revolutions that have each led to a fresh debate with a different contextual climate. Inventors also triggered social changes through the printing press, the astronomical and navigational devices that emboldened voyages of discovery and trade ultimately to the New World, the industrial revolution. In the nineteenth century, scientific and engineering excellence had led to electricity, mass manufacturing, steam and combustion engines, photography, wireless and telephones, and vacuum pumps. In the twentieth century we have witnessed many new frontiers represented by automobiles and aviation, by splitting the atom, penicillin, nylon, television, harnessing atomic energy, the transistor, computers, sputnik, lasers, landing on the moon and Dolly, the cloned sheep. While this is necessarily an illustrative list, the research and development (R&D) emerging from the laboratories around the world in the post-war period led to another step forward, at the time subtle but in reality dramatic, step forward by the 1980s. Quantum mechanics had entered the market place with laser diodes and data storage on disks. The role of quantum devices emerging from solid state physics and engineering physics, coupled to lasers and optical spectroscopies, plus microelectronics and advanced atomic and molecular materials, offered a potent mix of technologies for the rapid transmission of information between transmitters and receivers linked by copper cable, increasingly by fibre optics and by satellite. The developments of the microprocessor, and the DARPA research tool allowing scientists and engineers to communicate electronically across USA and later internationally (the forerunner of the Internet) also began to impact on journal publications and peer review protocols, as researchers exchanged valuable data and ideas across time zones and raced to scientific print to announce the next bold idea or discovery. Supercomputers, space and super-colliders prompted intense policy debate on resources directed towards 'little science' versus 'big science and engineering', let alone the evolving roles of genetics and medical research, ethics, interdisciplinary environmental studies, biotechnology, and funding for the social sciences and humanities. As university–industry interactions became stronger in some R&D areas, joint centres of excellence were established, including training at the graduate level and post-doctoral fellows in the emerging interdisciplinary areas.

In 1985, the US National Science Foundation established NSFNet to demonstrate the feasibility of networking outside the specific dedicated R&D networks in existence. This became a backbone service which undoubtedly presented an impetus to the present Internet growth for electronic communications, services and e-commerce offered by companies today. By the late 1990s, the marketplace consequences of the R&D and technology fusion is setting an awesome pace of change. The convergence of computers, video, optical technologies, television, telephone, wireless, telecommunications and satellite communications has produced an integrated if complex system of communications and information technologies. Global and regional networks affect us all, visibly or invisibly. The end is not in sight by any means, as the multi-billion communications and software industries now focus on broader bandwidths, high-definition television, three dimensional transmission of images and enhanced digital content in a once-upon-a-time analogue world. Distance learning is one of the major beneficiaries. Web-based learning has become a personal act of daily discovery for millions of children and adults around the globe.

The death of the long-distance monopolies, deregulation and opening up of cyberspace has indeed accelerated another more personal and social revolution, which had begun to be discussed in the 1980s as modern home conveniences and computers began to remove many of the routine and time-consuming daily tasks from our lives. Pundits promised a leisure society. The social challenge would be to use creatively all this spare time. Economists and social policy experts argued over the meaning and level of full employment, and the need for the dignity of work, were such an era to become reality. Levels of stress today and unemployment in some sectors argue the opposite! In fact, the clear distinctions between personal time (as self) and work time (as employee) seem to be blurring, as we are increasingly living, studying, working and at leisure in the world of virtual reality, namely cyberspace. Furthermore, the demand from the world of modern work for the employees to be computer-literate, and to possess knowledge and know-how with a degree of technological expertise that did not even exist a decade ago, has refocused attention on schools, curriculum, content, standards and employability. There is a mismatch. Gaps exist in students' knowledge and skills. Training and education today in comparison to the market demands are inflexible.

Higher education seeks to prepare and give confidence to a student for a lifetime, to learn how to learn. Training has traditionally been more vocational, and sometimes short-term in its horizon. However, these distinctions are blurring too, especially in technology-intensive manufacturing and services, because the specialist knowledge and practical know-how needed is changing so fast. If we observe the automotive and aerospace industry, and the impact of microprocessors, computers and communications technologies on their products today, General Motors now ships annually in its cars as much computing capacity as IBM. 'Big Blue' has reinvented itself from a mainframe manufacturer, through personal computers, into a software and services company by 2005. The division between manufacturing and services must also be re-examined. Is a software package a product or service?

Aeroplanes find their most complex and value-added components in integration, eg. aerodynamics design, composite wing technologies and avionics. The inventions and derring-do roots of aviation at the beginning of the twentieth century have evolved in a Darwinian way into massive systems-integration products or smart aeroplanes, which are in reality information management systems that fly. To gain that extra performance edge, aeroplane and car manufacturers invest in leading-edge aerodynamic design and wind tunnel testing, and R&D programmes on software timing and reliability. Test crash dummies and simulators explore passenger comfort and safety and pilot responses to neurophysiological levels. Since the average life cycle of a modern aeroplane exceeds 40 years, a premium is placed on smart maintenance and mid-life technological upgrades. Thus the demands on the workforce, from design to final production and certification on budget and on time to the customer, have increased dramatically.

It was in this context that in 1996 British Aerospace began to reappraise its internal efforts on training and education. A long and proud history of apprentices and graduates moving up through sequential learning experiences over several different major aerospace projects no longer matched the global reality of aggressive market competition. There was a need for multi-disciplinary skills and effective teamwork, particularly on the systems integration, to meet the customers schedules and maintain profitability across many diverse businesses and projects. Competitiveness was the issue. Education was the answer (Kenney-Wallace, 1997). A small senior advisory group worked with the Chief Executive, Sir Richard Evans, and proposed the concept of a company-based university as a strategic response to the company's challenges. On 3 March 1997 the Board of Directors approved the concept, and within a month the Director and Registrar, and Managing Director and Vice-Chancellor were in post. The mission was to develop and capitalize on the human, intellectual, technological and process resources of the company, as British Aerospace continued on its corporate quest to respond to the global competition by becoming the Benchmark Aerospace company (Evans and Price, 1999). The recollections and contributions of those involved internally and externally to British Aerospace, and the role of the Strategy Board as a governing body since 1997, will be recorded elsewhere. The journey has proved to be as challenging as any, as we set out to build a corporate university. Aerospace consolidation, mergers and acquisitions continue, and electronic commerce is reinventing business processes at a dizzying pace (Tapscott et al., 1998).

Traditional universities are no longer the dominant players in the creation and communication of knowledge, especially in cyberspace. Just-in-case education has moved to just-in-time and just-for-you, as self-managed computer-based learning plays an increasing and natural role for individuals and families. What to teach, how to learn and issues of quality are topical again. Plato.com has arrived.

This chapter offers a progress report up to September 1999 as we move from the complexity of a vast company into a coherent and cohesive strategy for learning and research, and build new strategic relationships with our partners in higher education (Kenney-Wallace and Howison, 1999).

British Aerospace and the Virtual University: Establishing the Framework

In a bold step publicly announced in May 1997, the company had set out to position education, training, technology, research and development within the core of the company's growth strategy. With knowledge acquisition and application now recognized as a key business strategy, the creation of the Virtual University (VU©) signalled the implementation phase of concept to operational reality. We set out to build an enhanced capacity and capability, across the whole workforce, to match the new competencies and competitiveness demands of a twenty-first century aerospace company. In this section, we focus on creating the first pan-BAe Framework, which comprised the foundation of the Virtual University's conceptual, intellectual and physical infrastructure. The Framework is now the enabler for present and future delivery of specific company-wide learning and research programmes and projects. It is also designed to be robust and adaptable to future expansion or shift in our business directions through mergers, acquisitions or spin-offs.

Corporate universities have grown considerably in number in America in recent years. There are now estimated to be 1600 in the USA in comparison to over 3,500 institutions of higher education aimed at the 18–24 year old population. This trend reflects a growing recognition across many sectors that people, knowledge and know-how are the most valuable and enduring company assets towards sustaining existing business activities, attracting investment, and winning new business, whether in global or local competition. The 'education industry' is referred to by investors as a $750 billion growth industry, in North America and Europe, of which the fastest growing segment is in USA in distance learning programmes and software. We will return to this topic in the final section of this chapter. The Virtual University has been designed in response to British Aerospace business needs by twinning academic and business excellence, through creative collaborations. The key policy decision we made in early 1997 to seek degree accreditation through the established universities also had the desired impact of shifting the then defensive and sometimes hostile response from academia to the VU as a substitution and threat to a more forward-looking progressive viewpoint of opportunity and partnership. Strategic partnerships between academia and enterprise can offer high-quality, co-designed programmes and innovative research projects, while maintaining appropriate academic standards, recognized routes for accreditation, and a flexible set of direct and distance learning courses (Kenney-Wallace and Howison, 1999).

Over two years after the concept emerged, and one year after the official launch and publication of the first Founding Prospectus in April 1998, it is clear not only that the Virtual University is unique to British Aerospace as an authentic mirror of the evolving business needs, cultural and organizational realities, but also that it is a very real window open to the external academic and world-wide opportunities to meet those needs. Furthermore, given the broad interest and scrutiny shown to date, it is also on the leading wave of change within the industrial and academic worlds in the UK. Increasingly decision-makers recognize that knowledge acquisition, knowledge management and life-long learning can converge to identify the fertile common ground for both public- and private-sector shared educational initiatives. Unlike many of the 'Corporate Universities' in the USA, which focus only on senior management groups, British Aerospace seeks to liberate the talents of its full workforce into a learning organization. Learning for what? A Systems Technology Powerhouse.

The answer captures a benchmark, global and innovative aerospace and systems company, which can meet the customers' demands for systems, and systems-of-systems, to be the integrated, cost-effective, and timely solution. The global aerospace and defence sector continues in 1999 to undergo restructuring in a series of mergers, acquisitions, alliances and consolidations. Eventually the new industry profile and players will emerge for the post-Cold War era and, increasingly, establish an information and communications technologies-driven aerospace business sector. British Aerospace as a systems company exceeded £8.6 billion sales in 1998 with over £27 billion in the order book and 46,500 employees. As UK's largest exporter with 89 per cent overseas sales to 70 customer countries, and a major player in 29 international partnerships, the company is keenly aware of the external economic market and regulatory climates in which we carry on business and build shareholder value. The largest aerospace company in Europe and the fourth largest in the world in 1998, British Aerospace is involved in over 50 major high technology aerospace and defence programmes worldwide. British Aerospace's merger with GEC Marconic Electronic Systems, projected to commence in late 1999, will create a new millennium company that is a truly global aerospace and defence company, the second largest in the world, operating across nine home countries with close to 100,000 employees. This is the global context of enhanced performance, collaboration and competition, which in aerospace often coexist among the players whose rich legacy and history go back to the early roots of aviation at the beginning of the twentieth century. How do we build on our intellectual assets for market performance?

The Virtual University has set up the present organizational framework within British Aerospace comprising the Faculty of Learning, the International Business School, the Faculty of Engineering and Manufacturing Technology, the Benchmarking and Best Practice Centre, and integrated the Sowerby Research Centre (originally established as the scientific research organization in 1982) to offer full educational, research, and benchmarking services to the company's business units, and in the longer term to the supplier chain, international partners and customers. In order to build the necessary infrastructure to apply knowledge across some 15 business units and over 30 locations in UK alone, to build upon any existing education and training activities within the various businesses, to optimize and then leverage on prior R&D partnerships and new R&D consortia, and to offer access and guidance to all employees wherever they worked, it soon became clear that there were two parallel priorities for the Virtual University during 1997 and 1998. First to establish the first company-wide view of all activities related to the Faculties' Missions and goals, and second to establish *de novo* and then integrate what we will call here the alignment and integration frameworks of the foundation for the Virtual University Framework.

In retrospect, the activities of the founding Vice-Chancellor, Directors and Deans have indeed been reminiscent of setting up a traditional university, where policies and procedures first have to be designed, discussed, agreed and finally put into place for access, enrolment, programmes, curricula, fees, etc. However, the students come from the employees, all of whom have full-time jobs. The logistics and affordability (in terms of financial and time investments of individuals and their business units) present real points of tension between the noble aspirations of learning and the blunt business realities of delivering airbus wings or aeroplanes to a tight schedule.

The company is complex, with a high degree of local business autonomy.

Moving from complexity to simplicity has long been one of the hallmarks of a paradigm shift in approach, an outside view. Whether at the molecular, business, human behavioural or planetary level, to move from complexity and apparent disorder, requires a sudden forcing function, from which a new structure and degree of order gradually appear. One sees the world through different eyes. Coherence emerges. Although some of the components may stay the same a new alignment is evident, and the components become integrated into a system. The system's capacity and dynamical response are now substantially higher, more productive and effective than ever before. Indeed, as we seek a coherent business strategy, information technologies (IT) sweep relentlessly through the workplace. Without user-friendly IT systems, integration to more efficient and effective linkages can be readily thwarted.

Synergy, cycle-time improvements, and reduction of ad hoc or fragmented activities and duplication can also lead to genuine cost savings, which may be reinvested in new priority activities. Cost savings are visible value, providing they are documented. The old adage of more-with-less becomes a reality as the stress and tensions of complexity are reduced, and behavioural resistance becomes acceptance. The rewards and visible value of the new model and approach gradually begin to receive a wider currency. However, as so often stated and experienced before, cultural changes do not happen overnight, nor without a huge investment of peoples' time, imagination and diplomacy as the old order gives way to the new. In fact, unless the company begins to evolve locally into critical masses of learning communities, the cultural changes will not be sustained, as we explain later.

Thus the Framework in place today is the result of such an investment of the Virtual University and other staff drawn across the company, who have worked in small but vital virtual teams during the implementation stage towards achieving the coherent learning and research strategy. We have built upon the existing educational and training components, wherever appropriate, and also created new foundations and then most recently integrated them into the overall Framework. Not surprisingly, there is always more work to do, more refinements to be made, as short- and longer-term business educational needs become more clearly articulated.

Led by the Faculty of Learning, the Learning Resource Centre Network is distributed across the major company sites in the UK. Now 33 locations are IT linked across the UK, with LRCs also the USA, France, Germany, Saudi Arabia and Australia. The Network also acts as a single procurement agent to take genuine advantage of economies of scale, single licensing fees for software, etc., and prompts the sharing of best practice. Access to the Virtual University and its programmes can now be offered to employees who take advantage of the local Learning Resource Centre, where the company's first comprehensive electronic prospectus, the Learning and Development Guide, is also available on the British Aerospace Intranet. As an internal academic prospectus and educational compass for people seeking to acquire qualifications, competencies and recognition of skills in the context of national standards, the Learning and

Development Guide will be updated regularly by the Faculties and the sponsors of the programmes in the business units. The shared responsibility should minimize the bureaucracy of keeping over 2000 courses up to date. It also offers guidance on career progression and job profiles, and reflects changing academic demands, new national standards or refined business needs. Finally, the guide offers employees an opportunity to self-assess their learning styles and thus enhance their confidence of a good cognitive match. The complexity of modes of learning is a fascinating and important subject for all of us to better understand, in order to ensure that the learning experience is effective and not just a short-term break from work.

The Integrated Development Framework thus now embraces the development of the people, the LRCs and the Integrated Core Curriculum. We sought an intellectually resilient, flexible and modular approach for and across the many professional disciplines that operate within the various business units. Coupled with specialist modules that reflect the latest yet different demands of, for example, finance, international marketing, the legal group or human resources, the core curriculum approach can also respond to the enhanced interdisciplinary requirements of procurement, interdisciplinary, project management or design and manufacturing. The overall Leadership Development policy framework within which individuals can progress to increasing levels of management, professional expertise and leadership within the company emerged under the initial design auspices of the International Business School. With the full involvement of the Faculty of Learning, Directors of Personnel and Engineering and the Business Units as major customers, we now have a full picture of the present programmes from apprenticeships to PhDs, and the missing gaps in professional programmes and qualifications needed for the future workforce capabilities in a global, multicultural aerospace and defence company. In response to the articulated business need for people's development, the certificate/diploma/degree programmes are jointly designed by the VU and university partners or HE/FE consortia, selected after a competitive bid process. Real strategic business issues can be introduced as case studies or research assignments, and workplace learning is combined with lectures and residential opportunities, adding value through the power of regular peer interactions.

The research and development activities comprise the substance of the Strategic Research and Technology Acquisition Framework, led by the Sowerby Research Centre for its corporate mission on Technology Acquisition, in conjunction with the Business Units, and the Strategic University Research Partnership policy for the extra-mural research and engineering education, led by the Faculty of Engineering and Manufacturing Technology. After reviewing the more than 70 partnerships contractually in place, and then analysing and rationalizing current relationships in the context of future business technology needs, the Faculty anticipates that a far smaller number of Centres of Excellence and Consortia will emerge. Finally, we designed the Benchmarking and Best Practice

Framework for the company. Whether best practice is to be identified, shared, catalysed, communicated, or embedded into tools, techniques and processes in the Business Units, it will be supported by the expertise within the Faculties and across the company. The Best Practice Forum launched in March 1998 acts as a round table for practitioners who, through the Virtual University's own strategic linkages, can access global benchmarking data and USA, Asian and European case studies from inside the company. Is Best Practice better promoted by behaviours or world-class content? In fact it is both. But passionate arguments support both sides and this is symptomatic of learning and sharing knowledge and ideas in the workplace or anywhere. Without positive attitudes and commitments to link learning to clearly defined academic or business goals, learning rapidly fades.

In summary, it is upon these new foundations integrated into the company-wide Framework that the VU has moved into a more comprehensive academic and accreditation focus in 1999. While the VU strives to foster a life-long learning culture and community, in which individuals are encouraged to be responsible for their own learning aspirations and career development, it is nevertheless true that incentives, rewards, and barriers felt at a personal level must be proactively monitored by line management and their senior executives on an ongoing basis. The next stage of policy discussion and direction is with HR and business units towards the explicit linkages of personal development plans for each employee to career progression, promotion, 'gateway issues' for senior positions and international assignments.

Many lessons have been learned during this start-up phase. Perhaps three stand out as vital to the potential success of a coherence strategy, based upon partnerships (Kenney-Wallace, 1998). First, there needs to be a magic mix of champions, trust and business savvy to ensure ideas move into actions. Second, with clear mutual objectives in place and an understanding of the synergy and savings to be gained by new initiatives, there is nevertheless a transitory period of 'constructive uncertainty' and resistance to changing roles and responsibilities. These roles do gradually emerge with desirable differences, and a deeper understanding of the value of the new strategy. New internal partnerships are created across the company. Finally, to sustain academic and business excellence through partnerships means not only agreeing what to start, but also what to stop. It is a matter of priorities and value returned from the investment. Partnerships that trust, openly share the risks and enhance the rewards will also have the confidence and astuteness to recognize, in time, the next level of complexity and competitiveness for which simplicity is once again part of the answer. We will now pursue the lessons learned from two aspects: the culture of change, and the complexity of large organizations.

Corporate Survival as a Learning Community

To be successful and to sustain its vitality in the workplace and the market-place, a corporation must also exhibit the social characteristics of a learning community. These might be identified as a sense of shared space and intimacy of contact, a shared set of values from which a common language and culture can grow, and shared experiences including myths that nurture the culture in a positive way. All of these culminate in a shared sense of 'purposeful belonging'.

Space defines boundaries, but values can transcend borders. Language defines meaning and ideas, which nevertheless can bring together two strangers, bound through common and shared experiences. A clash of values or conflict over territory or failure to communicate can begin to destroy any sense of common purpose within an organization. A global company positioning for the next millennium faces an even more complex challenge to ensure its global network of local communities is fully interconnected in human terms. If its market competitiveness is enhanced by a strong internal culture and performance, driven by continuous improvement, the company, its employees and shareholders will thrive. If the company is slow to respond to the new global challenges of trade liberalization and continues to operate on the old economic and management paradigms, then the seeds of failure are already internalized. The fate of dinosaurs is well known.

People, Partnerships, Customers, Innovation and Technology, and Performance. These terms today permeate the language of our business. British Aerospace had begun a change programme under Sir Richard Evans' leadership in 1994 (which has been written up elsewhere, see Evans and Price, 1999), which focused the company on delivering its performance through these five values. If the leadership of the company can see what dramatic change is required to move the business strategy and thus internal structure of the organization into a new paradigm for global performance, then the sense of community within the company can be the powerful focus and vehicle for this cultural shift. The most difficult change to tackle in any large organization is a cultural change. Survival through crisis is often the timely opportunity to begin such an important task. A far-sighted leader will see the need to adapt rapidly to unexpected markets, or to economics, consumer or government realities before the shockwave actually hits the company.

Over the past decade, the role of the corporate university in developing a learning community within the company has been directly linked to globalization and survival. Industrial sectors and country economies have been fundamentally restructured as a result of the rising importance of the knowledge-based economy and, in particular, as information technologies continue to sweep through every aspect of our lives. The final frontier is upon us: cyberspace, with growing attention on cyber-rights, intellectual responsibilities, electronic security and cyber-warfare, personal privacy versus unknown powers.

The demand for knowledge and expertise, education and training, research and development, knowledge management (and all the enabling technologies that underpin successful application and sharing of the results of these activities within and across a complex organization), is rising exponentially. For over 900 years, the focus for such activity had been the university. Paradoxically, in 1999 we must ask, is the university a true and contemporary learning organization? How has higher education evolved to offer flexibility or reflect a just-in-time demand, without abandoning the generation and communication of knowledge as its fundamental mission? Where are the vibrant university–industry interfaces? At the time of the Industrial Revolution, the societal response to the new capability of mass production and mass distribution for the markets of the Empire was also to create new types of institutes for adult education. In the phrase of the day, 'diffusion of knowledge' became the new ethos.

Over the late nineteenth and twentieth century, the public policy focus and initiatives that first led to mass education, then adult education, moved to higher education. New learning communities appeared. The number of universities grew dramatically after World War II, many growing and diversifying from the roots of the former 19th-century adult institutions or affiliated colleges. Management colleges for senior executives in business and government began to appear in the 1960s in many countries for the professional development of new governing elites, who would be well versed in contemporary business practices, as the early mainframe computers and time-management studies changed organizational behaviour. Distance education through correspondence has now evolved into distance learning with open universities as 'mega-universities', each offering several hundred thousand students access to a wide choice of disciplines (Daniels, 1997).

This was not enough, however. By the 1980s 'corporate universities' in the United States had become a curious new feature of the shifting educational landscape, offering education and training for their selected employees. Most had also grown from long-standing in-house management training programmes. However, the shift to 'corporate university' was a strategic signal about the importance of learning within the whole company, and the necessity for widespread cultural change. By 1998, over 1600 corporate universities had been identified in North America, and there were visible signs of similar initiatives in the UK. In 1997 the British Aerospace Virtual University was a pioneer within the UK in its comprehensive and strategic approach to learning and R&D. Many other companies are active, positioning or already have followed suit, some 37 by late 1999 in Europe. From the data available, we can draw certain generic conclusions about how a learning community works.

The corporate university is usually driven as a top-down strategic response to change, survival and then sustained market success. Since each corporation is a unique entity, possessing its own culture, legacy, customer base, markets, business challenges and profitability within static or volatile financial markets, the precise timing for the chief executive and the board of directors to make such a move is usually a singular and sudden event that triggers a long-standing proposal into an action plan. In a recent US Survey of Fortune 500 companies, 76 per cent of the organizations responding came into existence as a top-down strategy, and over 80 per cent of the executive heads appointed to the corporate university reported directly to the chief executive of the company.

The three major missions to be followed by a corporate university appear to be (1) strategic driver for change, (2) embedding of change and capture of best practice, and (3) global benchmarking for excellence under a kaizen (continuous change) philosophy. The learning and research programmes to be put into place, expanded, or rationalized and closed down will be in response to clearly articulated business needs. This requires collaborative leadership from the line managers and the corporate executives with the university staff. Thus the top-down strategic initiative must be accompanied by a grass roots and middle management acceptance, and a willingness to participate in the change and the new learning processes. If the shared values and experiences have already built a company community, then the task of the corporate university is vastly simpler, and it can focus on academic and business performance, which is hard enough anyway! Value will build naturally as the company grows into a learning organization through the energy, commitment, creativity and empowerment of a learning community striving for business performance.

However, in cases where the company or organization comprises many subcultures (for example, groups normally distinct or geographically disconnected from each other, populations in territorial or budget conflict, legacies from downsizing during the early 1990s recession, recent acquisitions from other companies, business divisions whose internal relations are as entirely autonomous units except in the annual report), then the ingredients of the learning community are not present. If present, they are fragmented and frail. The leadership required is one that brings about a cohesiveness, possibly by creating virtual working groups focused on mutually beneficial actions, in order to begin to build the linkages, shared experiences and trust that is needed.

Change management programmes based on the needs for behavioural and cultural shifts have become very common in the 1990s. This reflects the fact that very few global corporations had yet grappled successfully with being 'global' and the concomitant challenge of the development of a company-wide community. Years of downsizing, rightsizing, re-engineering and technological change had left their marks on the workforce, apprehensive in its response to yet another new initiative. Some exceptional companies had reorganized, and their improved performance in the marketplace illustrated the visible value from the focus and attention given to such 'soft issues'. Once derided as irrelevant in the boardrooms and as threatening on the factory floor, culture change and preparation for a global management are now hot topics. The lessons learned from companies is clear. Executive leadership is a necessary but not sufficiently persuasive condition to ensure that learning and sharing of knowledge and experience is a highly valued activity in a corporation. The attitudes of management and workplace in companies, and in different countries, must reflect that learning priority. The executive team must ensure that, in a widely recognized and well-communicated way, value is placed on intellectual capital as well as physical capital and infrastructure, and facilitate access to learning.

The overarching role of the true corporate university is thus to offer a strategic focus and an acceleration of such changes into an era when intellectual infrastructure and human capital will be measured, valued, reported to the analysts and in the annual report to the shareholder and stakeholders alongside the productivity, sales, R&D, capital and physical infrastructure investments of today. Creating and networking the learning community must be seen as a company's asset and competitive advantage. The corporate university is an innovative learning laboratory for a company in change.

The Corporate University as a Coherent Strategy for Competitiveness

Large companies by nature are rather like universities in the sense they are multi-disciplinary organizations. Thus within any campus or company community, it is important to accept some differences and distinctive features. Enforcing a homogeneity that is artificial will cause rejection. The challenge is in defining and coalescing the learning community. In linking communities across the campus or company, it is important to recognize the desirable differences and work productively with them, and to avoid the inevitable eddy currents of the not-invented-here syndrome or protectionism of turf under another guise.

Let us now presume that, in terms of human nature, the values, hierarchy of needs, and vested interests of a multi-disciplinary organization will be fairly similar (whether in universities, hospitals, companies and government departments or not-for-profit agencies), providing they are of a similar size and demographics, in terms of the staff population. My own experiences have yielded considerable empirical evidence to support this presumption over the past two decades (Kenney-Wallace and Bull, 1996). It is a reflection of the degree of complexity of an organization. The complexity can also be significantly enhanced by the very nature of the daily risks in the work of the employees. Perhaps, at first glance, there might be little to connect an aeroplane or car manufacturer, or pharmaceutical company, and a government agency, whose mission is food safety or environmental standards. But such connections are there when the risks are evaluated. Each is concerned with safety and human lives, each is subject to UK, European and World Trade Organization regulatory systems, and each invests substantial sums in research and product development over many years, prior to entry and acceptance in the marketplace. They are all in high public profile sectors in the sense their individual products and services touch our daily lives.

From this complexity and an understanding of the risks, a coherent learning and technology strategy must be developed by the corporate university to align with the company's strategic business and technological directions, and operational needs. This necessitates strong linkages for the VU into both the headquarters staff and line management operations. Naturally this is in the context of a strategy for competitiveness for the company. The more complex the organization, the more likely it is that the coherent strategy will finally lead to the creation of a company-wide set of strategies, policies and protocols which provide a global learning framework, within which different business divisions or departments can exercise some degree of local controls and accountability for actions. In this way, it is possible to reconcile and accurately reflect the desirable differences in business needs for learning, with local business risks and a realistic commitment of work time to learning, given the job profiles and demographics across the various subcultures. By analogy, the university senate policies and procedures offer a framework for the many faculties and degrees offered. Departments and the professoriate focus on the subject matter and delivery methods, from lectures and tutorials to modules and distance learning, and the intellectual progress and welfare of their students.

Is there a simple, albeit not simplistic, indicator to act as a proxy for complexity? From empirical evidence, we can illustrate usefully seven measures or profiles. Together, they are of fundamental importance in analysing and understanding the organization's complexity factor. Complexity in the end is a matter of objective facts, some scientific conclusions and human judgment. To be complete, many other measures could be added, which make sense to a particular business (retail) but not to another (biotechnology). The reader is invited to prepare another list for higher educational institutions.

- Number of employees world-wide (in home country, abroad, in headquarters [HQ]), over the past decade which will reveal patterns of workforce evolution.
- Number of business divisions, subsidiaries (all profit centres).
- Number of locations in home country, abroad.
- Demographics of workforce (age, gender, diversity, years of service).
- Competence profile of workforce (discipline, qualifications, mobility).
- Asset profile: source of profitable business, investments, pipeline of R&D, order book, brand name, etc.
- Prior existence and track record of company-wide strategy, or policy, reflecting degree of centralization/decentralization in business affairs.

The number of employees may be a self-evident indicator of complexity, but tracked over the past decade it will also reveal the degree of downsizing, hiring, and redistribution of jobs to different countries. A company of 30,000 employees with 20,000 abroad is a very different culture than one of 30,000 with only 2,000 abroad. A workforce of 60,000 may or may not be twice as complex as one of 30,000; it depends on the business and the other six measures. (The answer may be ten times more complicated if a merger has just taken place!) ABB, the international electrical engineering company, hires about 5,000 people annually, 30 per cent of whom are engineers. In the 1990s the total workforce of about 213,000 had experienced a decrease of 62,000 jobs in western Europe and an increase of 57,000 in Asia and emerging markets in eastern Europe, as the strategy moved more towards value-added high tech engineering and services, offered globally.

The number of business divisions indicates the number of possible isolated units or 'silos' in the organization. A company with three divisions is in principle less complex than one with 118 divisions; however, the internal structure of the divisions into departments can sometimes heighten isolation if very little mobility and inter-departmental communication takes place, or a cultural divide exists. A publishing company or bank usually has many divisions, branches, departments, and consequently their corporate university or institutes for learning will reflect this reality on a regional basis. Adding to the complexity is the geography of the company, best represented by the number and cultural distinctiveness of the locations in the home country and abroad. Geographical borders are not always the intuitively obvious barriers. Sometimes shared culture can overcome borders, for example the West Coast versus East Coast cultural work styles in North America. Toronto financiers in Canada work professionally in Boston and New York with no qualms, while Calgary and Vancouver entrepreneurs prefer to jostle in Silicon Valley and Los Angeles. A company in south-east England or Ireland may find more common cultural cause in major cities in southern Europe, while those in northern England and Scotland have had long-standing linkages into Scandinavia and The Netherlands. Naturally, personalities and social interactions play a role in keeping linkages strong and effective for business, hence new R&D linkages may appear in, say, Australia not simply through building on recognized expertise but also because a former business partner has been posted there.

Demographics reveal both the obvious in terms of the strength of the existing workforce and the degree of knowledge and know-how that will be at the fingertips of those serving longest in the company. How many times have we heard managers rue the day a certain individual left because 'when Charlie was here, we never had this production problem', or 'Sharon was the only one who ever understood this computer invoice programme'? It is the role of the corporate university to ensure that tacit and explicit knowledge are both captured and shared across the company, but the ways and means for a young software company are different from those appropriate to a venerable precision manufacturing operation.

Knowledge must be well documented before it can be shared. If the company hires a considerable number of graduates each year, then their retention rates are very important to track, as are the career progressions of the different specialist functions. Are there inadvertent or deliberate glass ceilings experienced (by women, men, and minority groups) at the senior levels? Unhelpful quota systems, if put into place, may lead to reverse discrimination. Poor morale demotivates if merit and experience are not seen as criteria for promotion and new job opportunities. These are certainly barriers to building a learning community within the company. Learning must be seen to pay back in terms of the individual's own personal development and career progress, as well as enhancing the company's overall capability. Policies determined by the human resource function, in conjunction with the corporate university, can assist in linking learning to personal career development, in the context of the overall business strategy.

The fifth measure of complexity is indeed the competence profile of the company. What businesses are we moving into for the future, and do we have the people with the competence and skills to get us there? Clearly the business strategy has to be in place first, with the people strategy then clearly linked to provide the competencies and capability of developing the results. This then defines the learning, research and development strategy of the company for which the corporate university will now seek to fulfil its mission. Next, the anatomy of the workforce must be overlaid by an understanding of the mobility within and between business divisions, disciplines and international locations. A company with major automotive manufacturing plants will have a very different competence profile to a financial management consulting company or a telecommunications software company. However, today each company is experiencing shortages of digital software and web designers, who are not only in demand but also very mobile. Their qualifications and experiences travel well in these days of increasing computer-aided design and production automation, in all sectors. The buoyancy of electronic commerce driven by the multimedia technologies and growth of the Internet applications has also captured many entrepreneurs before they even seek university qualifications. What does higher education mean to them? Remarkably little today.

The next measure is the asset profile. It is important in assessing complexity to understand how the company invests its capital. What is the risk-adjusted return on capital, and where does it generate profitable business? The import/export profile dependence on the supplier chain, the distribution of the customer base and the distribution of markets, all reveal whether or not there is a need to value some 'assets' more than others, eg. the future order book, the value of the backlog of orders, global market share, strategic market alliances, the linkages to R&D and innovation in the company, the physical plant and machinery, the overall brand name for outstanding quality and customer service, to name a few. This is a major focus for business schools and Masters of Business Administration (MBAs), and a paragraph does barely justice to the core assets of the company's future. It is critical to ensure that the company's learning and technology strategy capitalizes on and enhances the assets and resources of the company as the corporate university pursues its mission.

Finally, if this intrinsic complexity is truly to evolve into a coherent company-wide strategy for business competitiveness (as noted on p. 70, through the integration and alignment of a learning strategy, with the business strategy), what evidence is there of prior company-wide activities? What is the degree of centralization and prescribed policies and sanctions emerging from HQ compared to the decentralization and, ultimately, fully autonomous behaviour of the business divisions and subsidiaries? Of course, the balance between centrifugal (spinning-out) and centripetal (pulling-in) forces may well vary in any organization's history, as a consequence of business cycles, or the style of the chief executive. The change in management styles is clear as modern companies move increasingly from command-and-control architecture to more flattened layers in the corporation, 'coaching' from executives, and empowered and self-managed teams. Nevertheless, theory is so much more lucid than the actual reality of the workplace. Changing personalities can often bring degrees of personal comfort or discomfort to consensus making in the company. Matrix management groups, versus directive line-management within a given division, exhibit different dynamics and challenges for individuals. Similar statements are readily seen to be valid in higher education administration and government departments. Without a doubt, leadership is still needed. A decision must still be made, actions taken.

In summary, these are some of the generic lessons learned from the Virtual University's two years' experience and from my own previous executive administration. If the corporate university is to be effective as a vehicle to help drive the company from complexity into coherence and cohesiveness, then the above factors and others, such as political will and leadership, have to be taken into account. Therefore such a corporate initiative has to begin as a top-down strategy and be supported that way, above and across all functions and divisions, in order to prevent diminution of results and frustration with the inevitable three deadly sins: not in my backyard (NIMBY), not in my turn of office (NIMTO), and not invented here (NIH). By coupling the top-down approach with clear communications and a plan for involvement of people throughout the organization, the learning organization will begin also to grow from the grass roots upwards.

Plato.com: The Cyber World is Approaching Fast

Internet-related deals totalled £88 billion in 1998 and this was 30 per cent of all technology merger and acquisition activity, world-wide (Hill, 1999). In an era with only 20 per cent of the GDP contributed from manufacturing, and nearly 80 per cent from the service sector, it is notable that 69 per cent of manufacturing was exported compared to only 11 per cent in the service sector in the UK. This will undoubtedly change, as authors of educational content, and educational providers, meet the demand to satisfy learning in cyberspace. As trade liberalization underpins legitimate arguments in MBA classes over the existence of real or perceived trade blocs, the entrepreneurs move ahead. Protectionism, non-tariff barriers in tradable goods and services, the dollar, yen, euro and high-valued sterling, currency fluctuations, interest rates, derivatives, the tax climate and a number of other monetary and fiscal policy issues determine the economists' options and the national investment and business climates in which corporations are choosing to spend their money globally and on in-house educational activities to make more informed decisions.

To what extent do the cyber world and electronic commerce wait for these trade and climate issues to be resolved? Not at all. Virtuality can override national policy. Amazon.com is already a classic case, but not the only case as the financial impact of the cyber world begins to present a unprecedented degree of innovation, and opportunity (*Business Week*, 1999). Despite the hype, we are witnessing in real-time the discontinuity and risk characteristic of another paradigm shift to e-commerce. Education is not immune. The spin-offs from educational and cultural software industries are appearing almost daily with new initial public offerings (IPOs) as start-up companies. Business is entering a world that is traditionally the purview of universities, colleges, educationalists, animators, writers and publishers. From 1996 data, it is estimated that a 1 per cent shift of public funding to the private sector for educational delivery represents up to 12 per cent growth in market share of the increasing educational and cultural industry index and market. This is strong leverage upon investment. Should not the universities and colleges, particularly those in continuing education, be there?

By late 1999, over 180 million people world-wide were estimated to be actively using the Internet, not only as a global library and research database, but also as a route to book aeroplane tickets, buy books, or antiques, enter chat rooms before purchasing a car, buy CDs and videos of favourite stars, select insurance, make bank transactions, review companies' annual reports – and take academic courses for degree qualifications. Jones International University, a cable company pioneer since the 1970s in distance education in USA with Knowledge TV, now offers Internet degree instruction and received accreditation in 1999. Since data show over 100 million people in USA alone are interested in further educational development, and only 15 million traditional university and college places are available annually, the business case for distance learning is not difficult to make. (But neither is the infrastructure and investment simple or cheap.) Add the potential markets in China, India and other developing nations, and the potential for export markets is lucrative. However, dependency on specific regional export markets (such as students from an Asian Tiger country), could well be vulnerable to currency issues and changes in government educational investments, in a way that several UK universities have experienced during the Asian financial crises of the past two years.

To what extent is access to computers the main barrier? In Europe, estimates project 27 per cent of personal computers (PCs) to be present in homes compared to 45 per cent in North American households in 1998. Over 50 per cent of the global market's software programmes is now sold within North America. The USA buyers of 1998 software now have a mean income of $27,000, compared to earlier 1990 reported estimates of $62,000. Presumably, this is because the price of PCs has dropped as competition and volume increased. A similar observation will apply soon in UK, given current Department for Education and Employment and Department of Trade and Industry government policy initiatives through the University of Industry, and the March 1999 UK Budget. It is estimated that 92 per cent of the population in the United States has access to electronic multimedia, be it CDs, video, TVs, tapes or discs. The next trends are already on high streets in UK and USA. Speciality software shops are now being phased out or taken over by supermarkets as general distributors of software packages for the wider public. It is now possible for individuals to buy equipment to generate their own customized CD-Roms and videos, as digital photography, computing and electronics R&D of the early 1990s come to market at consumer prices.

This access to cyberspace is becoming a necessary part of our daily communications and an extension of our individual creativity. Admittedly, not all today wish to participate in this virtual reality and borderless experience. However, there are clear signs that the present generation of university and college students seeks 'cyber access' as an entitlement. What will future students expect from traditional universities? MIT has been surprised by the high response to its 1999 MBA in e-commerce. Wharton Business School is reaching out globally by satellite as Wharton Direct. The Open University and Law College in UK have joined forces on distance law. The Committee of Vice-Chancellors and Principles in the UK held a major conference on this subject in April 1999 to look at the opportunities and challenges of virtual and corporate universities, and the strategic implications for UK universities in the global education and research markets.

As we conclude this chapter, the list of corporate ventures in UK grows longer. Some 60 per cent of major industrial companies and 36 per cent of non-industrial groups experienced difficulties in meeting graduate requirements in 1998. There is a global tug-of-war for talent. Company-specific courses are seen as a response to this shortfall, as well as better-designed content, whether delivered in-house or in-partnerships. Some companies, such as General Electric Company (GEC) and British Telecom (BT) in late 1998, signalled their intentions to move in the virtual university partnerships direction. With over 125,000 employees, BT has complexity but is also committed to build a corporate university which in size could match Motorola University (USA) in its global operations. Unipart 'U', Ford, General Motors, Saturn Corporation, and most recently Daimler Benz Chrysler, have corporate university activities in the automotive sector, while IBM, ATT, Microsoft, Sun Microsystems, Dell Computers, KPMG, Ernst & Young, A.D. Little, Andersen Consulting and even McDonalds and Disney have new or well-established learning-responsive organizations too. Pharmaceutical companies (such as Pfizer, Inc., Bristol-Myers Squibb, Glaxo-Wellcome, Pharmacia & Upjohn, Inc., to name but a few) support Directors of Learning, and companies as diverse as The Body Shop to Anglian Water (or Universitas Aqua) have academies that focus on business training. Departments of government are considering similar strategies in USA. This is not an exhaustive list, but it is indicative of more than a passing trend. Over 40% of Fortune 500 firms also host a corporate university. Analysis shows that industry sectors most advanced in their development of corporate universities tend to be technologically-driven and experiencing global consolidation, such as healthcare, banking, telecoms, manufacturing, financial services and utilities.

The Open University (UK) now operates in many countries, as indeed do these corporate universities. Many traditional universities are involved in various international consortia to promote student exchange and R&D, through strategic alliances with local universities. Increasingly, private-sector training providers, or private universities such as De Montfort University and Phoenix University, are entering the marketplace. It is time perhaps to pause and reflect on the outcomes. The creation of knowledge is no longer the prerogative of the few. It has become the responsibility for a far wider population in our society and across the world, involving both the public and private sectors. How we intelligently share this task is the new agenda to be aggressively grasped, because without a clear articulation and understanding of the new roles, the results will be expensive confusion, loss of opportunity to exploit the knowledge-base for the new millennium, and ultimately by every organization attempting to do everything, loss of standards and quality. In an era of life-long learning, where the student population base is society, the entrepreneurial shift to self-employment is accompanied by support for teleworking (Mitel Telecom, 1998). Virtual chalk in the classroom (Johnston, 1999), also implies that the decision on where to learn may depend more on the value of an individual's time than the cost of the course. These are significant policy issues which will determine the shape of the academy for the next decade. Beyond that time, perhaps plato.com will need to be reviewed, to ensure that the law of unexpected consequences has not indeed changed the trajectory which appears so clear today.

References

Daniels, J. S. (1998) *Mega Universities and Knowledge Media*, London: Kogan Page.

Evans, Sir R. and Price, P. (1999) *Vertical Take-Off*, Nicolas Brealey Publishing, London.

Hill, C. et al. (1999) 'The Internet cuts the cord', *The Wall Street Journal Europe*, September 20.

Johnston, I. (1999) 'Virtual chalk: The future of work in higher education', *Perspectives*, 3(1) 28–33.

Kenney-Wallace, G. A. (1997) 'Creating the Virtual University – Education is the answer', London: *Parliamentary Brief,* 5(2) 20–21.

——(1998) 'Competitiveness and complexity: The Virtual University as a coherent strategy', London: *Parliamentary Monitor*, 6 (11) October.

Kenney-Wallace, G. A. and Bull, W. (1996) 'Partnerships for science-based development', in *Science-based Economic Development*, Annals of the New York Academy of Sciences, vol. 795, 302–313.

Kenney-Wallace, G. A. and Howison, S. et al. (1999) 'The future of distance learning', *Technology, Innovation and Society*, 15, 16–11.

Mitel Telecom (1998) *A Director's Guide to Teleworking in Britain*, London: Confederation of British Industry and Mitel Telecom.

Rebello, K., et al. (1999) 'Business Week e-biz', European Edition *Business Week*, 22 March.

Tapscott, D., Lowry, A. and Ticall, D. (eds) (1998) *Blueprint to the Digital Economy*, New York: McGraw Hill.

5   Students as Consumers

The Individualization of Competitive Advantage

David Robertson

Introduction

On a previous occasion, when colleagues came together to discuss the world in the year 2000, it was forecast that entire cities would develop whose principal business was knowledge and higher education. At that time, Boston was the model in view. It was assumed that students would be increasingly mobile, spending periods in different universities and in several university cities. Such mobility, it was argued, would inevitably be international, since by 2000 'London will be an hour's distance from New York' (Bell and Graubard, 1967: 189). Thirty years on we can smile a little ruefully at this. New 'knowledge cities' have not developed in the manner envisaged, although one day they might. A mainly postgraduate elite remains mobile between the great international universities as they always have been, while a lesser group in America and Europe manage some modest regional mobility. Generally, though, students are captured on entry and continue to remain at one university for better or worse.

London of course remains physically further than an hour's travel from New York, but interactive electronic communication has improved immeasurably over the period. In ways which were barely conceivable 30 years ago, Internet technology has ensured that universities in London and New York are now a 'mouse click' away, reducing the 'virtual' distance to zero, with obvious consequences for knowledge transfer and higher education. So predictions made even 30 years ago alert us to the hazards in any forecasting. The most significant changes are often surprises, and we feel more confident when forecasting events which have their roots in familiar conditions. In the case of higher education, of course, forecasting change – any change – is intrinsically hazardous as long as some universities retain the capacity to absorb centuries of change without much apparent impact on their behaviour.

This is particularly germane to this discussion of students as consumers. The latter part of the twentieth century was dominated by policy shifts towards the market across the range of public services. Institutional managers replaced professional voices as the guardians and promoters of consumer interests, which in turn came to define the purpose of organizations. To date, universities themselves have been reluctant to compromise the sovereignty of the academic guild for anything so fanciful as the student consumer. Market forces, the need to capture private funds, great diversity among providers and a more flexible curriculum have combined to sharpen the attention paid to the American student as consumer, but even in this most market-led and student-focused system, universities remain principally about supply – of research and new knowledge, of qualified leavers. Elsewhere progress towards extensive flexibility and diversity has been more restrained.

National policy communities in the United Kingdom and Australasia have begun to shift the higher learning market in the direction of greater accountability and responsiveness to student choices via funding formulae and the introduction of tuition fees. In Europe, however, progress in this direction has been mixed. Even where progress can be noted, as in the United Kingdom or New Zealand, changes to the internal culture and organization of universities have rarely followed suit. Life for academics and students in a British university continues much as it has done for years, departmentally focused with full-time and closely prescribed courses, a life interrupted these days by a management megaphone calling for more enterprise, flexibility and research in return for more bureaucracy, but an experience not that dissimilar in cultural terms from academic life 30 years before. Even if institutional funding 'follows the student' in some arcane formula, students are little more than 'income units', never themselves in a position directly to influence the nature of courses or suppliers.

A veneer of flexibility has been smeared across the underlying disciplinary structures of the curriculum with modularization, but this has been so artlessly applied that it has not dramatically improved students' capacity to change. Students themselves continue to follow courses largely according to the prescriptions handed down to them at entry – necessarily so in certain professional courses, but only because of local regulatory restrictions in many others. Even the national policy community in the United Kingdom is in confusion on the matter of student choice and flexibility. Both the Dearing Report on higher education and the government's response call for a more flexible curriculum and a national credit transfer system. Yet the newly established Quality Assurance Agency advises that it will scrutinize much more closely institutions which display high levels of modularization or credit-based curricula. It is hard to imagine a signal better calculated to impede the development of flexible curricula than one which warns universities that a course of action to which they were hardly committed will anyway result in greater scrutiny by the quality regulator. Nevertheless, despite these confusions and false starts, it is a principal argument of this discussion that the twenty-first century will bring changes in higher education which will place the student at the centre of the university, not just as the object of the university's attention in educational terms, but as the principal architect of the institution's character. Student choices and student behaviour overall will drive institutional responses in all but the most prestigious and well-funded research institutions.

The Changing Student Consumer – Beyond the Academic Playpen

We can forecast with reasonable certainty that the achievement of individual competitive advantage – that is, the ascendancy of merit over wealth or advantages of birth – will be more closely tied than ever to qualities of mind. To ensure that each individual secures the greatest possible return on their investment of time and money in higher education, students will be required to accept, and will seek, much greater personal responsibility for decisions precisely because higher education will become a commonplace experience for more people. Under such conditions, each individual will be required to extract the maximum possible benefits from the experience. These benefits will include, not just the quality of the credentials obtained – this will continue to remain important – but also qualities squeezed out of the social networks, human contacts and technological resources of the university.

Moreover, the constellation of factors influencing student choices will grow in scale and complexity. This means that students will plan their higher education from a much earlier age, not least because they will almost certainly be able to gain a place of some kind with a university or similar provider, but also because a cluster of educational, employment and financial decisions will have to be put together to make the experience beneficial. Hence our antique images of students will be reconstructed. David Reisman, contributing to the same Year 2000 forecasting exercise mentioned at the start, argued on that occasion that getting into the right college would be more important than working hard once there. Meritocratic pressures on students, he forecast, would produce countervailing releases – alcohol, drugs, travel, leisure (Bell and Graubard, 1967: 271). He was predicting with some foresight the emergence of that generation of students world-wide for whom entry to higher education was as much an extension of teenage and conspicuous consumption, as a rigorous preparation for adult life.

Participation in higher education, while no longer a luxury for the 1960s generation, was still a novelty to be enjoyed. Its consumption involved access to the conventional pleasures of youth, and universities organized and sometimes tacitly presented themselves as modest extensions of the recreation industry. In the United Kingdom, as elsewhere in Europe and America, the student generations of the late twentieth century became cultural symbols of rebellion, fashion, sexual and political freedom. Intelligent youth became an icon of innovation and freshness located in a discourse of personal identity and short-term hedonism. For a time, higher education enjoyed all the characteristics of 'the spectacle' – superficial and passive consumption of the relatively novel. But the binge is over. Patterns of consumption of this nature are sustainable as long as students, and those funding them, are sure graduates will find their way optimally in the labour market at some point. With participation levels at 10 per cent in the United Kingdom and Europe, or even at 25 per cent in America or Japan, youthful indulgence was tolerable since competitive pressure in the job market was not particularly severe. In purely economic terms, the university could be sustained as a middle-class 'academic playpen' for as long as the global economy remained predictable and therefore manageable. The moment economic conditions change, so too must our collective treatment of the higher education experience.

When participation levels rise as they have in the past decade – and I forecast below that they will rise still further – our images and expectations of the student as a consumer alter fundamentally. The image of the *ingénu*, dependent and feckless student which has conditioned policy and institutional responses over the last 50 years or more will shift radically over the next 50 years in favour of a student identity which emphasizes personal forward planning, intellectual polyvalency, and informed decision-taking. Some of this change will be the consequence of a changing demographic composition of the student body (students will be older, more experienced, and more likely to be in employment of some kind, returning to the university after a period of absence), but the most significant influence on student behaviour will be the need to manage learning in the context of earning.

This is not to imply that students will cease to be attracted by the familiar pleasures of youth, nor that circumstances will produce generations of worthy but joyless academic 'grinds'. Rather, the emphasis will shift dramatically in favour of attention to the core work of higher education as students learn to 'consume' the experience in ways which do not take their future prosperity for granted. A number of factors makes this kind of development likely. Principally, higher education as the 'knowledge industry' will be affected by precisely the same forces that are determining the shape of all other industries world-wide. Globalization, competitive advantage through knowledge application, information management within non-linear complexity, and universal credentialization will be the driving forces for much of the next century. The rest of the discussion is an attempt to substantiate this assessment.

The Universalization of Higher Education

To begin with, the new century will see a universalization of higher education similar to that witnessed in the twentieth century by secondary education. Higher education credentials will become the most sought after and highly valued social and economic assets for the vast majority. Within 50 years and certainly by the end of the first century of the new millennium, the total numbers experiencing higher education will have risen world-wide, so that 75 per cent of those living in the developed economies, and 50 per cent of those in the currently emerging economies, will have achieved some form of higher education qualification. The attraction to individuals is that successful higher education will become the principal passport to global citizenship, bestowing upon individuals the capacity to live, work, travel, communicate and participate actively in local and global affairs. It will be the main vehicle by which individuals will accumulate and direct their competitive advantages – critical skills, intellectual diversity, and above all social networks – to the pursuit of personal security and happiness.

The universalization of higher education will be opposed by established elites on grounds of quality or affordability. They face the prospects of historic social and economic advantages being eroded. Where popular pressure cannot be resisted, it will be distorted by attempts to protect exclusivity, sheltering elite advantages in specific institutions or in specific segments of the labour market. To this extent, universalization and stratification go hand-in-hand, but at least the majority of people in the advanced economies will enjoy some of the benefits of a complete education. The new emphasis will be upon ensuring that, however higher education systems are stratified, prospective students are able to enter and move within the system in a manner which reflects their abilities and overall welfare, and not in terms of the social or class prejudices of the institutions themselves (Scott, 1995). Because of the extrinsic rewards to the individual which flow from higher education, there are few natural limits to its growth. More than 20 years ago, Fred Hirsch (1977) pointed out the limitations of ever-expanding the supply of any 'positional' good. Higher education, he explained, was quintessentially a positional good to the extent that it bestowed socio-economic advantage on those who consumed it, but utility became futility once everyone could claim the benefits of the good. His conclusion was that no one gained relatively from the benefits of higher education if the labour market was saturated with graduates – wage premiums would erode – so there was an efficiency limit to the growth of positional goods. In sum, more meant worse.

This line of thinking tells us something about limits to the supply of positional goods, but it tells us less about demand for and consumption of sought-after goods such as higher education, because it undervalues the consequences to the individual of not obtaining the benefits. What fuels relentless demand for higher education is status competition, largely the desire of individuals and groups to possess those attributes which allow them to prosper relative to the next person or group. Of course, like any other product, the consumption of higher education will be influenced by price. In America, cost is rapidly becoming a key point of departure for speculations on the future of higher education in the twenty-first century, and access to higher education for some groups will continue to be sensitive to the availability of subsidies. Growth inhibitors and how to sidestep them will be addressed later in the discussion. Generally, however, consumption of higher education will increase if demand from prospective students and employers is the principal guide to policy. The reason is obvious.

Investment in higher education is closely tied to the collective prosperity which flows from economic growth. Unless demand is checked by politically artificial or crisis-driven interventions of a financial nature, higher education will shift in the next few decades from being a rationed to a freely available part of the social bargain in all but the poorest countries – and possibly for the very poorest sections of the advanced economies where special measures will be needed. Only if the connection between economic growth and educational investment is broken will the cycle of increased production and consumption of higher education be disturbed. The consumption of universalized higher education will be continuous, recurrent and necessarily life-long. The initial cycle will not be adequate to contain all available demand, nor to offer the range of relative credential advantages to a diverse population. In any event, the costs of full-time residential higher education will far exceed the ability of all but the rich to pay. Indeed, it is possible that full-time residential – and highly expensive – higher education will become the principal means by which elites will purchase their exclusivity. Under such conditions, the elite universities will become part of the 'privacy industry' along with securitized housing estates, exclusive holiday resorts and private clubs.

Credential Saturation of the Labour Market

Demand for higher education from social elites never has been contained by the initial undergraduate experience, and patterns of recurrent consumption will transfer to intermediate social groups throughout the twenty-first century. New forms of credential will emerge, many at a highly advanced level and focused on mid-career proficiency and achievement. The explosion of postgraduate programmes in the United Kingdom and Australasia, following the trajectory of American higher education, merely prefigures a more extensive expansion of higher level credentials, of which the Masters of Business Administration (MBA) rather than the research-based Masters is an example. Demand for higher credentials will come initially from that generation of graduates currently moving through the workforce with only a first degree. The impact on the consumption of higher education will be similar to that which drove the first expansion of the system after 1945 and again two decades later in America and Europe. On this occasion, the surge of demand will be global, with few societies having reason to lag since the programmes will almost all be financed not from public expenditure but by individuals or their employers. This will have consequences for the character of programmes, since fee-paying students will want to ensure, mid-career, that their costly new credential will guarantee returns in employment. These advanced credentials are therefore likely to be close to the labour market.

Thereafter, a scramble for reputational advantage will kick in. Demand will be self-generating as individuals seek to secure or preserve individual competitive position. And providers other than universities will move into the market to supply the necessary employment-based additionality which mid-career students will seek. This is not to suggest, however, that the new credentials will be vocational in any limited sense. Academic credentials will continue to outweigh vocational equivalents for as long as employers continue to offer better wage returns to the former, no matter what the exhortations to the contrary. For pessimists of this process, the 'diploma disease' will get worse (Dore, 1977) and credential inflation will become a cause of political concern (Collins, 1979), but the qualification epidemic will rage out of control. A majority of participants will achieve more than the basic graduate credential. Attempts to produce a cure for the 'diploma disease' via politically inspired rationing or increased state regulation of the supply of credentials will founder on upwards pressure from citizens for a stake in common prosperity and from employers seeking fresh sources of intellectual capital. Only if the state is able to persuade its citizens that their welfare can be advanced without advanced credentials will any form of acceptable 'inoculation' be possible.

Despite the pessimism of some labour market economists and workforce planners, the global economy will continue to absorb this hugely increased supply of skill until most market segments within the developed economies are fully saturated with highly qualified individuals. In the developing world, workforce graduate density will rise steadily until, by the end of the twenty-first century, differentials between developed and developing nations within the global economy will have narrowed considerably. The global labour market will be faced with the need to absorb an enormous increase in graduate supply by mid-century. China, India, other developing Asian nations, and the countries of South America and the former Soviet bloc will increase their production of highly qualified labour to current American and European levels. Apart from the social and political transformations this will engender in those countries, the competitive impact will be sufficient to force a further rise in the consumption of higher education within the developed economies themselves.

The Informational Division of Labour and the Knowledge Industry

We can be reasonably certain that the universalization of higher education will occur, if for no other reason than because it will be driven by panic. Both nations and individuals will quickly become aware in the early part of the twenty-first century that former divisions of labour within local and global economies are being replaced by a new informational division of labour. The dividing line between the 'information-rich' and the 'information-poor' will determine not just a nation's prosperity, but also its security and independence. The 'information-rich' nations will not merely be the most prosperous, they will also be the most powerful, enjoying extensive regional and global hegemony (Carnoy, 1993).

The informational division of labour is the product of what Manuel Castells has described as the 'network society' (1996, 1997). The emergence of a post-industrial economy in the developed world has been accompanied by dramatic shifts in the division of labour. Whereas the social division of labour was formerly based on the ownership of private property and labour power, the new informational division of labour will be based on ownership of, access to, and the management of information. Nations which maximize the connectedness of their information sources and which ensure that citizens have high levels of control over information technology will be the ones to triumph in the twenty-first century. It is for this reason that governments are now keen to introduce policies, for schoolchildren onwards, which ensure high levels of 'IT literacy' for their populations. The information economy, or the 'knowledge economy' more precisely perhaps, will place the greatest possible premiums on innovation, new research, and the creative application of ideas. Access to the latest communications technology will in the twenty-first century be the definitive characteristic of successful higher education systems, since universities cannot be without access to the complete stock of available knowledge. The hugely expanded constituency of highly qualified graduates and postgraduates will therefore be the natural product of a 'knowledge industry', an industry whose business is precisely the capture, management and application of knowledge.

Nations within the global economy will therefore scramble to ensure that they fall on the right side of the informational division of labour – the consequences of failure will be a low position in the global hierarchy. And what is true of societies as a whole will also be true for individuals. Within societies, the same informational division of labour will open up a colossal gap between the successful or the potentially successful and those whose lifetime chances of success and prosperity are minimal. Unless government policies and the local behaviour of universities and colleges ensures it, significant sections of even the most developed countries will be thrown into perpetual penury and dependence with incalculable consequences for social order. Hence, one of the biggest challenges of the twenty-first century will be to ensure that the consumption of higher education is not merely universalized but democratized also. This is likely to force governments to open up their systems of higher education in ways which may run counter to the preference of social elites for the preservation of prestigious and exclusive centres of excellence.

Demonopolization in the Knowledge Industry

The imperative to ensure that a nation and enough of its citizens fall on the right side of the informational division of labour will lead to a demonopolization of higher education and massive changes in the structure of the knowledge industry. Universities will lose their monopoly of degree-awarding powers, and alternative providers will enter the market, some on a 'for-profit' basis. Many universities of the conventional form will be both larger and smaller than the standard today. The largest will be formed either from global alliances between super-universities – Harvard–Cambridge or Stanford–Imperial; or by university–media corporation mergers – something like Microsoft–Beijing; or by technologically advanced mega-universities in the style of a global Open University. Nations which fear they may be left on the periphery of the global economic order may even promote transnational associations and alliances within the knowledge industry. So we may see universities in Cape Town, Auckland or Sydney in merger-alliance with universities in America, Europe, China or Japan. In addition, some of the large international consultancies and 'think tanks' – the RAND corporation is active in the market already – will begin to emerge as higher education providers in their own right, taking advantage of the demonopolization of the award of academic credentials.

Some nations will decide to 'out-source' their knowledge requirements. Instead of exporting their students to universities overseas and importing research, they may invite internationally prestigious university–business corporations to establish an 'on-shore' presence, either in physical terms or via Internet technology. Some of these developments are emergent today where there is evidence of a substantial international market, dominated by the English-speaking universities, in the supply of higher education. The expensive research function will remain beyond the capacity of most developing nations. The smallest constituents of the knowledge industry will scarcely be universities at all. They will be highly selective, prestigious and heavily financed research institutes. Here public–private interests will fuse, so that global businesses and governments will support and finance the most prestigious institutes, and an elite of postgraduate and highly qualified students will move transnationally to seek research opportunities within them.

The extensive fragmentation of higher education systems is a predictable consequence of the process of universalization. The twenty-first century will see a dazzling array of 'intermediate' providers: distributed and regional universities, big urban institutions, loosely coupled transnational alliances, corporate universities, and 'virtual' universities. Internet technology will of course play its part in rendering largely irrelevant the physical location of many providers. Students will become internationally electronically mobile as interactive video and video-mail replaces current forms of communication. Moreover, as the state has less interest in regulating the precise characteristics of higher education compared with secondary education, and less capacity for regulation in a globally accessible market, the traditional identity of the university will dissolve. Additional and alternative providers will swarm into a more open, less state-dominated market, offering an immense diversity of organized and self-constructed programmes under a variety of conditions, at a range of prices, and at times in the life-career cycle which we can barely imagine today. The market will be lucrative for those providers that are able to charge premiums for quality, or those that manage to contain costs by lowering the price of higher education to the learner. Although the University of Phoenix appears an aberration at the moment, demonopolization will result in the emergence of a business-focused 'for-profit' sector in global higher education.

Internet Technology and its Limits

While there is little doubt, in the absence of an unforeseen catastrophe, that the Internet will have an enormous impact on access to and distribution of knowledge on a global basis, claims for its influence have been extremely excited. Certainly it appears likely that the Internet will grant students access to higher education in forms, locations, and at prices which are substantially more varied than today. It is already possible for postgraduate students in the United Kingdom to study at an Australian university if they choose. The question becomes: what makes an on-line course at Deakin University any different from an on-line course at, say, the University of Leicester down the road? The answer of course has nothing to do with the excitement of communicating with the other side of the globe. An assignment travelling down the line does not distinguish Deakin from Leicester by distance or speed of transfer. The choice to the student therefore is only about relevance, quality and reputation – will the course and the credential add value to the individual's capacity to compete in the labour market? The Internet will therefore only complement existing judgments about the value of a university's quality in a reasonably informed market.

It has been claimed also that the Internet will open up the prospect that students world-wide will be able to access the world's finest universities. This may prove to be over-optimistic. The claim assumes that the most prestigious universities will offer courses via the Internet, driving out less favoured competitors. The most frequently cited example is the Harvard

MBA, widely accepted as the benchmark quality credential. Yet Harvard will need to have a reason to offer access to its MBA via the Internet, and whatever reason it finds, it is unlikely to include generalized access. The reason is obvious. The reputation of the Harvard MBA depends not just on its intellectual quality but also on its positional value – its scarcity and exclusiveness. Unless Harvard becomes a profit-maximizing organization – and it is hard to see why it should – the university will have little need to open up the market for its MBA on a general basis. If it wishes to improve the quality and influence of its graduates, it may use the Internet one day to target a global management elite, but not otherwise the wider international market for management development, lest over-selling should dilute the positional value of its MBA. Moreover, assuming demand for the Harvard MBA remains enormous, the university will always be able to maintain its income streams from the course, not by increasing numbers, but by increasing price. The Internet will not, therefore, produce a major flight to quality by students, because access to the very best will always be rationed. However, the Internet will allow students to improve the value of their credential by moving beyond those courses which are offered physically and locally. Students will not be hampered by brute misfortune because of geographical location in the manner to which we have been accustomed hitherto.

The Americanization of Higher Education – Consumer Sovereignty

The Internet will change the face of higher education in two other intercon-nected ways. It will lead to the emergence of an internationalized form of English as the common language of global higher learning, politics and business. In turn this will assist the Americanization of post-secondary education systems throughout the developed economies. By the mid-twenty-first century, the principal features of all major post-secondary and higher education systems world-wide will be American – perhaps with some local characteristics. American higher education will provide the inspiration in terms of quality and diversity. It generates the greatest number of policy innovations. And generalized political democracy will consolidate its influ-ence in a globalized system of advanced learning.

Consumer choice will drive the global system as costs continue to be transferred from society to the individual. This will be reflected in curriculum structures, pricing policies and information supply. The sovereign student consumer will exercise far greater purchasing power, and therefore have far greater impact on the structure of the learning market.

The emphasis on the student as a consumer will reflect more than just the ascendancy of markets over alternative distributional models. Students of the new millennium will face choices of enormous variety and complexity, needing to select from a bewildering range of providers and programmes, at varying prices, locations and delivery systems. The explosion of information sources alone will test the resilience of students and well-qualified citizens alike. In addition, students are likely to manage learning and earning trajectories in parallel, rather than in sequence as now. This will place new responsibilities on providers and the state to provide students with the information they require to judge outcomes which are optimal for their welfare.

Towards a Cut-and-paste Higher Education Curriculum

The influence of the student as consumer will be felt in a further way. Early in the new millennium the familiar pattern of the higher education curriculum will start to break up. Subject disciplines will begin to dissolve and recombine; the organization of the university will become more fluid as departments lose their hold on the disciplines which gave rise to them. In such an environment, student decisions on what and how to study will have an amplified impact on the emerging new curriculum. These changes will have a shattering impact on the culture and organization of higher education as we know it. Subject disciplines endure as the primary loyalty for most university teachers, anchoring them in the university. They constitute the intellectual preoccupations, professional routines and socio-economic linkages of academic colleagues within and between institutions. Books are written for disciplinary settings and they usually reflect the paradigms and discourses which dominate research.

The influence of the academic subject discipline on the character of university life has been sustained initially by the natural inclination of academics to impose intellectual coherence on the apparent chaos of the world. Thereafter this preference for mastery of complexity through discipline is reflected in the organizational arrangements of institutional life. Academic departments follow the contours of subject disciplines, and courses evolve as the property of departments. The effect is often to produce a cultural and organizational closure which militates against cross-disciplinary flexibility, inter-departmental mobility and expressions of informed student choice. Such arrangements are largely out of step with changes to the production and application of knowledge in the world beyond the university.

The signs of change are already with us. The conventional structures of the linear curriculum are being modified by the introduction, in the United Kingdom at least, of modular and American-style credit systems. Progress remains painfully slow, and the impact to date has been slight. By early in the twenty-first century, within a decade or so, the pace will quicken. A non-linear, 'cut-and-paste curriculum' will emerge in which students combine, assemble, and reassemble to their own design and for their own purposes components of learning from various disciplines and trans-disci-plines, and from local and global sources. Students will 'cut' learning components from one source, and 'paste' them into a personal portfolio of learning, a process subject only to reasonable assurances of quality and coherence. The motivation will come from the accessibility of learning via the Internet, and from students' interpretations of shifting signals from the labour market.

Currently we talk – rather dismissively in the United Kingdom, it must be said – of a 'cafeteria curriculum', implying that student choice involves a somewhat haphazard and fanciful selection of questionable quality. Others speak of the 'McDonaldization' of society generally, invoking images of mechanized consumption and routinized services (Ritzer, 1996). This is because we are working largely with the concept of an uninformed student, and mainly from the premise that disciplines represent something objective in the world. Neither will be true in the twenty-first century. The subject disciplines in all but the most technical areas such as medicine will dissolve, meld, and re-form in entirely novel ways. This will happen most swiftly in the 'soft' biological sciences and social sciences, and in areas close to infor-mation technology.

The new curriculum structure will emerge by force. It will be complex, fluid and non-linear. The subject discipline structure with which we are familiar is largely the product of nineteenth-century industrial society. It reflects the social and technological priorities of the time. It is questionably fit to manage the categories of knowledge and learning suitable for a post-industrial and information-driven economy in the twenty-first century. Already there are calls for a rethinking of relationships within the social sciences (Wallerstein, 1996). The development of biology as the discipline to unite neuroscience, genetics and computer science will further challenge the way we think of the conventional disciplinary arrangements (Wilson, 1998). Indeed, the emergence of complexity theory as the likely candidate to generate a General Theory of Everything will by mid-century have forced an entirely new way of seeing in both the social and natural sciences (Cilliers, 1998).

How will this affect the student as consumer? Gibbons et al. (1994) have correctly foreseen that we are edging away from the production of knowl-edge based on institutionally constructed academic disciplines towards forms of production based on the application of knowledge to specific prob-lems in specific social, economic and commercial settings. The latter form of knowledge production is increasingly taking place outside the university – in industrial laboratories, 'think tanks', consultancies and so forth. Distinguishing between 'Mode 1' and 'Mode 2' knowledge, Gibbons et al. explain that 'Mode 1' knowledge is academic, institutional, disciplinary, homogenous and hierarchical. Its integrity and utility are defined princi-pally by the judgments of the professional academic community. On the other hand, 'Mode 2' knowledge is application-centred, transdisciplinary, heterogenous, reflexive and transient. It is accountable beyond the professional academic community to diverse socio-commercial interests embracing a wider range of expertise.

Of course the transdisciplinary and application-focused character of 'new' knowledge raises profound questions for the long-term future of university-based disciplinary knowledge. An over-reliance on disciplinary-based knowledge will contribute to the demonopolization of higher education institutions in the learning market. As knowledge becomes a commodity to be traded by a variety of providers amongst a number of potential consumers, its transdisciplinary character will be precisely the quality which attracts student consumers and other partners of universities in the future. In this context, frameworks which promise to facilitate transdisciplinary knowledge production will be the best means of retaining for universities their competitive advantage. Frameworks which replace one form of disciplinary inflexibility with 'new' administrative rigidities, or with heavily bureaucratized quality assurance arrangements, will not release the potential of transdisciplinary learning. For this reason, curriculum frameworks will need to be developed more sensibly with the promotion of student choice, organizational flexibility and professional academic cross-fertilization in mind (Robertson, 1994).

Intellectual Capital as Personal Property – the Political Economy of Student Consumption

The most radical changes in the character of higher education in the new century will be a function of the political economy of student consumption. As the state continues to pass back the costs of higher education to the individual, individuals from an early age will need to be prepared by family and schooling for a more direct engagement in personal life-career planning. This is likely to involve the development of skills in both financial and information management – an acceleration of socio-economic maturation in the later teens which would have been natural a century earlier amongst young people obliged to leave school, work and start a family. On the other hand, higher education providers will come under pressure to see students as nothing more than consumers, as income to be earned. While the best providers will continue to defend their market position on grounds of quality, some others may choose to offer inducements of various kinds in order to attract the income that students bear. The threat to quality that this will imply is one reason why students themselves will need to be equipped with far better information and decision-making resources than now.

It is likely, therefore, that the biggest change to higher education in the twenty-first century will be the radical restructuring of its finances. Students will not only be required as a matter of course to pay for their tuition, they will also carry with them, for distribution at their discretion, an element of the income which hitherto has been paid by the state to the providers. This will be in the form of a voucher, educational credit, or as currently mooted in the United Kingdom, an Individual Learning Account. Both the Dearing Report in the United Kingdom and the West Report in Australia move in a similar direction, while ideas of this nature have been on the policy agenda in America and New Zealand for some time. No change will be more fiercely resisted by the established providers, and no change more welcomed by new market entrants. Moreover, a comprehensive system of vouchers or accounts will be initially difficult to manage – students themselves make reluctant consumers of higher education in the manner proposed. Yet it is likely the state will have little choice. It will need to open up the higher education market to new entrants for three reasons: to contain upward drift in costs; to recognize the impact of the Internet and 'off-shore' suppliers on the supply of learning; and to establish a different kind of contract with students over a learning lifetime.

It is impossible to foresee at this distance how profoundly radical such a departure will be. It will be opposed by established institutions as a reckless destabilizing of their organizational integrity, and it will be resisted by those who see any extension of sovereignty to the student as an inappropriate shift in the balance of power in higher learning. Students as we conceive them today may not even be ready or willing to shoulder the responsibilities implied by their newly enhanced role. But this is the point. Students will not be as we conceive them today. The assertion at the start of this discussion was the social composition of the student body will change as universalized higher education becomes the norm. The image of the student as a young undergraduate will change in favour of the student as citizen, engaged in higher education throughout adult life. If we doubt this, then we should reflect on the fact that our image of the student has changed radically over the past half century; it will change dramatically over the next 50 years.

What will be the impact of financially empowered students on higher education, and why should they benefit? First, whatever the mechanisms used to recognize or contain the fact, students will become less predictable, and less easily captured by institutions. Their behaviour will increasingly recognize that intellectual capital is a personal property to be developed in terms which reflect their own preferences and life-career points. Its development need not fit conveniently into the organizational and professional values of the university. This will truly challenge the power of the academic guild more fundamentally than any incursion by the state in the past century. Yet the academic guild need fear little if it recognizes that autonomy is better secured via alliances with freely acting students than with an unbiddable regulating state.

Conclusion

The student consumer of the twenty-first century will have an autonomy which was earlier difficult to imagine. Higher education systems in the twentieth century encouraged a notion of the dependent student-in-deficit for which attendance at a university is a compensation. In this regard, higher education remains like the Church – where the students' sin is ignorance, and salvation can be achieved via a limited number of rituals under the gaze of the powerful academic clerisy. This will change in the twenty-first century. Students will not of course be born well-tutored, but they will grow to understand what belongs to them and what does not. And they will learn that the one thing, apart from their health, which belongs to them alone is their intellectual capital. After a certain point, its development is their own responsibility.

The consumption of higher education will continue rapidly in the twenty-first century, but it will be a more varied experience, more closely integrated into employment and the rhythms of family life. The losses incurred by the decline of the sheltered world of the academy will be over-whelmingly made good by the explosion of fresh ideas and sound judgment. Higher education will become the principal means of achieving personal prosperity, but it will also be the means by which more people world-wide gain access to social justice. The twenty-first century will not, however, find an answer to the problems of those globally and locally who fall on the wrong side of the informational division of labour. That is likely to become the great burden of the twety-first century.

References

Bell, D. and Graubard, S. (eds) (1967) *Towards the Year 2000: Work in Progress*, Cambridge, MA: MIT Press.

Carnoy, M. (ed) (1993) *The New Global Economy in the Information Age*, London: Macmillan.

Castells, M. (1996) *The Rise of the Network Society: The Information Age – Economy, Society and Culture*, vol. I, Oxford: Blackwell.

——(1997) *The Power of Identity: The Information Age – Economy, Society and Culture*, vol. II, Oxford: Blackwell.

Cilliers, P. (1998) *Complexity and Postmodernism: Understanding Complex Systems*, London: Routledge.

Collins, R. (1979) *The Credential Society*, New York: Academic Press.

Dore, R. (1977) *The Diploma Disease*, London: Allen and Unwin.

Gibbons, M., et al. (1994) *The New Production of Knowledge*, London: Sage.

Hirsch, F. (1977) *The Social Limits to Growth*, London: Routledge.

Ritzer, G. (1996) *The McDonaldisation of Society*, Thousand Oaks: Pine Forge Press.

Robertson, D. (1994) *Choosing to Change: Extending Access, Choice, and Mobility in Higher Education*, London: HEQC.

David Robertson

Scott, P. (1995) *The Meanings of Mass Higher Education*, SRHE/Open University Press.

Wallerstein, I. (1996) *Open the Social Sciences*, report of the Gulbenkian Commission, Stanford: Stanford University Press.

Wilson, E. (1998) *Consilience: The Unity of Knowledge*, New York: Alfred Knopf.

6 The Globalization of Higher Education

*Denis Blight, Dorothy Davis
and Alan Olsen*

Introduction

In the year 2000, 66 million students globally, 1 per cent of the world's population of 6.2 billion people, will be at universities (Blight, 1995: 22). As the new millennium starts, 16.5 million students globally will embark on the first year of a first degree, with an average time at university of around four years, including postgraduate study for some. Universities offer these first-year, first-degree places every year, as new age cohorts move through the education system. The best measure of participation in higher education involves a comparison of the number of new undergraduate places with the size of a relevant age cohort. The access rate is the ratio of the number of first-year, first-degree places to the number of 18-year-olds. The number of 18-year-olds can be smoothed by averaging the 18- to 21-year-olds or the 15- to 19-year-olds.

Globally the access rate in the year 2000 will be 16 per cent. This average masks a diverse range from 6 per cent in Africa and 11 per cent in Asia to 32 per cent in Europe, 34 per cent in the Americas and 35 per cent in Oceania (unpublished data from models prepared for Blight, 1995; see Figure 6.1). At the level of individual countries, differences are more pronounced. In the year 2000, access rates will range from 5 per cent in China, 9 per cent in Malaysia and India, 29 per cent in Singapore and 42 per cent in Japan to 59 per cent in Canada and 62 per cent in the United States (unpublished data from models prepared for Blight, 1995).

Drivers of Change in the University of the New Millennium

International growth in demand for higher education will be the principal driver in changes in the nature of universities in the new millennium. There will be other drivers of change. Although harder to forecast than the growth in demand for university places, there will be growth in demand for

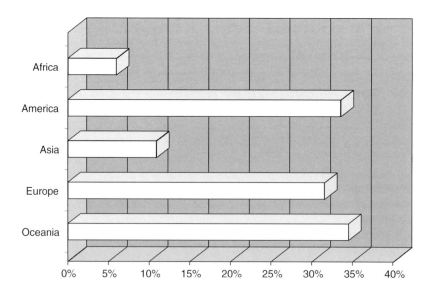

Figure 6.1   *University access rates by region: Year 2000*

university research. These changes are already under way; they are irreversible. Policy-makers, institutions, corporations and individuals will respond to the growth in demand in various ways.

The least likely option is increased allocation of public resources, given current trends. More likely options include:

- Internationalization of universities, particularly in English-speaking OECD countries: international student programmes are central to internationalization of higher education institutions, but the scope of internationalization at the start of the new millennium means much more than an international student programme.
- Offshore campuses, including twinning programmes and franchised operations, often permitting private investment in university enterprises.
- The combination of information technologies and telecommunications technology to enable the global transmission of information, leading to the potential for virtual universities, perhaps in partnerships with global media networks, and facilitating corporate universities linked to conventional campuses – the 'porous' universities.
- Consortia and strategic alliances involving universities as a response to perceptions about globalization and other perceived twenty-first century challenges.

Implementation of these options will give rise to issues of accreditation and quality assurance, threats of globalization and homogeneity, the potential and the demise of national university systems and the risk of cultural imperialism

This chapter explores these issues of internationalization, offshore campuses, technology, consortia and accreditation and quality assurance. Finally, it proposes a vision of the culture of a university in the new millennium. But first, we explore global massification in demand for higher education, and the increasing demand in the new millennium for international university places.

Demand for Higher Education

IDP Education Australia in 1995 (Blight, 1995) developed models for world, regional and country demand for university places. These models enable top-down forecasts of student numbers to be made on a global scale. Changes in enrolments over time are driven by two factors – changes in population and changes in access rates. The 1995 study modelled population changes and access rates to the year 2010, and further out to 2025. The fundamental proposition in the 1995 study is that access rates vary with changes in per capita income. As incomes rise, demand for higher education places grows. Population growth will not have a major impact on enrolments, contributing around 0.4 per cent growth each year. Changes in access rates will make a much greater contribution, adding around 2.9 per cent growth each year. Aggregated, global demand for university places will grow at 3.5 per cent per year in the first 25 years of the new millennium. By 2010, the global access rate will be up from 16 per cent to 20 per cent, with 97 million students at universities throughout the world including 45 million from Asia. By 2025, the global access rate will be 31 per cent with 159 million students at universities throughout the world including 87 million from Asia (Blight, 1995: 22; see Figure 6.2).

Most students go to universities in their home countries. But there is a global flow of students. Malaysia and Hong Kong provide useful case studies. Malaysia's economy grew at 8 per cent or 9 per cent per annum for most of the 1980s and 1990s, transforming Malaysia over a period of 15 years from a low-technology, commodity-based economy to one where manufacturing and the services sectors employ higher and more sophisticated technology. The professional workforce plays the pivotal role in Malaysia's competitive edge. Yet Malaysia provides first-year, first-degree places for an estimated 9 per cent of its 18-year-olds, a quarter the OECD average. Malaysia's *2020 Vision* is to become a fully developed economy by the year 2020. As articulated by Prime Minister Dr Mahathir bin Mohamad (1992: 196):

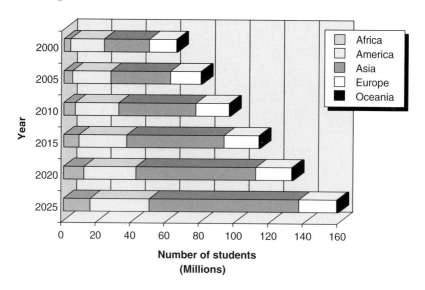

Figure 6.2   *Global demand for higher education: 2000 to 2025*

We would be a developed country in our own mould. Malaysia should not be developed only in the economic sense. It must be a nation that is fully developed along all dimensions: economically, politically, socially, spiritually, psychologically and culturally. By the year 2020, Malaysia can be a united nation, with a confident Malaysian society, infused by strong moral and ethical values, living in a society that is democratic, liberal and tolerant, caring, economically just and equitable, progressive and prosperous and in full possession of an economy that is competitive, dynamic, robust and resilient.

Implicit in this *2020 Vision* is that access to higher education in Malaysia will be on a par with OECD countries by the year 2020. At the *fin de siècle*, Malaysia was going through tough times economically and politically. Nevertheless, short of Islamic fundamentalism, Malaysia will achieve its *Vision* to become fully developed, perhaps a few years after 2020. Malaysia in 2020 will have 390,000 18-year-olds. To provide access to higher education on a par with OECD countries, Malaysia needs to provide university places for 40 per cent of its 18-year-olds. By 2020, or shortly after, Malaysia needs 156,000 first-year, first-degree places each year. This would imply a higher education sector of 600,000 students. Blight (1995: 36) estimated 137,000 students in universities in Malaysia in the year 2000. To achieve its *2020 Vision*, Malaysia needs to increase the size of its university sector four-fold in the first 20 years of the new millennium. Demand for university places in

Malaysia will continue to outstrip supply. Many students from Malaysia in the first years of the new millennium will seek their degrees from overseas universities.

Structurally, Hong Kong needs half its workforce to be trained overseas. The Hong Kong Special Administrative Region Government provides first-year, first-degree places each year for 18 per cent of its 18-year-olds, less than half the OECD average of 40 per cent. Hong Kong's Projections of Manpower Supply and Requirements for 2001 indicated in 1994 that 116,600 new graduates would join the workforce between 1997 and 2001: 48 per cent local graduates, 30 per cent immigrants and returned emigrants, and 22 per cent overseas trained graduates (Education and Manpower Branch, 1994: 14).

In its Statistical Yearbooks, UNESCO estimates that from 1970 to the mid-1980s the number of students in higher education outside their own countries grew from 500,000 to 1 million and by the mid-1990s to 1.5 million. In the mid-1990s, 46 per cent of these students were from countries in Asia and 63 per cent of these students from Asia travelled to English-language destinations. The 1995 study (Blight, 1995: 26) concluded that the growth of international student enrolments is closely related to the growth of total student numbers. In each region, domestic and international enrolments in higher education grow at about the same pace. Since it is regions with relatively high growth rates of total students that are the main sources of international students, growth in international student numbers globally will be higher than growth in domestic student numbers globally. The models behind the 1995 study provided for the inclusion of such factors as changes in the attitudes of source countries towards their students studying abroad.

The IDP Education Australia study in 1995 suggested a figure of 1.78 million international higher education students in the year 2000, with 47 per cent from Asia (Blight 1995: 29). This study predicted that the number of international students would rise to 2.75 million by 2010, with 53 per cent from Asia. In the first ten years of the new millennium, Asia would demand an additional 600,000 international university places. Further out, total numbers of international students would grow to 4.9 million in 2025, with 58 per cent from Asia (Blight, 1995: 29; see Figure 6.3). While there might be some short-term impact from the Asian economic crises of the last few years of the twentieth century, it is expected that the longer-term projections will stay firm.

IDP Education Australia carried out the 1995 study to support Australian education institutions in developing export markets. The first measurable output from the study was the forecast that Australia's universities would be host to 89,000 international students by the year 2000 (Figure 6.4). Australia is well on the way to achieving this forecast, in spite of a drop in demand from several countries in Asia.

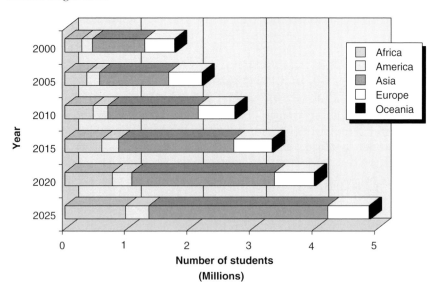

Figure 6.3   *Global demand for international higher education: 2000 to 2025*

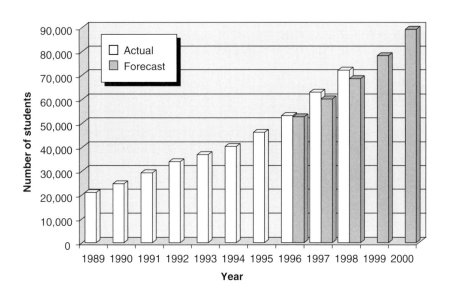

Figure 6.4   *International students in Australian universities*

Official figures from Australia's Department of Education, Training and Youth Affairs (DETYA) report that there were 72,183 students in Australian universities in 1998, up 14.6 per cent on a year earlier (DETYA, 1998: 146). Australia's figure of 72,183 international students in 1998 compares with the US figure of 481,280 in 1997/98 (Institute of International Education, 1998: ix) and the UK figure of 198,400 in 1996/97 (Higher Education Statistics Agency, 1997: 5). Interim 1997/98 figures provided by the Higher Education Statistics Agency (HESA) indicate 207,771 international students in UK universities as at 1 December 1997.

Internationalization of Universities

International student programmes are central to internationalization of higher education institutions. They add diversity to institutions and to their local communities. They influence the research interests of staff, and over time influence the curriculum. They may start a flow of funds to other internationalization programmes. The scope of internationalization at the start of the new millennium, however, means much more than an international student programme.

Knight (1997) suggests a process approach to internationalization of the core functions of a university where 'internationalization of higher education is the process of integrating an international/intercultural dimension into the teaching, research and service of the institution' (Knight, 1997: 8). Consistent with this process approach, Back, Davis and Olsen identified six programme strategies for internationalization: (1) international student programme; (2) international student support services; (3) offshore delivery of education and international delivery of distance education; (4) internationalization of teaching, through internationalization of the content and form of the curriculum and through international experiences such as exchanges; (5) international technical assistance and training, including short courses and customized training; and (6) internationalization in research. They also emphasize the over-arching need for an organizational strategy for internationalization (Back et al., 1996: 16).

Why do stakeholders in higher education world-wide – governments, institutions, including staff and students, and community, including business and industry – seek to internationalize universities? Knight (1997: 9) categorizes the reasons for internationalization into four groups – political, economic, academic, and cultural/social. Governments of nations have political incentives, including the commitment of the nation to a global economy and society, its openness to the world, its commitment to its region and its commitment to development assistance to the world. Economic incentives for a nation include the value of education as a service export and, for the community also, the labour market need to train students to operate in international and intercultural contexts. At the level of the individual institution there are financial incentives through international student fees.

The institution and the community, including business and industry, have education incentives for internationalization. Knight (1997: 11) argues that 'by enhancing the international dimension of teaching, research and service there is value added to the quality of our higher education systems.' An international academic approach attempts to avoid parochialism. An interaction with other cultures is important in the development of students. Universities have the opportunity to increase awareness and understanding of the new and changing phenomena that affect the political, economic and cultural/multicultural developments within and among nations (Knight and de Wit, 1995: 12–13). The nation's own students and the community benefit from an international curriculum. The institution and the community also have cultural and social incentives for internationalization. Internationalization of the student population adds cultural diversity to an institution and its community, leads to a demand for international exchanges and familiarizes the nation's own students with the world and with their region.

Offshore Campuses

Official figures probably do not capture fully the numbers of international students enrolled at offshore campuses. These figures include: 'all international students appearing in university databases as normal mode (on campus) or external (distance education) students. The extent to which on-campus mode students refer to offshore students is not clear, and subject to individual university interpretation' (Adams, 1998a: 4). A study by the Australian Vice-Chancellors' Committee found that 34 of Australia's 38 universities report offshore programmes with a total of 493 individual degree, diploma or similar programmes in 24 countries. IDP Education Australia in first semester 1999 surveyed Australia's universities on numbers of international students enrolled, specifically seeking data on international students on campus in Australia, off campus (studying by distance education or flexible delivery) and at offshore campuses. Universities reported a total of 93,400 international students, including 25,150 (27 per cent) at offshore campuses (IDP, 1999: 1).

The total of international students in overseas validated courses (OVCs) run by United Kingdom and Australian universities also can only be estimated. But there has been a rapid increase in the number of individuals from developing countries who are studying for foreign qualifications without travelling overseas. According to Bennell and Pearce:

> This can be done on their own by enrolling in pure distance education courses or, increasingly, by studying (on a full or part time basis) at local

public or private education institutions which have established collaborative links or partnerships with one or more universities/colleges overseas and/or have been accredited by overseas examination bodies.

Just as the Coca-Cola and McDonald corporations award franchises to companies and entrepreneurs in overseas countries to produce their products under tightly defined and rigorously enforced conditions, so too are a rapidly growing number of universities franchising other overseas institutions to offer their degrees and other qualifications.

(Bennell and Pearce, 1998: 9)

They further suggest that total OVC enrolments for all UK universities were probably in the region of 135–140,000 during the 1996/97 academic year. They add:

Not only is the magnitude of this form of education very impressive in absolute terms, but OVC enrolments were equivalent to two-thirds of the overseas student population in the UK in 1996/97. Taken together, the total number of overseas students either studying in the UK or as part of OVCs comprised 19.2 per cent of all (i.e. national and foreign) students registered in UK university courses in that year.

They estimate that OVC enrolments for all Australian universities were around 22,500 in 1997.

A transnational programme has been defined by Adams as any teaching or learning activity in which the students are in a different country (the host country) to that in which the institution providing the education is based (the home country). His typology of transnational programmes (Adams, 1998a: 8–12) includes twinning programmes; distance learning programmes, directly supported from the Australian university or with some local support; franchised programmes where a local institution teaches an Australian university's programme, with quality assurance by the Australian university; moderated programmes, where a local institution teaches its own programmes with quality assurance from an Australian university which is likely to offer advanced standing on completion of the local programme; offshore campuses; joint award programmes; and delivery in cyberspace.

Professor Adams has also highlighted a further development, the emergence of regional universities. He writes:

With multiple programs in Singapore, Malaysia and the Hong Kong SAR, and with a growing commitment to China, Vietnam and Japan, Australian universities such as Monash, RMIT, Curtin and Deakin may be positioning themselves for a future as regional universities. In this scenario, these universities may see themselves as having a similar or even greater number of students offshore than on their home campuses, as having direct investments and incorporated joint ventures offshore and being the subject of specific legislation to establish themselves in other countries as they have in Australia.

In remarks at the closing of the Twelfth Australian International Education Conference in Canberra in 1998, he even speculated about the emergence of the world's first global university:

> My guess is that it most likely will be a series of hubs and spokes. Some of the hubs will take on the character of the host university. Some of them may be semi-autonomous, with links to a host university or university systems and host cultures. Twinning programs, centres for flexible delivery, community services, recruiting of students will spin off these hubs.
>
> Such a network may be a series of joint ventures of many types, will be subject to legislation in a dozen countries and will have more students in host countries than in [the home country]. One thing I am very sure of is that this network, the global university, will be of bricks and mortar and not of virtual reality, although information technology will be very important to its operation. It will also be very culturally diverse and because it will allow students to drop in and out of locations it will be the ultimate way of ensuring an international experience for our students.
>
> (Adams, 1998b: 2)

Technology

One of the most frequently asked questions about the future of higher education is whether the virtual university will dominate the new millennium. At the end of the old millennium, IDP Education Australia commissioned research on Technology in International Education which highlighted the merging of information technology and telecommunications. It concluded:

> The combination of information technologies and telecommunications has meant that world events are no longer localised, but spread around the world within a split second via technologies ranging from Email to satellite video links. For those with access to these technologies, the global village has arrived.
>
> This global transmission of information is not restricted to current events, but extended to learners from kindergarten to senior citizens who, although they may live in the United Kingdom, participate in

learning experiences delivered from other countries in Europe, the United States or Australia, for example.

Information technologies and telecommunications build on existing distance education courses by adding value to the design of internationalised learning experiences.

(Alexander and Blight, 1996: 20)

Another Australian study examined the available evidence for the interest and involvement of global media and communication networks in higher education provision across borders, against the background of world-wide trends towards globalization of markets, communication, and culture. This report reached similar conclusions:

While there is a good deal of 'hype' relating to the involvement of global media networks in higher education, there is currently little evidence of this involvement, and, at least in the declared strategies of many of the global media networks, little intention of involvement beyond current interests in the carriage of educational content produced and controlled by other providers.

The greatest single involvement by large corporations is via the 'corporate university' model. Rather than global media networks penetrating the higher education sector, this model describes the provision of training (distinguished from education) within a large and often international corporation which may result in the growth of a sector increasingly competing with higher education for lucrative programs.

(Cunningham et al., 1997: xiii–xv)

Of course, demand for both education and training by 'large and often international' corporations provides opportunities as well as challenges for the traditional higher education sector. Cunningham et al. also found that, although the involvement of global media networks in providing higher education has been overstated, there was ample evidence of individual projects and a gathering focus on the use of new media and technology in higher education by established and new higher education institutions, and clear indications that this use would continue to grow. The use of technology and new media was in many cases still in its experimental stages. While technology was facilitating expansion into distance education by many higher education providers (including traditional universities) and brokers, such as the Western Governors University in the United States, and although the rhetoric was global, the focus was still on a local or at best national market.

Nevertheless, Cunningham found evidence of major segmentation of the market, with new providers targeting the 'life-long learning' cohort (25 years and up), and also a widespread perception that traditional institutions were not meeting the needs of the life-long learning cohort, and that the field was open for new providers to meet market demands. One obvious, and problematic, outcome of this segmentation could be that traditional institutions might be left serving the less profitable traditional undergraduate market (18–24), largely government-funded or family-funded, in a time when governments are increasingly endeavouring to cut public outlays. Cunningham concluded:

> Converging technologies and the potential for global reach have led some to assume the existence of one 'global market'. Conversely, this investigation would support the notion of the fragmentation of world markets and the development of numerous niche markets on an international and regional, rather than global scale.
>
> (Cunningham et al., 1997: xv)

Universitas 21

One response to the twenty-first-century challenges to traditional higher education, from globalization, from an increasingly competitive and differentiating higher education sector, and from perceived initiatives of information technology and media companies, has been the launch in 1997 of Universitas 21. Universitas 21 is an association of major, research-intensive, international universities. Its objective is to assist its members to become global universities and to advance their plans for internationalization. It operates as a network, where autonomous members with strong research bases maximize their strengths through a collective internationalization of such activities as research, curricula, recruitment and marketing of intellectual property. It provides a framework for benchmarking of performance and quality of its members, and also assists in development of arrangements for student and staff exchanges. Universitas 21 currently (1999) has 16 member universities – four in the United Kingdom, four in North America, four in Asia, and four in Australia and New Zealand.

This association of world-class research universities has established a number of projects. One is the development of profiles of Universitas 21 members to differentiate them from other universities characterized by a less developed or less comprehensive involvement in research. A second stresses capability, focusing on the combined range, scope and performance characteristics of Universitas 21 as a means of identifying the value-added for potential clients who work with the network. A third project is designed to exploit new teaching and learning technologies, modalities and delivery systems, including cooperation in providing mutual access to multimedia courseware. A fourth project aims to broaden the basis of professional recognition through international collaboration in curriculum development and delivery, with an initial focus on international recognition of accountancy qualifications from Universitas 21 universities. There are also two projects that focus on student and staff mobility. The former is designed to develop an enabling framework for student mobility and mutual course recognition between member universities, and the latter to establish fellowships between members for outstanding and innovative university teachers and administrators.

In response to the challenges of the twenty-first century, Universitas 21 chose its network strategy in preference to alternative strategies, such as attempting to go it alone, opting out from the world stage to regional or national stages or replicating themselves in a number of national, regional and international contexts. The contention is that a strategic alliance with a university in Singapore is a better strategy for, say, a university in New Zealand than an attempt to go it alone in the Singapore market, the heroic option; withdrawal from the Singapore market, the defeatist option; or a replication of itself by building a Singapore campus, the expensive option.

Accreditation and Quality Assurance

Cunningham et al. have highlighted world-wide concerns about accreditation and articulation, with many governments, institutions and educational organizations struggling to identify possible solutions to the problems of identifying, assessing, ranking and accrediting awards in a borderless market (1997: xvi). In such a borderless higher education market, there are two fundamentally different approaches to accreditation. The two approaches involve the relationship between globalization and internationalization. For example, Knight draws on some of her earlier work to draw a distinction between the two that is relevant to the higher education sector. She sees globalization as the flow of technology, economy, knowledge, people, values, ideas across borders; it affects each country in a different way due to a nation's individual history, traditions, culture and priorities. The internationalization of higher education, in contrast, she defines as one of the ways in which a country responds to the impact of globalization, yet at the same time respects the individuality of the nation. In her view, globalization and internationalization are different but dynamically linked concepts.

> Globalisation can be thought of as the catalyst while internationalisation is the response, albeit a response in a proactive way. The key element in the term internationalisation is the notion of between or among nations and cultural identities. A country's unique history, indigenous culture(s), resources, priorities, etc., shape its response to and relationship with other countries. Thus national identity and culture is key to internationalisation. The homogenisation of culture is

often cited as a critical concern or effect of globalisation; internationalisation, by respecting and perhaps even strengthening local, regional and national priorities and culture is therefore seen as a very different concept.

(Knight, 1997: 6)

Technology often goes hand in hand with globalization, magnifying concerns: because technology makes possible the delivery of education services on a global scale, the perception is that technology will lead to globalization with the threat of cultural imperialism. In the context of transnational education, an internationalization approach involves quality assurance and accreditation by the home institution. Accreditation by the home institution may be supplemented by a process such as the International Quality Review Process (IQRP) piloted by the International Management of Higher Education (IMHE) programme of the OECD. The process aims to have the university provide a critical self-evaluation, against the IQRP framework, and to subject this to an external peer review process.

Consistent with internationalization, host countries will then decide the rules for their importation of transnational education. For example, the Hong Kong SAR Government's regulation of non-local academic and professional courses taught in Hong Kong, through the Non-local Higher and Professional Education Ordinance, relies on accreditation in home countries. In accordance with Hong Kong's Bill of Rights, which gives the people of the Special Administrative Region the freedom to seek, receive and impart information and ideas, purely distance learning courses are exempt from the requirement to register, but are subject to restrictions on advertising. Other courses, which involve the physical presence of the non-local institution or its agent in Hong Kong for lectures, tutorials or examinations, must go through a registration process. The registration process is designed to ensure that courses offered in Hong Kong are offered by accredited institutions, that the courses offered are accredited in home countries, and that the courses offered are the same as those offered in home countries. In examining courses for registration, the Hong Kong Council for Academic Accreditation has been concerned to ensure that courses offered in Hong Kong have the same spreads of electives as those offered in home countries, and that any advanced standing offered to students in Hong Kong would be offered on an identical basis in the home country. Consistent with 'one country, two systems', courses from institutions in the People's Republic of China are covered by the Hong Kong Ordinance.

On the other hand, the Global Alliance for Transnational Education (GATE) takes a globalization approach to accreditation. The alliance is described in the following terms:

The global marketplace and new technology are contributing to the rapid globalization of higher education. Today's business environment draws its professional work force from all corners of the globe. Human resource development divisions of multi-national corporations face the increasing challenge of evaluating courses and degrees from other countries when identifying personnel. Further, higher education is no longer provided solely within national borders. Provided both by the higher education and corporate sectors, transnational education can be found in multiple forms, provided both electronically and through traditional instruction and training programs. Issues of quality, purpose and responsibility abound in this new borderless educational arena and the time is ripe for an international alliance of business, higher education and government dedicated to principled advocacy for transnational educational programs. This new alliance is GATE – the Global Alliance for Transnational Education.

(www.edugate.org)

GATE's primary purpose is to address the assurance and improvement of the quality of education that crosses national borders. It offers GATE certification to higher education institutions, suggesting that the institution may find certification valuable for a number of reasons – for example, to demonstrate commitment to quality education; where certification is required by a country to permit a foreign institution to offer a programme; where certification is accepted by a country for the purpose of recognizing the institution's graduates; to ensure or enhance the employability of graduates; to provide international comparability; to promote international mobility; to permit transportability of qualifications and partial qualifications; to permit international credit accumulation; to gain exemption from other forms of accreditation; or to attract students. Based on the recommendations of a review panel, it is the GATE Board that decides certification. Just as increasing mobility of human capital, demands for mutual recognition and globalization of higher education are requiring new approaches to accreditation, global accreditation systems themselves straddle national boundaries and may threaten national accreditation systems.

A Vision of the Culture of the University in the New Millennium

Australia, philosophically and ideologically, is open to the world, part of the global economy and society. It has a formal immigration programme with a humanitarian component. It argues in international forums for open trade and economic cooperation. Australia has a long history of providing development assistance to its region. Australia is culturally diverse. After 50 years of a formal immigration programme, nearly a quarter of the Australian population was born overseas. Australia does not collect data on the ethnicity of its people, other than for its indigenous people, who made up 2 per cent of Australia's population at the 1996 census (Australian Bureau of Statistics [ABS], 1997: 1). The best proxy Australia has for cultural diversity is the language spoken at home. At the census, 15 per cent of Australia's population spoke a language other than English at home (ABS, 1997: 41). Multiculturalism is Australian government policy. Australia's universities reflect this cultural diversity, with the addition of large numbers of international students. Australia has been sponsoring students to study in Australia since 1950, when the Colombo Plan was launched. Australia's intentions are to equip students to contribute to economic progress in their home countries and to provide these students with an understanding of Australia and Australians.

In the context of work rather than of higher education, Cope and Kalantzis have developed the concept of productive diversity as a system of production that uses diversity as a resource.

> Productive Diversity is by no means an idea that we invented alone. Its immediate genesis was in the work of the Office of Multicultural Affairs which developed in consultation with some of Australia's leading businesspeople and business thinkers. The agenda was focused on working effectively with an immigrant workforce, and putting a positive spin on multiculturalism – a policy designed primarily to promote the welfare of immigrants.
>
> Our argument is that productive diversity is much bigger than this. The origins of the idea must be understood more broadly. It is a distinctly optimistic and ingenious Australian idea, born of an irreducibly diverse society of immigrants and indigenous peoples and an economy that must be export-oriented.
>
> (Cope and Kalantzis, 1997: ix)

This concept can also be used to define a vision of Australia's internationalized universities at the start of the new millennium. The concept is developed in the Australian context but clearly has broader application. In 1998, Australia's university student population was already diverse (DETYA, 1998). A total of 1.2 per cent were indigenous people; 10.7 per cent international students, of whom 86 per cent were from Asia; 0.6 per cent New Zealanders; 13.0 per cent Australians, or Australian permanent residents, who spoke languages other than English at home, essentially reflecting 50 years of formal immigration programmes including a humanitarian component; 74.5 per cent English-speaking non-indigenous Australians or Australian permanent residents.

But the concept of productive diversity, and this vision of internationization, can be applied to academic programmes as well as student origins, with teaching and research reflecting this diversity of access. Again Cope and Kalantzis have written about work in ways that can be applied to higher education.

> Until now, dealing with diversity has been one of those soft edge, low priority business strategies that involves patronising 'touchy-feely' training on how to be nice to strange people that is based on the dubious assumption that training can make us nice. Or, perhaps, workplace policies to deal with marginal minority groups in order to avoid irritating things such as claims of harassment or discrimination.
>
> This is where our larger version of productive diversity comes in. Diversity is not a problem. Nor is it just a matter of attitudes. In our view, workforces are most effective when they are as diverse as the local and global environments in which the organisation lives. The advantages include the range of language skills, communication styles, international networks, country knowledge and life experience that people bring to organisations.
>
> (Cope and Kalantzis, 1997: x)

Similarly, universities in the new millennium will be most effective when they are as diverse, in terms of both access and programmes, as the local and global environments in which they live. These universities will be productively diverse. Such universities will have a number of new characteristics in the new millennium. First, international students will no longer need to adapt to the dominant culture to maintain standards of academic excellence; rather, all students will be valued for the diversity of their education, work experience, language skills and country knowledge. Second, student services will no longer be provided to overcome deficiencies and problems; rather student services will be provided to encourage self-sufficiency and diversity. Third, there will no longer be an assumption that all international students are the same, with all international students, especially Asian students, sharing common characteristics including approaches to learning, study patterns and support requirements; rather, among all students, there will be a continuum of attitudes to knowledge and learning strategies. Fourth, there will no longer be an assumption that academic staff must be offered training, including cross-cultural programmes, to ensure they are competent to deal with students' special circumstances; rather, the diversity of student populations will provide opportunities for staff to broaden and enrich their teaching and research experience. Fifth, there will no longer be an assumption that curricula are by their nature international; the research and policy inputs of a diverse range of students are valued as elements of programmes to internationalize curricula.

Reflecting the concept of 'productive diversity', some universities are focusing on internationalization of the curriculum using the cultural diversity of students as a resource. The focus on internationalization of the curriculum is having an impact not only on course content but also on the dynamics of interaction between local and international students and on the kinds of programmes needed to enhance the total learning experience. One Australian university which has set up a faculty-based working-group to develop a strategy for the internationalization of the curriculum has described the process as,

> teachers and students learning from each other, meeting the needs of overseas, offshore and local students, creating interdependence between students, viewing our professional practice from diverse perspectives, using culturally inclusive teaching practices, accessing teaching and learning resources which reflect diversity and offering high quality courses which are internationally relevant.
>
> (Patrick, 1997: 6)

In the twenty-first century, the value of cultural diversity will underpin the teaching and learning of the university and its links with other education organizations, the corporate world and the community. The idea of productive diversity will signify far more than the cultural diversity of the student population. Instead diversity will be manifested in student objectives and outcomes; teaching and learning approaches, styles and interactions between teachers and learners; location of research, teaching and learning, including home, work, industry and community sites, and the tendency to blur distinctions between locations; forms of delivery including multimedia and Internet programs, and flexibility between forms; the content of curricula; relationships and interactions with global, local and regional communities; forms of institutions from multi-campus international universities to predominantly 'virtual' universities to university–industry partnerships; and linkages across countries, regions and globally. This diversity in universities will not only contribute towards meeting the demand for international education but will also provide a richer, more flexible, tolerant, responsive and innovative higher education, preparing students effectively for work and living in a more globally interactive world.

References

Adams, A. (1998a) 'The operation of transnational degree and diploma programs: the Australian case', *Journal of Studies in International Education*, 2 (1) Spring 1998.
——(1998b) 'Answers in uncertain times: the global university', remarks at the closing session of the 12th Australian International Education Conference, Canberra.

Alexander, S. and Blight, D. (1996) *Technology in International Education*, research paper presented to the 10th Australian International Education Conference on Technologies for the New Millennium, Adelaide.

Australian Bureau of Statistics (1997) *1996 Census of Population and Housing: Selected Social and Housing Characteristics Australia*, Canberra: Australian Bureau of Statistics.

Back, K., Davis, D. and Olsen, A. (1996) *Internationalisation and Higher Education: Goals and Strategies*, Canberra: Department of Education, Training and Youth Affairs (DETYA).

Bennell, D, and Pearce, T. (1998) *The Internationalisation of Higher Education: Exporting Education to Developing and Transitional Economies*, Brighton (University of Sussex): Institute of Development Studies.

Blight, D. (1995) 'International education: Australia's potential demand and supply', research paper presented to the 1995 International Education Conference, Brisbane, October.

Cope, B. and Kalantzis, M. (1997) *Productive Diversity: A New, Australian Model for Work and Management*, Sydney: Pluto Press.

Cunningham, S., Tapsall, S., Ryan, Y., Stedman, L., Bagdon, K. and Flew, T. (1998) *New Media and Borderless Education: A Review of the Convergence between Global Media Networks and Higher Education Provision*, Canberra: Higher Education Division, DETYA, Evaluations and Investigations Program, 97/22, January.

Department of Education, Training and Youth Affairs (1998) *Selected Higher Education Student Statistics 1998*, Canberra: DETYA.

Education and Manpower Branch, Government Secretariat (1994) *Manpower 2001 Revisited: A Revised Projection of Manpower Supply and Requirements for 2001*, Hong Kong.

Higher Education Statistics Agency (HESA) (1997) *Data Report: Students in Higher Education Institutions 1996/97*, Cheltenham: HESA.

IDP Education Australia (1999) *International Students in Australian Universities: First Semester 1999*, Canberra: IDP Education Australia.

Institute of International Education (1998) *Open Doors 1997/98: Report on International Educational Exchange*, New York.

Knight, J. (1997) 'Internationalisation of higher education: a conceptual framework', in J. Knight and H. de Wit (eds) *Internationalisation of Higher Education in Asian Pacific Countries*, Amsterdam: European Association for International Education/IDP Education Australia.

Knight, J. and de Wit, H. (1995) 'Strategies for internationalisation of higher education: historical and conceptual perspectives', in H. de Wit (ed.) (1995) *Strategies for Internationalisation of Higher Education: A Comparative Study of Australia, Canada, Europe and the United States of America*, Amsterdam: EAIE.

Mahathir, M. (1992) 'Malaysia: the way forward', paper presented to the Malaysian Business Council, Kuala Lumpur.

Patrick, K. (1997) *Internationalising the University: Implications for Teaching and Learning at RMIT*, Melbourne: Royal Melbourne Institute of Technology.

UNESCO (1997) and earlier editions) *UNESCO Statistical Yearbook*, Paris: UNESCO.

7 Reconfiguring the University

Ronald Barnett

The fall?

> There has been too much comment of late that refers to the death of the university.
>
> (Webster, 1998: 69)

To my knowledge, no book has appeared with the title 'the death of the university'. Admittedly, Webster's comment appeared in a symposium focused on a paper from Gerard Delanty on 'the end of knowledge'; there was, though, a question mark at the end of Delanty's title. Admittedly, too, a book recently appeared with the title *Universities in Ruins* (Readings, 1997). Furthermore, in essays on the universities and postmodernity, there have been some skirmishes on the general theme (eg. Smith and Webster, 1998). But we are not being overwhelmed by an avalanche of texts claiming the death of the university. Is the alleged death real or not?

We can see universities. They are solid stuff, increasingly so, despite the rise of the Internet and the possible emergence of the university in cyberspace. The buildings keep going up, notwithstanding the shortfall (in the UK) of several hundreds of millions of pounds to maintain the sector in anything approaching the way to which it has become accustomed (National Committee of Inquiry into Higher Education [NCIHE], 1997). The student numbers remain high, give or take a blip at either end (as would-be entrants pause to calculate the personal return on their investment and enrolled students find it harder to stay the course and the non-completion rates rise). The numbers of papers and academic books being published continue to increase. The university sector, in other words, seems more robust than ever. Apparently, it is wanted by different constituencies more than ever before, constituencies which are prepared to invest heavily in it. Universities, far from being near death, are fully alive.

Nor is this a matter of investing in old memories. New demands and expectations come the way of the university and universities collectively continue to adapt. It may be that the level and direction of that adaptation is not to everyone's taste. Pockets of resistance will be found: a chemistry degree course at an 'elite' university in the 1990s may bear many similarities to its predecessor course in the same department a generation before. But even there, change is to be found, in the new instrumentation, in the use of computers, in the importation of 'transferable skills' and in the new mix of modules reflecting the shifts in global technologies. So change, liveliness and demand are all in evidence. This is hardly a sector at its end.

Busy-ness, however, does not entail direction; activity does not entail purpose; change does not entail reasoning. It is in this sense that we are entitled to use the language of the end of the university. We use the term 'university' but we no longer have any clear sense as to what it might stand for: we no longer have a concept of 'university'. Less a death than a fall from grace: the university has lost any purity that it might have had. 'The entrepreneurial university' (Clark, 1998) simply becomes what it can fashion for itself. It has lost any sense that knowledge and inquiry generated value positions in themselves; but it has also lost a sense as to what it is to be a university. Or, rather, the sense is just created by the university for itself amid the opportunities that present themselves.

Epistemologically and ontologically adrift, then; this is the state of the modern university. It will be said that there will be winners and losers in the resulting struggle for survival. But against what criteria are we to judge the winners? Will the league tables supply the answer? In this chapter, I shall argue that the higher education system is the loser for not possessing an idea of the university; that, indeed, a new idea of the university is within reach, and one that would find widespread approval; and that its serious adoption would call for radical changes in the management and leadership of universities and in their central activities. A new state of grace is available.

Supercomplexity[1]

A situation of complexity exists when there is a surfeit of data, ideas or resource demands *within* a relatively given situation. A doctor is bombarded with information on new drugs, or is hazily aware of new possibilities of medical intervention or feels there to be too many patients to see in the time available. By contrast, a situation of *supercomplexity* – as I wish to term it – exists when the basic framework governing the situation is challenged. The same doctor is asked to see herself as a manager of expensive resources on behalf of the state; she is urged to reconsider the doctor–patient relationship, seeing it more as a market transaction; she is called upon to revalue her medical training and give greater weight to 'alternative medicine'; and she is urged to reconceptualize medicine as a practice that maintains health (so that her main client group is the healthy rather than the sick). All these are examples of challenges to the basic framework of what constitutes medicine and what it means to practise medicine. Categories of medicine, doctor, health, hospital and even patient do not evaporate; they become elastic and are extended.

The frameworks by which we understand medicine multiply; and, in the process, they conflict. Accountability rivals care, resource management runs against 'excellence', skill appears to supplant knowledge. This multiplication of frameworks, it will be clear from the examples just given, is not simply or even in major part, a technological matter. What is at issue here is not the assimilation of new technologies or even the repercussions of new technologies. What is at issue are matters of understanding: how do we understand ourselves, our world and our actions in the world? All of these fundamental matters of understanding, including our self-understanding, are continually being challenged by new and rival frameworks. This process of framework multiplication and framework conflict – this supercomplexity – is now becoming endemic, not just to professional life but to life itself. There is no hiding place from this turmoil.

The university is implicated in supercomplexity in three ways. First, the university is partly responsible for producing supercomplexity. There is much talk these days about the university losing its monopoly as a producer of knowledge (Gibbons et al., 1994). Be that as it may, the university both has been in the past a major producer of new frameworks of understanding and continues to be so in the present. That is the character of research of any significance: it offers us new frameworks through which to understand ourselves, the world around us and our relationship to that world.

Second, the university is being asked to prepare its students to develop the human qualities capable of withstanding a world of supercomplexity and of making purposive interventions within it. The talk of self-reliance, adaptability and flexibility that accompanies much of the rhetoric befalling the university in relation to its educational role is testimony to the emerging ubiquity of supercomplexity. These terms point, it will be noticed, not to the knowledge that graduates are supposed to acquire, nor even to their 'competences'. They point – to repeat – to certain kinds of human quality, to certain modes of being for which the handling of multiple frameworks calls. The educational problem of supercomplexity is not one of knowledge but of being.

Third, supercomplexity invites the university to reconsider what might be termed its civic or even – to put it grandly – its enlightenment role. Supercomplexity is a general, indeed a global, phenomenon. It constitutes the modern age. There arises, as a result, a general opportunity, if not to say need, for the university to assist the general assimilation of supercomplexity. The general call for the university to play its part in 'the learning age' (Department for Education and Employment [DfEE], 1998) can be seen just as part of this newly emerging role.

Well over a hundred years ago, the university considered that it had a role to play in advancing the level of general understanding in society. In the so-called 'extension' movement, scholars and scientists took it as part of their responsibility to carry the fruits of their intellectual labours into the wider society (Gordon and White, 1979). As academics came to have comfortable livings in the university, the sense of that wider responsibility was lost. Now, amid supercomplexity, a new educative role opens involving both the general expansion of frames of understanding in the wider society and the general easing of the perplexity that results precisely from the proliferation of frameworks of understanding.

Supercomplexity is a new phenomenon and has implications for the university as such. It undermines the traditional value background of the university since it attacks all frameworks. No longer can we talk in a cavalier fashion about the university upholding the value of knowledge or democracy or emancipation or even work. All such large ideas are contestable and are contested. But, at a metalevel as it were, supercomplexity provides not just a new rationale for the university but a new set of responsibilities. Especially since the university has been partly responsible for the emergence of super-complexity, it can hardly evade responsibility for attending to its repercussions.

A Leadership for Supercomplexity

Supercomplexity, it will be clear, bestows a new set of responsibilities upon the university. But if universities are going to accept this set of responsibili-ties, they will have to become different kinds of places. In the first place, therefore, university leadership has to be recast. There are, perhaps, three present models of university leadership. None of them will do as a response to supercomplexity. First, there is the chief executive model in which it is assumed both that it is right and that it is possible to direct and manage institutional change from the centre. Second, as a conflation of a profession-alist model with a postmodern model, is the action-at-a-distance model. Essentially, this takes a more modest view of the leadership role, and considers that both professional life and the complexities of the late-modern world grossly limit the scope of any direct control from the centre. It will monitor performance, it will try to anticipate crises – financial or otherwise – and it will do what it can to nudge the university up the league tables. Basically, it accepts a limited role: a gentle hand on the tiller so as not to rock the boat is the order of the day. Third, is the entrepreneurial model. Here, the motto is seize the main chance. All kinds of opportunities are opening for the university in the modern world: largely, its intellectual capital is under-utilized. Let us, therefore, find what markets we can for it.

The entrepreneurial model, much vaunted of late, is but a hybrid on the way to a model of institutional leadership appropriate to conditions of supercomplexity. It may offer some of the collective spontaneity, the engage-ment with multiple constituencies, and the institutional responsiveness that is required. It may even go some way to encouraging its scholars and researchers to project themselves into more public arenas. And it may not be displeased if, in the formation of new projects, academics are collaborating with each other across the disciplines. All this is required for a serious response to supercomplexity. But more is needed.

We may take a university to be a mosaic. In a mosaic, each piece is in contact with only a limited number of other pieces. Furthermore, in the mosaic that constitutes the university, the pieces are invested with energy: they are all shimmering. Some pieces, however, are shimmering more brightly than others. In a university for supercomplexity, there are two challenges: first, to bring pieces into contact with as many others as possible (since, amid supercomplexity, one never knows what epistemic alliances are going to prosper); second, to enable those pieces with less lustre to gain extra energy (since one never knows what intellectual resources may be helpful). Amid supercomplexity, therefore, university leadership has to contend with its intellectual forces. It has to seize them, to bring them into contiguity with each other, and to encourage them to engage in fruitful contact with each other. Not to do so would be to limit the resourcefulness available to the university. If the university is going to produce revolutionary frames of new understanding, they are especially likely to be forthcoming if epistemic groupings that customarily have little or no interaction are brought into contact.

It may be thought that what is being urged here is a plea for interdisciplinarity. Currently, such a plea tends to spring from on e of two considerations. First, it is said that the interesting intellectual problems lie at the conjunction of different forms of thought. Second, and quite separately, it is said that the problems of the contemporary world do not come neatly sliced up according to the disciplinary formations of the academic world: problem solving 'in the real world' calls for an integration of intellectual forces. Both of these considerations may have a point, separate as they are, but they are not at issue here. What *is* at issue is the maximizing of the intellectual energy and frames of thinking and of action that lie in the interstices of the university. Why should we expect that any configuration, any mode of interaction and any degree of collaboration across the epistemic units that comprise a university represent, by sheer happenchance, the ideal configuration appropriate to the conditions of supercomplexity that confront the university? No such assumption should be entertained. On the contrary, since the extent of interaction, communication and collaboration will be limited, a much more plausible assumption is that the actual configuration represents a less than optimal set of arrangements in the circumstances facing the university.

What emerges from these reflections is that university leadership, amid supercomplexity, has to concern itself with the disposition of the intellectual forces at its disposal. 'At its disposal' is, of course, question-begging. The phrase implies that university leaders have at least some degree of influence over the shape and dynamics of the intellectual resources that constitute the university. Just that is at issue. By and large, university leaders have shrunk from such a definition of their role. Certainly, they engage, from time to time, in structural changes: they create faculties by bringing together departments; or they disaggregate them, very often in cycles of fusion and fission. But, apart from the quite legitimate financial, resourcing and managerial considerations that enter into such reframings, the extent to which such reconfiguring is conducted with any eye to the intellectual opportunities that it offers is limited. Even where they do so, it is a case of light the blue touch paper and retire. Almost certainly, the normal assumption is that the mere cohabitation of individuals will bring about the required degree of collaboration.

Here, I am less interested in the actual extent of restructuring than in its motives. I am raising the possibility that academic leadership might include two dimensions. First, to return to our analogy, it might include a concern to ensure that the pieces of the mosaic that comprise the university are in contact with as many other pieces as possible. This is not a matter of restructuring but of interaction. Academics would sooner speak to another academic in the same field on the other side of the world before they would speak to an academic in an entirely different field in the same institution. If the university is to be best placed to withstand the forces of supercomplexity that surround it, the academics across the disciplines have first to start to get to know each other. Opportunities have to be created, excuses have to be found and chances have to be taken to require colleagues to interact. Once names have been exchanged, something may happen.

The second dimension goes beyond mere interaction. It is that of the promotion of substantial communication and even of collaboration. Collaboration would be a bonus; out of communication may come collaboration. Cross-disciplinary communication of substance is itself a major achievement. Very often, for mutual comprehension to occur, mutual antipathy if not downright hostility has to be overcome. Communication involves understanding; it requires give and take. It is not just a case of: I shall not prevent you from having a hearing. It is more a case of: I allow that what you say may have some substance to it, even though I do not understand it. Communication also involves not just active listening but an attempt to shape one's utterances in a form in which they might be intelligible to the listener.

For all this to take place, for academics to spark off each other and for the intellectual energy contained within the mosaic to grow, institutional leadership – at all levels – has to concern itself with processes of communication and engagement across the university. It is not just a matter of bringing staff together on joint ventures, diverse as these may be (for example, to explore jointly ways of engaging with the local region; or to utilize the computer for educational purposes; or to develop a university-wide learning and teaching strategy). It is also a matter of enabling staff to communicate more easily with each other. For example, an intellectual and professional audit of the expertise and networks of all staff might be conducted and made available to all members of staff (to enable team-building in relation to particular issues); a university magazine might be set up to encourage cross-university debate between groups and centres over academic and educational issues; all academic staff might be required to produce a 'Web' page about themselves.

'Who is there?' is a key unspoken question in university life. Unless and until staff develop lateral communication across the university – and they will need to be helped in doing so – the university's intellectual forces will fail to produce their potential energy level and fail, therefore, to be in a position to offer maximum responsiveness to the challenges and opportunities that present in a supercomplex environment.

Research for Supercomplexity

Amid supercomplexity, research is faced with three challenges. First, a world characterized by multiple frames of knowledge is paradoxically calling for those frames to multiply. Of the multiplication of frameworks, there should be no end. That is plain enough. A world of globalization, data creation and saturation via the Internet, an increasingly literate and demanding consumer society, and economic and cultural effervescence, has built into it forms of human exchange and contestability that willy-nilly go on producing new frameworks of interpretation and of action at an accelerating rate. Certainly, a common response at the personal level is: enough. Let me find stability. But at the global, societal and corporate levels, there are, as stated, propulsions at work both that call for new frameworks and that seek to generate new frameworks.

Admittedly, as is now common currency, the university has lost any pretence that it might have had that it possessed a monopoly of the legitimacy to produce new frameworks of understanding. Nevertheless, that role and that calling are there, placed upon the university but now with increasing urgency and insistence. The world calls for challenges to our frameworks by being offered new frameworks; and a responsibility falls upon the university to make its contribution to that requirement.

One reason that the university now has rivals in the supply of new frameworks of understanding is that the modern university has failed to live up to its rhetoric about itself in this respect. It has projected a sense of itself as 'pushing back the frontiers of our knowledge' but, in practice, has stood back while the academics have developed a massive infrastructure of warehousing and maintaining knowledge, rather than being mainly concerned with its continual reframing. 'Conjectures and Refutations' there may be (Popper, 1963), but they tend to be more concerned with the character of the infilling mortar rather than the shape and framework of the edifice of knowledge itself. This was the implication of Kuhn's (1970) analysis: that knowledge production focused more on refining the dominant paradigms than on overthrowing them. Feyerabend's later (1978) suggestion that 'anything goes' was more an exhortation than a commentary. For the most part, even though they might talk of 'risk' and 'chaos', academics like to enjoy as much stability and reliability in their professional lives as possible.

The result has been that a world that demands an increasing supply of ever-more daring innovations in its frames of comprehending the world has spawned all manner of knowledge producers. In the process, knowledge production widens to embrace image production, metaphor production, technology production, strategy production and data production. The very definitions of knowledge enshrined in the academics' infrastructure – varied as they believe them to be across the different academic tribes and territories (Becher, 1989) – turn out to be far too limited for a fast-moving, global world in which economy, culture, action and technology intermesh. The challenge here facing the university, accordingly, is not simply that it can no longer even pretend to be the main producer of knowledge, but that its framing of the frames of knowing is being left behind. The knowledge infrastructure that universities have developed or, more accurately, have allowed to develop, not only acts as a brake on creativity and innovation in knowledge production per se but also acts to exert inertia on the sense of what are to be counted as frames of knowing and understanding in the modern, global age.

Against this background, opportunities and challenges face the university at both the structural and the personal levels. Let us take the two levels in turn. Some are saying that the university should act as 'the conscience of society' (NCIHE, 1997). A less value-laden way of putting the point, and one that is more realizable, is to say that there is a new readiness for the university to expand the pool of ideas and frameworks that circulate in the wider society. Some of those ideas are bound to be critical rather than simply extending the already known. To fulfil such a role, conditions have to be put in place likely to engender the maximum outpouring of radical, innovatory and revolutionary ideas. 'Ideas' has to be understood in the broadest possible terms. It includes artefacts, methodologies and services; any knowledge product and service that the university might offer the wider world. We can term all such forms of research 'reframing' in character. Rather than 'refining' existing paradigms, this research seeks to challenge existing frameworks of knowing.

Within the university, the structural conditions of maximizing such reframing potential are three. First, academics have to engage with the widest possible range of academic networks. Research of a reframing character calls for the ability to stand outside of conventional frameworks, an ability that is likely to be prompted by interaction and communication across existing networks. Second, the criteria of success in the research 'game' have themselves to be widened to encourage both interdisciplinary work and unconventional forms of knowledge production. Third, reframing products have to take on a public character, such that they can add to the public circulation of knowing frameworks. A university for supercomplexity has to widen its self-conception to embrace that of enhancing the frameworks by which the world is understood and experienced beyond the university.

All this calls for enlightened knowledge policies and knowledge strategies at both the national and institutional levels. Academics have their identities anchored in their 'Tribes and Territories' (Becher, 1989), where the main consideration is not to rock the boat. If academics are to (1) engage systematically with others in contrasting networks; (2) promote their knowledge products to wider audiences in a comprehensible language; and (3) dare to imagine quite new orderings of knowledge, they need to be encouraged to do so. Institutional leaders will have to engender lateral communication in their universities; internal and external performance indicators should embrace an ever-widening range of knowledge products and processes; and space and time have to be allowed for transmitting those outcomes of inquiry into public spaces.

There is a difficulty here; that of performance indicators in general. Performance indicators are retrospective in their effects, looking back into past performance, and enshrine at best current presuppositions as to good practice. But in an age of supercomplexity, which calls for thinking and knowledge products that break through the boundaries of the given and to create new frames of knowing and experiencing, bureaucratically enforced performance indicators condemn higher education always to be behind the game. This is one field of academic endeavour where the application of market principles has a point. Let the academics try their knowledge products on the open market; at least, they should be permitted and encouraged to do so. Such an extension of academic activities will also serve to encourage academics to engage with the wider society, and so in turn encourage academics to make available their knowledge products to new and multiple audiences.

In this way, an enlightenment role for the university is regained; and in three senses. First, the university is released from its narrow sense that there are boundaries to what counts as knowledge and as knowing: processes, products, methodologies, action learning, knowing-in-action, as well as revolutionary theoretical frameworks are just some of the many possibilities that serve to expand the conventional definitions of bona fide academic activities. Second, the acceptance by wider audiences of such products and processes becomes a legitimate criterion in their validity. As a result, the university is encouraged to place ever more of its imaginary creations in the public domain.

Thirdly, the acts of translation, mediation and negotiation that such communication calls for bring with it a wider pedagogical role for the university, a role that the university has a particular responsibility to meet. The university has helped to bring about supercomplexity through the knowledge frameworks that it has put into the world; and it is faced with the challenge of doing even more of that. In turn, there emerges in the wider public an angst, a longing for a stability that is no longer available. Accordingly, the academy has the responsibility to help society live with the unease that it has helped to bring about. This is to take seriously its long-heralded role as a critical commentator.

It would be tempting to say that there is and that there should be a division of labour at work, that the sciences and technologies have the responsibility of increasing ideas, frameworks and understandings in the public domain, and that the humanities have the task of enabling the wider world to comprehend the resulting world of uncertainty. Adding to supercomplexity on the one hand; helping us to live with supercomplexity on the other hand: these are the two challenges that the wider world is putting to the university, and they fall neatly on the science–humanities divide, with the social sciences playing a dual role. Such neatness does not and cannot work. As a matter of fact, the scientists are already well engaged in the second role of articulating their new frameworks to a wider public: evolution, genetic manipulation, the cosmos, and even chaos theory find ready markets in the widening of the public consciousness. On the other hand, the emerging frameworks of the humanists and the social scientists directly add to the frameworks of self-understanding in the public domain. Not just grand theories of postmodernization, globalization and feminism are articulated from an academic base, but more localized ideas – for example, a concern with discourse, genre and signs – spill out into the public sphere, informing debates about communication and the media. Semiotics has a use value.

So, as a matter of fact, all domains of academic endeavour have increasing opportunities to place their imaginings in the public domain. But, in an age of supercomplexity, not only do they all have a responsibility to do so, but the academics in turn have the further task of assisting the ensuing public debate. They have the pedagogical role of enabling the wider public to make sense of the new framings and to live purposively amid the crazy experience of supercomplexity that they themselves have helped to bring about. In this sense, the academics are only helping to meet the bill that they have partly landed us all with. Many academics will shrink from such a public role. The idea of the public intellectual is afoot but, insofar as it is exemplified, it is taken up sparingly by individuals and given a narrow interpretation. Much as they talk of risk, chaos and change, the academics would rather seek the relative stability of the inner-oriented academic life. Nor will they change unless both pressure and rewards work in the requisite directions.

Teaching for Supercomplexity

The fundamental educational problem posed by supercomplexity is not one of knowledge, or even of the transmission of knowledge. It is, as already stated, one of *being*. It is to assist students in developing dispositions appropriate to the conditions of supercomplexity. Supercomplexity is a global matter and, therefore, bears on individuals across society. The conditions of supercomplexity, it will be recalled, are those of uncertainty, unpredictability, contestability and challengeability. But this constellation of fragility bears less on technological change than, more crucially, on changes in and challenges to the frames by which we understand the world, understand ourselves and our relations to the world and our actions in it. This is a problematic of being, not of knowledge.

Although it constitutes a universal framing of modern life, supercomplexity shows itself unevenly across society. In particular, it strikes at professional and corporate life at the levels to which graduates aspire. At those levels, they not merely have to handle supercomplexity: they have to add to it, they have to enable others (both those who work with them and their external clients) to comprehend the conditions of supercomplexity with which they are immediately faced, and they have to assist those others in living and working purposively amid those circumstances. These are modes of being, not of knowing; and they are modes of being that place professionals and senior managers in quasi-pedagogical roles.

To repeat, then, a higher education has to take seriously the world of supercomplexity into which its graduates will move. Bodies of knowledge, theoretical frameworks, and technical concepts and all their associated knowledge processes do not have to be abandoned but they have to be reshaped. Courses have to become less programmes of study and even inquiry and more programmes of confrontation and engagement. The required confrontation is not with theories and concepts as such but with the conditions of uncertainty and contestability that surround them. This is not a plea for relativism or postmodernism. Rather, it is an urging that the very conditions of uncertainty and contestability that surround both the original creation of those theories and concepts and their associated methodologies be presented to the students. In addition, the conditions of uncertainty and contestability that surround their utility and valuing in the wider world should also be revealed to the students.

In this way, research and teaching can be brought together; and the relationship can also be taken to a new level. The personal challenge that lies in the research endeavour is experienced first-hand by the students; and it will be said that that pedagogical approach has been used – especially in the sciences – for some time. But much less in evidence is the wider personal challenge that accompanies the presentation of that research in the wider world. The chemistry student who proceeds into the chemical industry needs not only to have experienced the personal unsettling that is part of the research process but needs also the personal wherewithal to withstand the critical questioning and even hostility that is aimed at the corporate projection of chemistry (for instance, in its impact on the natural and increasingly on the human environment).

A pedagogy for supercomplexity, accordingly, puts weight on the associated pedagogical relationships. Students will develop the dispositions for handling uncertainty and for living through uncertainty only if they are given the pedagogical space to experience and work through situations of uncertainty. To repeat, this uncertainty cannot merely be a matter of uncertainty in relation to knowing; it has to challenge students in their self-understanding, in their capacities to act and to value. The pedagogical situation has to be widened beyond its conventional narrow concerns with knowing within given frameworks. The frameworks themselves have to be put under scrutiny; the students have to feel – not just know – that there is no resting place. There can be no 'problem solving', only further and unending problems opened up by the inquiry process.

In a pedagogy for supercomplexity, accordingly, the pedagogical relationships have to be turned upside down. Students have to be put on the spot to come forth with their own offerings, within a developing sense that there is no given end-point and that the inquiry is, necessarily, a matter of some risk. Nothing ventured, nothing gained. The students have to make themselves in the process of formulating their offerings. Those offerings require a commitment from them. The students have to make their identity, even though any such identity must inevitably have a degree of fragility attached to it. For such a student to be realized, for the student to have space to make their own interventions and to come to their own offerings, their lecturers have, to a significant degree, to fade into the background. This does not represent an abandonment of the authority of the lecturer, still less of his or her responsibilities. But that authority has to be made and remade continually, and in numerous ways.

Indeed, the role of lecturer has to be displaced. The lecture has itself to be radically diminished, if not abandoned altogether. The pedagogical relationship that it sustains is one of fixed boundaries between the lecturer and the audience. The boundaries enable the recipient to stay outside of the utterances. The student is transformed into voyeur rather than being obliged to engage with the knowing frames that are being proffered. Still less are students required to sense the intractability of the issues raised and to feel their way to forming their own position in that situation. That a lecture may expose uncertainty and contestability, that a student may experience an unsettling, and that a student may even begin to frame his or her own responses do nothing to change the constituents of the pedagogical relationship systematically enshrined in the lecture. The lecture confers on the lecturer an authority that he or she cannot maintain in an age of supercomplexity. What is required is a pedagogy that allows the student to come to terms with uncertainty, where there are no ultimate authorities; and no ultimate authority residing in any framework.

Against this analysis, a number of currently espoused strategies for teaching and learning have to be given short shrift. Skills, whether domain-specific or transferable, are entirely inadequate as a response to supercomplexity. Skills assume fixity in presenting situations, however loosely they may be defined. Amid supercomplexity, skills are both changing and are challengeable. They are an impoverished attempt to provide security where no security is to be had. The use of information and communications technology may offer enhanced accessibility to higher education. It may even allow wider forms of uncertainty to be presented to students and, in that sense, can contribute to a pedagogy for uncertainty. And it may encourage the formation of Socratic dialogue both between teacher and student and, more tellingly, between students themselves. But the issues remain to be addressed: what are the presenting conditions of supercomplexity and how do we encourage the formation of those dispositions that are likely to carry the students forward in that milieu? Information and communications technology is neither necessary nor sufficient for realizing that kind of pedagogy.

A third strategy being mooted is that of defining the learning objectives and ensuring that the curriculum and the learning environment are given the best chance for their realization. One immediate response is that the specification of learning outcomes forecloses on just that should be in question; namely, the outcomes of learning for a unknown world, which themselves have to contain some degree of uncertainty. The main problem with learning outcomes, however, is that they smuggle in a technological pedagogy: they treat students as means on which pedagogical devices are to be wrought. They deny that students have their own beings, however fragile, that have to be nurtured. The encouragement of a certain kind of being is an outcome to be achieved not by educators but by students themselves. Their resilience, fortitude, willingness to stand up to the enemy, preparedness to have a go, to place their own imaginings into the world, and to engage with the world are not outcomes, in the way that my arriving at Glasgow is an outcome of my getting on a certain train from Euston. They are qualities, into the fashioning of which students have had to invest themselves.

A pedagogy for supercomplexity has to be unsettling, open and full of risk. Those conditions hold not just for students but also for their lecturers. Their lecturers have to become educators. But lecturers and students have, in the present climate, both motivations and encouragement to opt for a learning environment devoid of risk, one indeed that will yield stated learning outcomes. It is less a joint conspiracy and more a subtle agreement in favour of safety where boundaries, expectations and criteria of judgment are all known in advance. Certainly, some features of a pedagogy for supercomplexity are embryonically in place: information technology, learning resource centres, action in the community and self-reflection and self-assessment: all these can be ingredients of the appropriate learning environment. But they will, at best, fall short of the mark without a fundamental appreciation of the pedagogical challenge of supercomplexity. Certainly, some worthwhile forms of human development may result. But, unless a curriculum is systematically constructed to produce the qualities and propensities to engage with the consistent personal and conceptual challenge that a world of supercomplexity represents, it is extremely unlikely that they will emerge.

Conclusion: A University for Supercomplexity

'The entrepreneurial university'; 'the service university'; 'the corporate university'; 'the virtual university'; a 'university for the learning society'; a university characterized by 'excellence': these are just some of the current visions of the university for the twenty-first century. They each have their own appeal and their own attractions. Each implies a greater set of linkages between the university and its wider environment, although that wider environment is seen quite differently. Indeed, 'the corporate university' almost implies a reversal back to a university under the control of the producers; only, this time, the producers are the current consumers. Despite their differences, however, they share a common weakness in that they are each addressing a particular set of issues and each, in turn, offers a narrow view of the university.

As a shorthand description, a university for supercomplexity may not have the immediate appeal or accessibility of those five others. Its character is less obvious; its purposes are less evident; its client group is less clear. Its strength, however, is that it is built on a diagnosis of our age and of the challenges to humanity that the age is presenting. To a large degree, it embraces all those other conceptions and goes beyond them. For example, the entrepreneurial university is but a halfway stage to the university for supercomplexity. It has some of the openness, dynamic and preparedness to adapt that is characteristic of the university for supercomplexity; but it lacks a sense of its responsibilities to the wider community and is relatively silent about its pedagogical role. The sheer pragmatism built into the entrepreneurial university will not deliver a university that will meet its responsibilities to the wider world that supercomplexity presents us with.

On the other hand, the university for supercomplexity contends against some of the elements in those other conceptions of the university. The corporate university – or even a 'conventional' university that was significantly oriented towards the corporate sector – has, by definition, a limited mission – that of corporate well-being at most. But, almost paradoxically, the definitions of corporate well-being are likely to be so constrained in time and scope that even that set of aims has to be in doubt. Skills and knowledges, doubtless of an advanced technical kind, are likely to come to the fore just at the time when those skills and knowledges are every day being seen globally to be an inadequate defence against a changing, uncertain and contested world.

Less glitz and more honest toil may seem to be the message for a university to be realized amid conditions of supercomplexity. But this would sell short the character of the university for the twenty-first century. Constructing a university that both understands its responsibilities to the wider world and delivers on them has to involve the construction of uncertainty itself, and at two levels. The university has the responsibility to inject further uncertainty into an already uncertain world; and it has itself to comprehend that role and itself to take on the conditions of uncertainty of the wider world. Universities have for too long been safe havens. In an age of uncertainty, the universities have to abandon the idea of knowledge as an emblem. Instead, they should help us to revel in uncertainty for that is the condition of our age.

Note

1   The concept of supercomplexity and the general argument of this chapter is developed more fully in my book *Realizing the University* (Barnett, 1999).

References

Barnett, R. (1999) *Realizing the University in an Age of Supercomplexity*, Buckingham: Open University Press.

Becher, T. (1989) *Academic Tribes and Territories*, Milton Keynes: Open University Press.

Clark, B. R. (1998) *Creating Entrepreneurial Universities: Organizational Pathways of Transformation*, Oxford: Pergamon.

Department for Education and Employment (1998) *The Learning Age: A Renaissance for a New Britain*, London: HMSO.

Feyerabend, P. (1978) *Against Method*, London: Verso.

Gibbons, M., Limoges, C., Nowotny, H., Schwartzman, S., Scott, P. and Trow, M. (1994) *The New Production of Knowledge: The Dynamics of Science and Research in Contemporary Societies*, London: Sage.

Gordon, P. and White, J. (1979) *Philosophers and Educational Reformers*, London: Routledge and Kegan Paul.

Kuhn, T. (1970) *The Structure of Scientific Revolutions*, London: University of Chicago.

National Committee of Inquiry into Higher Education (1997) *Higher Education in the Learning Society*, Report of the National Committee of Inquiry, London: HMSO.

Popper, K. (1963) *Conjectures and Refutations*, London: Routledge and Kegan Paul.

Readings, B. (1997) *The University in Ruins*, Massachusetts: Harvard University Press.

Smith, A. and Webster, F. (eds) (1998) *The Postmodern University? Contested Visions of Higher Education in Society*, Buckingham: Open University Press.

Webster, F. (1998) 'The idea of a university: a response to Delanty', *Social Epistemology*, 12 (1) 67–72.

Part II
Future Knowledge

8 New Technologies, Students and the Curriculum

The Impact of Communications and Information Technology on Higher Education

Diana Laurillard

The challenge for this chapter is to speculate on the changes that new technology will bring to higher education. It is a task to be approached with great care, as technology, that 'great growling engine of change', as Toffler (1970) memorably described it, has a way of continually surprising us. It is reasonable to expect that the potential of new technology to change the way we teach and do research will be realized eventually in some way. The question is, whether it will be universities doing it on their own terms, or whether it will be more successfully exploited by others first.

The shape this chapter takes is to begin by clarifying the fundamental role and purpose of a university, against which we can test the directions in which we may be driven. It is important to be able to distinguish the ways in which the technology is a positive driver towards improving higher education, from the ways it could undermine its mission. Technology is rarely designed for education, so the technology we use in education may have either a positive or negative effect on educational objectives: it is the way we use it that makes the difference. The chapter goes on to identify some of the ways in which new technology will impact on higher education, and analyses why universities tend to resist these changes, thereby sacrificing the potential positive effects. It then concludes by suggesting how universities could set about modulating the impact of technology in order to drive change towards a higher education system that is more successful, in its own terms.

The Role and Purposes of the University

The recent review of United Kingdom higher education, conducted by Lord Dearing's National Committee of Inquiry into Higher Education (NCIHE, 1997), revisited the purposes of higher education as defined by the Robbins Report in 1963. After a thorough analysis of how best to express these in the very different political and economic context of the 1990s, the new list of four main purposes was very similar, except the last, which under Robbins was cast as 'transmitting a common culture':

- inspiring and enabling individuals to develop their capabilities to the highest levels
- increasing knowledge and understanding
- serving the needs of the economy
- shaping a democratic and civilised society.

We now recognize the importance of multiple cultures within our society, and see university students as participating in the development of, rather than merely receiving, those cultural values. It is an important change, and probably an irreversible one, that will itself help to shape the way universities operate in the future, but the other core purposes are likely to remain unchanged. The first testifies to the university's commitment to the long-term personal development of the individual, in contrast to the focus on employment needs that inevitably drives other forms of post-school education, such as industrial training. The second purpose links the twin activities of research and teaching in the development and dissemination of knowledge. The third expresses the economic value of this, and the fourth its cultural value to the society it serves.

The unique role of the university in society, embracing these purposes, we defined as being 'to enable society to maintain an independent understanding of itself and its world'. Each word in that definition was carefully chosen.

- 'Society' does not confine the university's role to service of the nation state. This is one of the key changes now in the way that universities relate to their context – once an organ of the nation state, a university now crosses national boundaries in teaching in the way it has always done in research.
- 'Maintain' suggests a continuing responsibility, but one that is responsive to change, because of what is being maintained – an understanding of society itself, in continual flux, and of its world, for which our theories are in continual development.
- 'Of itself' requires that the understanding reached must be consensual, widely owned, fully disseminated, not located with some elite, but with society itself, thereby enabling it to become, in the fullest sense, a learning society.
- 'Independent' is there to express the unique position of universities as creators of understanding. There will be many claimants for the role of understanding our society and its world in our new 'knowledge society', but most – the media, industrial research units, corporate universities – cannot claim independence from political and commercial interest. The

- individualistic and disinterested nature of university research and teaching remains unique.
- 'Understanding' expresses the epistemology of a university as knowledge acquired with a sense of responsibility for how it comes to be known, and with the purpose of enabling enhanced action.

This portmanteau definition of the unique role of universities will be necessary for the analysis of the direction they must now take. It is essential that universities and academics lift themselves above the riot of change that is affecting the conduct of both research and teaching. To do that, we must hold on to a clear vision of the role and purposes of the university, and use it to modify the political, economic, and technological pressures we are now experiencing. For the task set for this chapter, therefore, I take the above definitions from the Dearing Report, as an appropriate benchmark against which to test any future model of the university – it must meet the role and purposes defined there.

Technology Drivers – Academic Brakes

Where is the 'great growling engine' taking us? The academic profession has been quick to embrace new technology in its research, but hardly at all in its approach to teaching. After some 25 years of fragmented experimentation with what computers might contribute to the teaching process, we still have rather little progress, or understanding of how to drive, rather than be driven by, the new learning technologies. This would be nothing worse than a lost opportunity were it not for the fact that the new technology is also driving the world outside universities. Some of its most successful effects are in areas that impinge directly on how universities operate, and they do not always respond well. In this section, we examine those effects, and how they may develop.

Information Access

The development of the Internet and the world-wide Web has left commentators weltering in a mire of superlatives and hyperbole in an effort to capture its meaning and effects for our society. It is probably the technology driver that attracts most comment, and the one that most easily generates adverse comparisons for universities. The argument derives from the idea that university teaching is essentially the transmission of information from teachers to students. Now that lecture notes can be available on the Web, there is no reason for the student to go to the lecture, and moreover, every student can have access to the best lecturer in the field. This quote is a typical form of the claim:

> Education on CD and on-line is a reality and a threat to the established institutions ... there is real pressure to return to the 'guide on the side' ... When a good Master class ... is available on-line or on CD, there will be little room for a second. We might thus expect to see very few really great teachers and an awful lot more coaches.
>
> (Cochrane, 1999: 75)

It is a useful principle in evaluating the stupendous claims made for new technology to translate them into the equivalent claim that might have been made some centuries ago for the new technology of printing. 'When a good master class is available in a book there will be little room for a second.' Our knowledge of the world of print renders that last sentence an utter absurdity, and yet it is an analogous claim to the one made by Cochrane and others. The arrival of the printed book made it possible for the 'master' to be widely reproduced, and widely read, and yet it was almost contemporaneous with the inauguration of universities in Europe and their principal, and enduring, mode of teaching, the lecture. The claim betrays a simplistic understanding of how the process of learning operates, and indeed how power structures within a culture determine individual behaviours. The characteristics of the technology itself must be understood as *potential* drivers, modulated by many other constraints and drivers within the culture. In the case of books, the power of the Church, of access to written language, of educational institutions, all modified the potential effects of the widely distributed availability of books. Eventually, the book itself became a performance indicator for scholars, and an effective income-generator for publishers, rendering impossible the idea that there would ever be just one great book on any one subject. Why should the CD or the Internet be so radically different? The conditions may be slightly different, but in general our cultural and economic pressures promote proliferation, competition, and pluralism, as far as content is concerned, not convergence to a single standard.

It is not simply the inevitable proliferation of multiple versions of the master class that undermines the claim, however. The process of learning, to be effective, demands a more sophisticated approach than mere access to the information, no matter how masterly the teaching. This is the natural brake that academe applies to runaway notions about the value of information access for all. Information is one aspect of knowledge, which is itself only part of what constitutes understanding. The purpose of the university is to enable understanding. Whereas information may be transmitted, understanding cannot be. The process of learning for understanding requires a succession of cognitive activities in which the learner engages with ideas in several different ways, in theory and in practice, successively engaging in attention, enactment, reflection, critique, adaptation, articulation. Elsewhere, I have proposed the most minimal possible description of this process of learning as a 'conversational framework', operating on the levels of theory and practice, between student and teacher (Laurillard, 1993). It is an iterative process, a dialogue with oneself and others, progressively moving towards a shared understanding, a critical distance, and eventually a personal perspective in which the learners finally assume responsibility for what they know, how they came to know it, and where they may apply it. This is what William Perry described as the development of a personal epistemology during the college years (Perry, 1970). The most important ideas in our cultures have developed over time, and are difficult enough for us to need this kind of progressive iteration to grasp them. They provide the framework into which the information we gain access to can be slotted and thereby made useful. There is no shortcut to developing the framework. It needs time and guidance, and cannot be transmitted. The university teaching process offers that time in a way that information access systems cannot.

Guidance is key. When lecturers recommend a list of textbooks to their students, they are acting, in a sense, as the 'guide on the side'. This is a good model for all forms of teaching. The teacher's role in the 'conversation' is essentially to guide the student towards a shared understanding, while developing in them the capability to go beyond what is given, and build their own perspective. The teacher, as guide, exercises control during the process of learning through selection, sequence, mode of presentation, pace, and testing. Without selection, the learners would waste time on inappropriate and irrelevant material; without sequence, they would be building on sand; they would benefit from choice of mode, because some learn better from books, others from people, but in practice there is a range of modes; learners benefit from some self-pacing, but they also need to be paced to prevent procrastination and to concentrate the study; and they need testing to assure themselves that they have made progress, and to enable the teacher to accredit them. The purpose of the university is to enable 'individuals to develop their capabilities to the highest levels', and that entails all the cognitive activities defined above for learners, and all the guidance activities defined here for teachers.

The information access that new technology enables is important for updating and informing those who have already developed the framework that makes the information usable. That will include students. But they will not be using it as the principal way to develop their intellectual perspective. That comes from a different route, from engagement with others in the gradual development of their personal understanding.

New technology provides significantly wider information access, but it also offers much more valuable support for the kind of learning experience to which universities aspire. The learning process entails high-level cognitive activity by the learner, and supportive guidance by the teacher, both of which can be delivered through the learning technologies. The next section discusses this in more detail.

Diana Laurillard

Curricular Change

Universities have traditionally been founded on discipline-based knowledge, its development and dissemination. The academic profession trains and rewards its members for the optimal development of the discipline areas, and the dissemination of foundational knowledge in those areas to students who will maintain the tradition. When the university served the elite of the nation state, the practice was effective for the development of knowledge and understanding within that small interconnected elite. Universities still serve the minority, but a very large minority. And they now also serve 'the economy'. The prosperity of the modern nation depends not just on its ownership of land and resources, but also on the productivity of its people. In the knowledge economy productivity will relate closely to the effectiveness of education at all levels. In the nineteenth century, universities had to adjust to the needs of the industrial society, and recast their curricula towards greater emphasis on science and engineering. In the latter part of the twentieth century they had to adjust to the rise of managerialism, and introduce more economics and management theory. The pace of change has quickened, with the inevitable result that management theory does not have the same level of sophistication that science and engineering achieved when the university had more control of the curriculum, and teaching could more easily follow where research led. Again, we find a natural brake on the external drivers of change, deriving from the way the university must operate. There is no question that universities must be responsive to the needs of the developing economy, but they must also respond to the demands of the discipline. The economy needs management theory to be taught, but what is it? who knows it? It is a developing discipline, which, like any other, makes its own natural demands on the academic. It requires a particular kind of methodology – the means by which the discipline develops and shares a usable understanding of organizational behaviour – and there is a natural rhythm to discovery and validation, as in every discipline, that does not necessarily obey the requirements of external pressures.

Universities have always offered a provider-led curriculum, and internal procedures governing teaching, research and staffing, have developed accordingly. But this is no longer sustainable if they are to play their proper role in responding to the needs of the economy and society as a whole. It is a difficult dilemma. The curriculum and the way it is taught must become more responsive to external pressures. At the same time, universities must continue to follow the demands of their disciplines, because that is the insurance for our futures – that the development of independent understandings of our society and its world will continue. We will not achieve that by being driven only by the current requirements of the market. It is in this sense that universities are not businesses, and neither students, nor the other stakeholders in our society, are customers. Or, they are businesses in which the customer is not always right. The resolution of this dilemma could rest

138

on the way we teach, as much as what we teach. In the next section, we consider how the technology could be used to provide for a more responsive curriculum.

Expert Teams

The technological drivers of change do not always create compatible effects. The Web now offers a universal publishing mechanism for the individual, which is highly compatible with the scholar's drive to disseminate his or her ideas to the world. However, new technology tends to require new skills, and these have been acquired by very few of today's generation of academics. The result is an uncomfortable clash of media styles, which characterizes every new form of technological medium: the proscenium arch that graced every early silent film as it mimicked theatre; the stately Victorian family photographs that recalled eighteenth-century portraiture; the Gutenberg typeface that carefully reproduced the forms of thirteenth-century script. We use the Web in a way that transfers as many of the conventions of print as is possible for such a radically different medium – Web-pages, titles, alphabetical indexes, menus of content, margins, logos, paragraphs ... almost the only convention not carried over is readable line length, which would have been a useful one to keep. The CD fares no better. The unique adaptive power of the computer is ignored in favour of its capacity to store and retrieve acres of text and pictures. Both CD and Web are most frequently used only to the extent that they enhance what the individual academic can do with print. It requires a team of experts to exploit fully the new technologies, but this is incompatible with the way academics work.

Teaching through membership of a team is not something that comes easily to academics. The development and dissemination of ideas is a highly individual process, for which it is more satisfying to take responsibility, albeit responding to others' contributions, than to share responsibility. The close relationship between medium and message becomes synergistic for the academic who is fully in control of their medium, as in the lecture, and to a great extent in print. When the medium is the unfamiliar combination of audio-visual, adaptive interaction, and software, the close relationship between medium and message remains, but the academic can only be one member of a team in control of the medium. So whose message emerges?

It is ironic that the technology which offers such freedom of creative expression to the individual academic, as well as freedom from the stranglehold of the publisher as distributor, should at the same time demand the discipline of collaborative teamwork to realize its potential. Under-exploitation of a new technology is not a brake on its development that either can or should be maintained. If academics do not find a way to meet the challenges of the new media, then they will be outclassed by other providers, and deservedly so. In the next section, we consider an alternative solution.

Alternative Providers

Although I have argued that universities have a unique role in our societies which cannot be imitated by other providers, it is a claim that will be challenged. The new media enable any companies trading in the information industry to offer 'expert' teaching to the growing audiences for higher education. If they provide what appears to be a more attractive product, then no matter how legitimate the claim of the universities, the new audiences for higher education could take their custom elsewhere. If post-experience employees want a professional course in a specialist field that updates their knowledge and skill, and the choice is between a university whose level is too high, or duration too long, and a commercial course at a time, pace and level of their choosing, there will have to be some powerful marketing to ensure they choose the former. And universities are not yet very good at marketing.

Universities do have an effective weapon against commercial rivals in higher education. The unique selling point for university teaching, and the most enduring, is its link to research. University research is too often regarded as a kind of indulgence by academics that should be restrained if the government is to get good value for money for its expenditure on universities. There are persistent calls for 'teaching-only' universities, and selectivity in research. The reasons advanced are that: (1) most academics do not need to do research to be able to teach well – 'scholarship' is sufficient; and (2) we must maintain our world-class research at all costs. Are these sound?

The first argument runs counter to the idea that university-level teaching provides a learning experience that is qualitatively different from, say, further education, which aims to give students a grounding in the practice of a skill or subject area. The university is meant to be 'inspiring and enabling individuals to develop their capabilities to the highest levels', which entails them taking personal responsibility for what they know and how it comes to be known. This essentially epistemological aim is crucial in a time when the individual throughout their working life must be able to draw on their own intellectual resources to evaluate critically the way that knowledge is being generated and used. The foundational knowledge they begin with will change and develop, and they must adapt their understanding and use of it accordingly. So knowledge alone is insufficient; they will need an understanding of the nature of knowledge as well. It will be important for all graduates to understand that knowledge is neither static, nor discrete. It is continually developing, and they must keep abreast of that; it is relational, context-dependent, and complex to transfer from one context to another. This is why they must take personal responsibility for what they know, how it comes to be known, and how, therefore, it is to be used. If the expansion of higher education dilutes the ambition of university teaching to achieve this for its students, then there is no point in expansion at that level. Expansion of university teaching should be commensurate with the society's need for people who can apply independent thinking to both the theory and practice of their work and culture.

To the extent that we expand university teaching – and the Dearing Report suggested the United Kingdom should aim for 45 per cent participation – we should expect to maintain its value. Teaching at this level should be done by people who are capable of building in the student the intellectual capabilities necessary for them to sustain their own epistemological development. Academics who are engaged in the process of critiquing and developing knowledge in their field are better equipped to do this than those who are only following the developments. There will always be a range of research involvement among academics, as there always has been, but it should be the responsibility of the university to ensure that all its students are taught by people who are able to 'develop their capabilities to the highest levels'. If it can do that, then it maintains its clear distinction from the commercial provider, who cannot expect to link teaching to research. Students coming to higher education do so because they want to have the sense of intellectual excitement, to be close to the cutting edge, to be empowered to think for themselves in their chosen field. Universities must be able to provide that. Students who simply wish to be told – 'just tell me' is a common enough plea – are not asking for a university education.

The second argument for teaching-only universities, that we must be selective in order to maintain our world-class research, is persuasive, because we do want to achieve the best. But perhaps not at all costs. We can use selectivity to focus the funding needed for the best research while still maintaining basic funding for all academics to engage in research at some level. This is the value of our dual-funding system, which Dearing recommended should continue. The Funding Councils enable all university departments to do research, while the Research Councils fund the best. Dual-funding is the system that enables nascent disciplines to flourish in academic backwaters until the central funders realize their importance. Artificial Intelligence is a good example. It is the system that enables the individual academic to pursue an abiding interest in the study of molluscs while the oil industry only belatedly discovers its importance for exploration. Academics tend to become academics because of a love of their subject, so it is scarcely possible to prevent them from doing research. For most, the opportunity to do it overrides the material advantage of alternative professions. Every study of academic time management has shown that, on average, academics work significantly longer hours than the 'standard' working week, and much of that additional time is spent on research. Academic research represents very good value for money, which it would be absurd to ignore. We could hardly claim that society does not need more research – the pace of change is such that we cannot hope to keep up with what is needed in any case. Selectivity yes, but not at the cost of teaching-only universities. More research is needed. Academics are able and willing to do it, and cheaply too. And it is highly synergistic with university teaching.

Alternative providers of higher education will be able to use technology to simulate the provision of high-level knowledge and information, but that does not achieve for the individual what a university education will offer, as long as universities maintain their distinctive adherence to the close relationship between teaching and research. The argument for teaching-only universities will continue, however, because it appears to be such an attractive way to reduce the cost of higher education to the public purse. Only academics are likely to defend the status quo, and they will have to work hard to do it in the face of strong opposition.

If universities can remain competitive with respect to teaching in the face of the opportunities created by new technology, there is still the question of competitiveness with respect to research. There is much greater potential for the dissemination of research to potential users and beneficiaries than universities and academic researchers have achieved so far. This must be a key area for development in the coming decades, and would itself help to stabilize the funding of university research. Academics have traditionally relied on conferences and academic journal publishers to disseminate their work to other researchers, and on book publishing to reach the wider audience. This route provides a slow diffusion rate in comparison with what new technology could offer. There is no natural brake being exercised here, other than inertia. Publishers are not likely to suggest to academics that they would be more effective in dissemination to, say, government administrators, if they made summaries of their research findings available on the Web. At present, it is far easier for civil servants to use other civil service reports, than to trawl through academic publishing for the analyses they need. Academic research would get a better press if it were more accessible, and new technology makes that more feasible than ever before. We return to this in the next section.

Wider Participation in Higher Education

The knowledge economy will need a much higher participation rate in higher education than we are currently producing. Over the last three decades, the 'knowledge workforce as a percentage of the total United States workforce' has increased 5 per cent every decade (Jonscher, 1999). In the decade to 1998, the age participation rate in higher education has doubled from 15 per cent to over 30 per cent in the UK. That is an impressive leap, and the higher education system has struggled under the strain of it, but it has to continue. The conclusion of the Dearing Report was that it should be expected to increase further to 45 per cent within the next 20 years (NCIHE, 1997). The report identified several sources of the pressure to expand:

- the developing competitive environment
- adverse consequences of not responding to investment by competitor countries
- economic benefits for individuals and society
- improving achievements at school level
- graduates in the workforce refreshing their learning.

None of these pressures is likely to diminish over that period. Thus wider participation in higher education has now become government policy in the United Kingdom. The 1998 Labour Government offered funding for increased participation, but this will not be done by maintaining the per capita cost of higher education, even at the reduced levels at which it is now funded. Wider participation cannot be publicly funded at the same level as the narrow elitism of the traditional university. The Dearing solution was to introduce 'income-contingent contributions paid by graduates in work', as a fairer way of funding higher education than we have ever had in the United Kingdom. The Government's response was to introduce 'tuition fees', which results in a tax on education instead of a tax on the financial benefits of higher education, which was the imaginative solution recommended by Dearing. If 35 per cent of the age group are receiving publicly funded higher education, it means that the other 65 per cent are paying for it, and the ratio gets ever less fair as the proportion in higher education increases. It is an inevitable consequence of wider participation that a greater proportion of the per capita cost is paid for by the recipient who benefits – *when* they benefit, which is what makes the 'income-contingent' aspect of the contribution feasible for all students, no matter what their background.

Universities cannot escape the need for expansion, although they must certainly defend the importance of expanding on their own terms. But there is another natural brake that academe will exercise on the scale of expansion. The university learning experience has particular characteristics that are difficult to preserve when the scale increases. The nature of the learning experience that universities aim for has already been outlined above, and a key part of that is the focus on the needs of the individual learner. It could be argued that universities have already forfeited any pretension to this in their accommodation of rapid expansion with no commensurate resource throughout the 1980s and 1990s. There has been progressive dilution of the teacher–student relationship, with many students now experiencing very little sense of the development of their individual capabilities to the highest levels. Students have remained tolerant of this, unprotesting in the face of the changes, most of which are only noticeable over longer timescales than the three years it takes to graduate. But universities will not escape the long-term effects forever. The loss of enduring teacher–student relationships has long-term effects that cannot be detected by our internal quality processes, nor by the self-referential standards that universities maintain through the external examiner system. The effects will be noticed by employers, who already complain of the ill-equipped graduates they receive, who are still unskilled in the areas of communication, IT literacy, project management, and entrepreneurship. If universities cannot even create graduates with personal commitment to what they know, which has been a valuable by-product of the elite system of small-group teaching, then the loss of confidence in them will reach the critical point at which other providers look more attractive.

This particular driver of change is complex. The natural brake on widening participation, the labour-intensive task of developing the individual, has been weakened already. For universities to sustain any credibility as uniquely successful providers of highly-trained graduates, they must find some way of reversing the trend away from individual teaching – while at the same time meeting the need for increased participation. New technology has not created this situation, although it is certainly one of the drivers of the need for more graduates. However, it can help to provide a solution to the problem of how to provide more small-group teaching with wider participation and with no increase in unit costs. The next section turns to the new directions universities must take, and the ways that new technology can assist the process.

New Directions

The previous section outlined some of the key drivers of change in higher education, each of which works against some aspect of the mission of universities. To summarize: new technology has increased access to information, but university teaching requires a much more complex model than this; new technology is driving curricular change towards skill development rather than knowledge, but universities must maintain their focus on the development of knowledge; it requires expert teams to exploit new technology, but academics are driven by individual creativity in their teaching; it creates a variety of alternative providers of post-school teaching, whereas for universities teaching must be linked to research; it creates demand for wider participation in higher education, but universities must provide a close teacher–student relationship to achieve their objectives. This section must now resolve the dilemmas, and we will see that in each case, new technology can be part of the solution, even as it creates the problem.

Countering the Mere Access to Information with a Conversational Model

The learning process at university level is not a unidirectional transfer of information, but an active engagement of the student in the operational aspects of the subject matter, and in the articulation of its theoretical aspects. The two together provide a reflective, adaptive understanding that enhances practice. The new learning technologies can serve both aspects through the two different kinds of interactivity – adaptive manipulation, and communication with other people.

Adaptive manipulation means using a computer program to enable the student to drive some exploration or investigation of content, and to give meaningful feedback on their actions. In an example from business studies, it may be an exercise to find the combination of initial conditions that gives the optimal cash flow for a company; in art history the student could be asked to match the composition of a painting by arranging its component elements (see Figure 8.2); in technology it could be a spreadsheet exercise to develop the energy model that fits a set of temperature readings for a house … in each case the student's actions drive the program's behaviour to produce an output that either matches the target, or fails in a meaningful way. The feedback is 'intrinsic', ie. it shows the students the results of their actions, and can show them in relation to their respective targets, which makes it possible to derive the revised actions they need to take. Intrinsic feedback is in this sense far more meaningful than 'extrinsic feedback', which evaluates their work as right or wrong. Goal-oriented adaptive manipulation is one of the most powerful ways in which IT can be used to enhance understanding through experimentation and practice, and yet it is still seriously under-used. Part of the reason is the difficulty of producing such programs, and we return to this later.

Interpersonal communication is already well understood as an important feature of the Internet, but its use for university teaching has to be carefully structured to be useful. Asynchronous written communication is the most straightforward, using discussion environments that assist the process by maintaining some structure for successive messages and changing topics. Figure 8.1 shows an example from the *Journal of Interactive Media in Education*. In this case, the discussion is focused around an article, so that sections of the article form the first level of topic structure for the discussion, and titles of the points being made form a second level. A new participant can add a comment to an existing topic, or start a new one. Used as an attenuated 'reading group' format, this kind of application gives students motivation to articulate their ideas, participate in discussion and negotiation, and request advice and assistance. The asynchronous feature reduces the pressure that exists in a face-to-face group, and enables even the most reticent students to take part. It is now an accepted characteristic of this medium that it turns normally silent students into soap-box orators.

The asynchronous discussion environment could also focus on an adaptive program, and Figure 8.2 shows the art history composition task, mentioned above, with its associated dialogue. With a task of this kind, the dialogue may well be more about how to do the task in the first instance, but the tutor would still have the opportunity to turn the discussion to, for example,

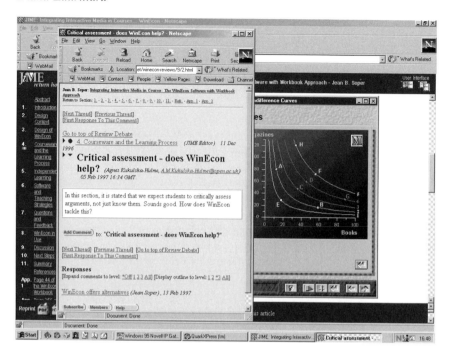

Figure 8.1   *A Web-based document discussion environment, showing the discussion entered in relation to a section of the article*

what made the task so difficult, or what solutions different artists have brought to the problems of composition. It is the ideal environment to support both the practical and theoretical aspects of the learning process.

As the Web begins to support audio of reasonable quality, it will become more common for this kind of learning conversation to be conducted in real time. Asynchronous communication will always have its own value, not least for the greater opportunity for reflection that it affords, but synchronous forms will become far more widely used as bandwidth increases.

The learning technology solutions described here are not futuristic, they are here now. But they are scarcely used in higher education, and have made no impact on the way higher education is conducted, because they do not fit with the way academics work. What should be clear, is that the new technology is not just about wider access to information. It supports a complex framework for university-level learning, that can provide sophisticated support and guidance in both theory and practice to the individual student, even working at a distance across a network. My first strong prediction for the future of higher education therefore has to be:

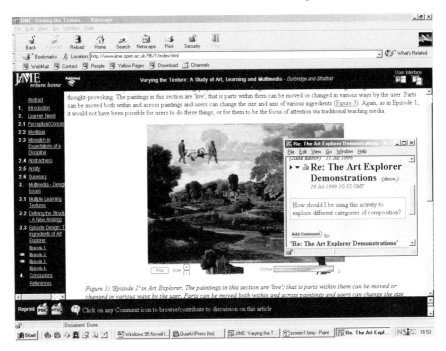

Figure 8.2   *An interactive Web-based task enabling students to experiment with the composition of movable objects in a painting*

Academics will be using adaptive programs and on-line discussion environments integrated with existing teaching methods to support student learning more effectively than is possible via the traditional campus teaching methods alone.

Delivering Individual Teaching to Larger Numbers

Both forms of interaction described above provide individualized teaching. This is important because it means that open learning, built around resource-based learning supported by individual guidance, becomes feasible for a wider range of students. This is the new direction being taken by the Open University. The original OU model used print as the principal medium of resource, with some audio-visual material, and combined this with tutorial support so that each student had individual guidance in the development of their understanding, through small-group teaching and through comment on their individual assignments. The reliance on resource-based learning for a high proportion (at least 80 per cent) of study time, meant that unit costs could be lower and numbers could be increased more easily. Many OU courses are delivered to hundreds or thousands of students, whereas campus university courses frequently average tens of students. And individual teaching is preserved. Open University courses are now increasingly using adaptive programs instead of print, and Internet-based discussion groups instead of tutorials. This is a model that all universities could use to preserve individual teaching, even in the face of large student populations.

Individualized guidance is a natural part of the adaptive program, because the feedback offered is so well-targeted on what the learner needs. This is not the form of individual adaptation that programmed learning aspired to, because that required the production of canned extrinsic feedback for every form of mistake. The intrinsic feedback offered by an interactive model requires far less production effort for greater value to the student. A larger proportion of the student learning time can be given to resource-based learning if it takes this form. The reliance on print alone is tough for the learner, because it provides little incentive to practice, and no feedback when they do.

Internet-based discussion groups are important for individualized teaching, but the network connection between teacher and student has an additional important property that no other form of communication possesses: the automatic capture of an interaction for future reference. The synchronous and asynchronous discussions cited above can be captured and replayed. This deceptively simple feature transforms the ability of academics to support larger numbers of students, and this is as important for campus universities as it is for distance teaching. The teaching developed to support one group of learners through a difficult asynchronous on-line task is there as a resource for other groups as well. The discussion environment in Figure 8.2 can be replayed, edited and indexed if necessary, as a resource for other students meeting the same kinds of difficulties as they tackle the same task. It is not the same as having the tutor commenting on your own problem, but it will act as a filter insofar as your problem has already been addressed. Where it has not, the tutor is still available, but his or her responsiveness to individual difficulties has been enhanced considerably by this kind of filtering device. It makes it feasible for a tutor to support with genuinely individualized teaching a much larger group of students. My next strong prediction therefore is:

Individual academics will support larger groups of students with individualized teaching via adaptive programs and discussion environment tools, while also relying on greater use of resource-based learning using print, audio-visual, and IT methods.

Disseminating Research-based Teaching

In exactly the same way that academics can support large numbers of students in developing their understanding, so they can offer the same kind of support to professionals in the dissemination of research. At present there are only very weak links between university research and the potential users and beneficiaries of that research. The research councils in the United Kingdom are taking steps to ensure that the audience is considered at all stages of the research, not just in the final phase, and this innovation alone will help the dissemination process. But a more mature partnership between research groups and their audiences will need to develop because the diffusion process we currently have takes too long and is too uncertain. It is increasingly difficult for professionals to keep up to date with research in their field, partly because it develops so fast, and partly because personal workloads are continually increasing. They cannot expect to attend academic conferences, and find all the relevant material in academic journals, as well as make the appropriate interpretations. The long chain from research paper to review article to book to mass media coverage creates selectivity at every stage.

It could be replaced by a more efficient route via the Web: the research summary goes on to a Web-page, an on-line asynchronous structured debate is opened up to all interested members of the profession, it culminates after a defined period in a synchronous audio-graphic event, where speakers illustrate points with reference to slides, extracts from the published research, relevant video clips, etc., and audience questions can be put via audio on the Web or via email, through a moderator, and the whole interaction remains captured as a replayable event for those who could not 'attend' at the time. Moreover, it generates further interaction in the asynchronous mode. There are a number of such 'conferences' now in operation within the academic community (see, for example, http://kmi.open.ac.uk/learning.org/). Again, this is not futuristic. The academic community must begin to exploit this application of the Web for highly valued access to its research results, even though this is not the way that research communities typically behave – they talk to each other. Indeed they created the Web for exactly that purpose. Research is becoming more action-oriented, with more focus on partnership with its users and beneficiaries. This will encourage industry to offer more funding. The cycle of mutual benefit will move faster with improved communication. So my third prediction is:

Successful academic research communities will open up Web-based conferences to disseminate their work to wider groups of professional users, in ways that fit with the way those professionals need to work.

Creating the Responsive Curriculum

From individualized undergraduate teaching to research-based support for professionals, there is a seamless continuum of ways of using the learning technologies to improve the functionality of the university. The same approach can be used to enable universities to be more responsive to the curriculum demands of students and employers. The difficulty for academics of moving from a provider-led curriculum to one that is more market-led, especially in the context of using resource-based learning, lies in the time it takes to develop the teaching approach, to assemble the materials, to construct a curriculum that meets the particular needs of a student group. The Web-based approaches already described in this section lend themselves equally to creating a curriculum that is responsive to the needs of returning graduates, or for mature undergraduates studying at degree level for the first time. In many cases, these people will have a clear idea of what they need from their study, and will be ready to negotiate the nature of the curriculum they want. Universities will rightly determine the exact content, sequence and objectives of the courses they offer, but equally, they will become more accustomed to responding to requests, as mature post-experience students become more discerning in their demands.

The combination of Internet, Web and CD-Roms comes close to making it feasible for academics to put together a new curriculum by weaving these resources into a structured set of materials for students to work through, and providing discussion-based support and guidance of the kind already covered above. The material is there, and can be edited to the lecturer's requirements, since it is electronic. The adaptive tasks would not be available for a new curriculum, because they need to be developed in relation to the objectives specified for it. The discussion-based support is on-line and requires little preparation beyond the scholarship needed to teach the subject in the first place. The student–tutor exchange of assignment and commentary on it via the Web create non-trivial, but soluble problems for the academic, and this will soon be commonplace. We are close to meeting the conditions for offering the fully responsive curriculum, but there are gaps that are still difficult to bridge. One is finding and re-using the material, which is difficult because it exists in multiple formats, and is usually not designed for re-use (see http://www.imsproject.org for a project which addresses this). Another is copyright – the permission to use Web-based or CD-based material for teaching purposes has to be acquired, and the procedures for doing this are still lengthy and difficult. Another is the difficulty of creating the adaptive tasks – it still takes expert teams many months to create such programs. My next prediction, therefore, is that the conditions needed for creating more responsive curricula and courses will have to be met:

Academics will be able to use Web-based tools and libraries to select and edit educational resource material to their own teaching objectives, acquire and pay for copyright permission, run guided discussion environments, create their own versions of relevant adaptive tasks, and operate on-line assessment methods.

Enabling Individual Creativity through Adaptable Learning Activity Modules

The development of tools and resources to enable academics fully to exploit learning technology is the key to its extensive use. It is unusual for academics to work in teams to teach. The course team has been at the core of the success of the Open University. It brings together academics, designers, editors, software designers, educational technologists, and audio-visual producers, each of whom brings specific expertise to the creation of high-quality learning materials. This mode of working was designed to meet the unusual conditions of creating individual teaching for students studying alone, at a distance. It is not typical of undergraduate teaching, however, as most academics work independently as far as the detail of their teaching is concerned. Course boards, examination committees, and syllabuses will set the framework within which they operate, but there is no equivalent of the course team – which brings together academics and production experts – giving detailed feedback on an academic's draft course unit, or the educational technologist reporting on the developmental testing of a prototype computer program, or an audio-visual team reworking the specification for a TV programme. These examples from the OU context represent the kind of quality assurance process that resource-based teaching demands. In the campus context there is a much higher ratio of academic to learning support staff, so it is more difficult to make the resource-based learning model work. Academics cannot spend all their time in team-working when they have to be teaching students face-to-face. Campus universities will need to restructure their staffing on similar lines if they are to shift to greater use of learning technology.

The alternative to expert teams is customizable tools and resources. Most attempts to bring learning technologies to academics have taken one of two extreme forms: the authoring tool, which provides a framework in which the teacher can sequence stored content and design multiple-choice tests; and the fully developed multimedia program, which provides a complete teaching resource which they can change very little. The first necessarily diminishes the power of the interactive program to make it simple, and yet requires the teacher to spend too much time on design. The second requires very little work from the teacher, and thereby allows no opportunity for customizing it to local needs, so that the teacher loses control over the content and how it is taught. Neither has succeeded. A better compromise will be new kinds of tools and resources, targeted on particular kinds of learning objective, and derived from learning programs whose interactive form has been shown to be effective (see http://mathetics.open.ac.uk/source/ for a project developing such tools). In the examples mentioned above, it should be possible for the academic to take the economic model, and relabel the parameters, edit in their own introduction and feedback comments, and link it to their own case studies; the art history program should be re-usable for discovering the right arrangement of design features of a building, with the teacher editing in their own comments on alternative arrangements; the discussion environment could be conducted around any article or program that the teacher cares to insert – in all cases the format remains the same, and the academic contributes the content, which is where their expertise lies. The advantage of the approach is that the form of learning interaction is crafted to match the nature of the learning objective, and this is done for them, by an expert team. It is therefore not as general as the authoring tool. There will be many of these adaptable learning modules, or similar learning design tools, each targeted on a different kind of learning interaction.

Tools or teams – it has to be one or the other; preferably both. Technology requires teamwork to do it well, but it also requires radical organizational change to achieve that. Embodying the team's design expertise in the format of a range of customizable tools for academics offers a more plausible solution. My final prediction therefore is:

The transferable currency of learning technology-based materials will be libraries of customizable learning activity formats, and adaptable media resources, to enable academics to exploit fully the technology while retaining creative control over what they are teaching.

Concluding Points

It is vital that university academics and managers understand the pressures on higher education and where they are likely to take us because the new directions will not necessarily be compatible with the cherished mission of universities. The role of the university in the twenty-first century will develop according to how we define it and conduct it. In this chapter I have selected some of the key drivers of change deriving from the new technologies, and concluded that, without careful and attentive control by the academic community, they could seriously undermine the role of the university. Each of the predictions outlined here implies a need for action to be taken, at different levels in the academic hierarchy. They are not wild predictions. They describe the optimistic future in which universities adjust to change while maintaining academic values, but they are difficult to manage effectively.

To summarize: the impact of Communications and Information Technology on higher education will see academics using adaptive programs, on-line discussion environments and customizable IT-based tools and resources, integrated with a range of other media-based teaching resources, to achieve individualized teaching with larger groups of students, to disseminate their research more efficiently to prospective users, and to make their curricula more rapidly responsive to students' needs. There is an alternative, more pessimistic scenario: the apparent value of ease of access to information, and the rapid responsiveness of commercial providers on a large scale, will send universities back to small-scale elitism, and an opportunity truly to 'enable individuals to develop their capabilities to the highest levels' will have been lost. Unless the academic community takes more control of its destiny than it has been prepared to do in recent years, the more depressing scenario will be visited upon us.

References

Cochrane, P. (1999) 'The global grid of chaos', in A. Leer (ed.) *Masters of the Wired World*, London: Pitman.

Jonscher, C. (1999) 'The economics of cyberspace', in A. Leer (ed.) *Masters of the Wired World,* London: Pitman.

Laurillard, D. (1993) *Rethinking University Teaching: A Framework for the Effective Use of Educational Technology*, London: Routledge.

National Committee of Inquiry into Higher Education (1997) *Higher Education in the Learning Society*, London: HMSO.

Perry, W. (1970) *The Forms of Intellectual and Ethical Development in the College Years*, New York: Holt, Rhinehart and Winston.

Toffler, A. (1970) *Future Shock*, London: Pan Books.

http://www-jime.open.ac.uk
http://kmi.open.ac.uk/learning.org/
http://mathetics.open.ac.uk/source/
http://www.imsproject.org

9 A Profession for the New Millennium?

John Randall

Is university teaching a truly professional activity? Most will say that the answer is self-evident. The problem is that to those within higher education the answer is self-evidently 'yes'; whilst to many outside, nurtured in the belief that 'those who can, do, those who can't, teach', the answer is, equally self-evidently, 'no'. The answer to the question matters for two reasons. First, to respond to those who doubt the professionalism of university teachers, some analysis of the nature of professional responsibility within higher education is needed. Second, whether the activity has the characteristics of a profession will be a major consideration in determining the way in which it is regulated. In short, is it an activity in respect of which the public interest requires inspection to check compliance with externally generated norms? Or can the public interest be satisfied by a peer-driven system of quality assurance operating in a transparent and accountable manner?

What are the characteristics of a profession? Mr Justice Brandeis, of the United States Supreme Court, writing in 1933, defined them as follows: 'First, a profession is an occupation for which the necessary preliminary training is intellectual in character, involving knowledge and to some extent learning, as distinguished from mere skill. Second, it is an occupation which is pursued largely for others and not merely for oneself. Third, it is an occupation in which the amount of financial return is not the accepted measure of success.' So far, so good. It is not difficult to fit university teaching within those definitions. However, they do not, of themselves, address the three practical elements of professional regulation: competence, conduct and compliance. There is a reasonable expectation that a professional person will hold a qualification attesting to competence in their field, will abide by rules of conduct, and will be subject to some form of monitoring of compliance with those rules.

Possession of a qualification alone is a necessary, but not a sufficient requirement of professional status. It is the existence and enforcement of a code of professional ethics that is the defining characteristic of a true profession. The seminal writing on this matter is by Sir Roger Ormrod (as he then was). Ormrod was both a doctor and a lawyer, and his 1967 paper 'Medical

Ethics' is a standard text on professional conduct for students of both disciplines. He said:

> The existence of a code of ethics is often regarded as one of the most important characteristics which distinguish the occupations known as professions from all others. So clearly is this recognised that one of the first steps taken by any body or group which aspires to recognition as a profession is to establish one, and to set up some form of disciplinary tribunal to deal with members who offend against it and then to seek from Parliament statutory powers to inflict sanctions on them.

Codes of professional ethics are often regarded with suspicion by laymen, sometimes being seen as a manifestation of Shaw's conclusion that 'all professions are conspiracies against the laity'. Dicey's scathing comments about legal etiquette in the *Fortnightly Review* in August 1867 support that conclusion:

> The Bar rules are regulations which have a two fold aim: firstly to promote honourable conduct; secondly to check competition. All the rules which have the first aim may be summed up under the one law – thou shalt not hug attorneys. Under this head must be brought many minor regulations, such as rules against frequenting public coffee rooms, or unduly cultivating the society of attorneys during circuit. No doubt these rules are extremely indefinite. No two lawyers will agree as to exactly what they are. Pedants and purists will enumerate a hundred little rules of etiquette, some of which they impose upon themselves, and all of which they are ready to impose on the less experienced and more docile members of circuit. Men of more sense and vigour do not pay much attention to the minutiae of the professional code. Still, all persons will acknowledge that there are some social rules of the kind referred to which it would be well for any barrister to observe who did not wish to incur considerable odium.

Not much recognizable public interest there, rather rules of etiquette concerning the social graces necessary to ensure that the professional classes behaved with a dignity appropriate to their rank. That, at least, is the charitable explanation. Dicey was right to observe that the rules were as much about inhibiting competition as anything else. It was not mixing socially with a lesser breed of lawyer that was the real offence, it was using that mixing to steal a march on the competition by touting for business. For an articulation of the public interest case for a code of professional conduct we must return to Ormrod. He observed:

Firstly, a professional man does not meet his patients or clients on equal terms. He is consulted for his special knowledge and experience by people who are in no position to make an informed or valid judgement about his skill or ability or integrity. Secondly, the discipline of the market, which, at least in theory, controls the conduct of the trader, is quite inappropriate to control though not by any means wholly without effect on the conduct of the professional man.

From this statement of the inherent inequality between the professional person and the client Ormrod defined the true function of a code of conduct:

The primary function of a code of professional ethics is to adjust the balance of power so as to protect the patient or client against the practitioner who has the immense advantages which are derived from knowledge and experience. A secondary but no less important function of a code of ethics is to protect the main body of practitioners who comply with its provisions against exploitation by the black sheep who are prepared to defy them.

He concluded:

This, then, is the real stuff of professional ethics. They are codes emanating from a general consensus of each profession and reflect the profession's own sense of the need for a discipline, primarily to prevent exploitation of the public by its superior power of knowledge and secondarily of the profession itself by its dissident members.

Why should it be that, unlike other learned occupations, university teaching has never developed the explicit code of ethical conduct that is the defining characteristic of a profession? Several explanations may be advanced. The quasi-monastic origins of universities were such that there was no need for the development of rules of engagement with a wider community. Study involved a retreat from, rather than an engagement with society. The conduct of individuals was largely an institutional matter. Rules defined the way in which each community of scholars would operate by setting out the rights, privileges and obligations of scholars *qua* members of an academic community. Duties were owed to the institution, to the community within rather than to the community outside. The best parody has reality recognizable within it. Cornford reflected the inward-looking nature of academic rules in his satire on Edwardian Cambridge, *Microcosmographia Academica*: 'The merit of such regulations is that, having nothing to do with right or wrong, they help to obscure these troublesome considerations in other cases, and to relieve the mind of all sense of obligation towards society.'

As universities developed away from their confessional origins, they turned not to a new relationship with society, but to the worship of a secular god – research. Chaucer's Clerk of Oxenford who 'found no preferment in the church and … was too unworldly to make search for secular employment', was nevertheless one who 'would gladly learn, and gladly teach.' Teaching gladly for its own sake across a wide range of disciplines might well have developed a growing awareness of a need for a code of conduct to regulate dealings between teachers and those they taught. But that was not the object of the exercise. Teaching was a means of disseminating the new knowledge that research created. Above all, it was the means of training the next genera-tion of university researchers. The measure of academic success came to be research, and measurement of undergraduates took the form of assessments of their suitability to embark upon a research career. Duties were owed first to the furtherance of the discipline, and only secondarily to the student.

All of this could be, and was justified by reference to the skills of inquiry and disciplined thought that were of use in many walks of life as well as in pure research. But it left university teachers defining their responsibilities by reference to their academic discipline, and to the pursuit of knowledge and truth within it. That may be an intellectually respectable approach, but it is some way removed from a profession seeking to regulate its dealings with the society it serves. Ironically, pure research possesses more of the characteristics of a profession than does teaching. There is an entry qualifica-tion (the good honours degree), clearly understood methodologies designed to maintain standards, peer evaluation of results, and a recognition of the responsibilities owed to lay users of research findings.

If a professional code were to develop, what might it cover? The starting point must be Ormrod's definition of the primary function of such a code – to adjust the balance of power in a relationship where the practitioner has the immense advantages which are derived from knowledge and experience. In these circumstances the practitioner cannot account to the client for his actions, for the client cannot make an informed or valid judgment about them. Accountability must be, in the first instance, to those who can make such a judgment, the professional peers of the practitioner. In the academic setting the primary client is, clearly, the student. It is the student who is unable to make the valid judgment about what it is they are taught. However, the inequality in the relationship is neither absolute nor fixed. In the process of learning the student will come to make critical judgments about the subject matter of the discipline, and may properly question the judgment of the teacher. In the course of medical treatment the patient is unlikely to acquire the means of questioning the judgment of the doctor. By contrast, a mark of success in academic study is the acquisition by the student of the ability to appraise critically that which is taught.

A professional code might have as a prime aim the discharge of the responsibility of ensuring that the student has the opportunity to develop critical judgment in the disciplines being studied. This suggests that there could be two components of it. The first would concern itself with learning opportunities, and would place upon the individual academic practitioner an obligation to discharge the pedagogic responsibilities that are beginning to be articulated in student charters and general codes of good practice. The second component would concern the validity of the academic programme itself, and the extent to which it was adequate to develop the critical faculties associated, generally, with a graduate level education and, specifically, with study to graduate level in a particular discipline. This second component is beginning to be developed through the benchmarking work facilitated by the Quality Assurance Agency for Higher Education (QAA).

That work has its origins in the report of the Committee of Inquiry into Higher Education (Dearing Report) of 1997. Dearing proposed the establishment of expert panels in the main subject areas, and pointed to Australian experience where: 'the interaction between academics has enabled views to crystallise on the essentials of an honours degree and the appropriate standards that ought to be applied.' There is a remarkable similarity between that approach and the classical definition of professional codes offered by Ormrod, namely 'codes emanating from a general consensus of each profession'. Substitute 'academic discipline' for 'profession' in Ormrod's definition, and it is possible to regard subject benchmarking as an activity directly comparable to the preparation of a professional code of conduct. Not only is the motivation similar, there are comparable methodology and similar beneficiaries. Professional codes are prepared by expert groups of senior practitioners, for adoption by the profession as a whole.

Benchmark information is being developed by expert groups of academics, and is subject to similar consultation within the discipline. Professional codes are there to protect the client; Dearing saw benchmarking as safeguarding the standing and meaning of awards that was: 'owed to the student – who is typically committing three or more years of life, spending money on higher education and foregoing years of potential earnings'. Just as the best and most effective professional codes deal with the principles of conduct rather than minutiae; so the best benchmarks will be those that address the higher level intellectual skills that programmes should deliver rather than attempting to tabulate detailed course content.

Ormrod's approach to professional conduct places an emphasis on the personal relationship between the professional person and a current client. There is a wider aspect to professional conduct that must also be addressed. This was articulated by Lord Diplock in his *dicta* in the Swain case in the House of Lords in 1982. This case related to the way in which the Council of the Law Society of England and Wales exercised the rule-making powers that Parliament had granted to it. Diplock said: 'The purpose for which these statutory functions are vested in the Law Society and the Council is the protection of the public or, more specifically, that section of the public that may be in need of legal advice, assistance or representation.'

In a real sense, Diplock identified a wider stakeholder interest in professional rules. Those whose interests were to be taken into account were not just the current users of the professional service. They were those of an entire 'section of the public that may be in need' at that time or in the future of such services. The Courts deliberately drew widely the scope of the public interest to be served. Applying that definition of scope to the academic world, it must include not only current and future students, but also those who have an interest in quality and standards as the future employers of graduates. That employer interest cannot be satisfied solely through the development of skills intended primarily to facilitate a career in research. Vocational needs, however defined, must be addressed directly not incidentally. This can be done through benchmark information, and the specifications of individual programmes identifying specifically those intellectual and other skills that are transferable into contexts other than the academic one in which they were first developed.

If it is possible to envisage some codification of the professional duties that university teachers owe to their students and to the wider community, where should the responsibility for that codification lie? Adjusting the balance of power so as to protect the client against the practitioner is not exclusively a professional problem, nor is it in any way new. Ormrod observed that one of the functions of city guilds in medieval times was to protect the public from exploitation by the various tradesmen on whom it was dependent. However, he said: 'What really distinguishes the professions seems to be the fact that they have developed their codes spontaneously in response to a general feeling in the professions themselves of the need for a professional discipline.'

That will strike a chord with anyone concerned with quality of provision. Quality cannot be imposed from outside, it must be generated internally. It is the combination of spontaneous development of codes, and the need for peer review to ensure effective compliance with them, that gives professional self-regulation its importance. However, self-regulation has had a bad press in recent years. Is it an option that is available to the academic community? Self-regulation fails where it lacks accountability, or has insufficient regard for the wider public interest. There are lessons that universities can usefully learn from the experience of others. There was a time when self-regulation was seen to place a body beyond the reach of any outside influence. In 1875, the House of Commons Select Committee on Foreign Loans observed of the London Stock Exchange: 'So long as the Stock Exchange has the power of expelling one of its members without appeal or redress, it can be bound by no law which it does not choose to obey. When it loses that power its means of self government are gone.'

That view would not be acceptable today. For example Professor Gower in his Review of Investor Protection, the 1982 discussion document that led to the Financial Services Act 1986 said: 'In this day and age it is just not acceptable ... that people can be excluded from bodies, which are not mere social clubs but agencies on which their livelihood depends, without a right to seek to persuade an independent arbiter that they were wrongly excluded.' Not everyone shares a selfless desire to be regulated. In 1973 a report of the Securities Subcommittee of the United States Senate described the limitations inherent in allowing an industry to regulate itself:

> The natural lack of enthusiasm for regulation on the part of the group to be regulated, the temptation to use a façade of industry regulation as a shield to ward off more meaningful regulation, the tendency for businessmen to use collective action to advance their interests through the imposition of purely anti-competitive restraints as opposed to those justified by regulatory needs, and a resistance to changes in the regulatory pattern because of vested economic interests in its preservation.

Thus, a century after Dicey commented on the restrictive practices of the English Bar, the criticism of the anti-competitive nature of self-regulation remained. It may be too much to expect a saint-like perfection from professionals, but one could reasonably expect a conscious effort to uphold the primacy of the client interest. Zander put it well: 'It is probably naïve to suppose that any profession could be expected to prefer the public interest to its own, but service to the public interest is one of the central elements of the professional man's ethic and one is entitled to expect the professions to try to conquer the natural temptation to put their own interests first.' Self-regulation does not exist in isolation, nor is it an absolute alternative to direct regulation by government or its agencies. As Professor Alan Page put it:

> Self-regulation is a matter of degree. To treat it otherwise would be to ignore the inter-penetration of the private and public sectors. Government has been heavily involved not only in the formation of self-regulatory regimes but also in their monitoring and adjustment.

The reality is that self-regulation is only effective if there are meaningful sanctions available to the regulator. Such sanctions, particularly those that may deny a person the opportunity to earn their living from professional practice, can be made available only by Parliament. That is why Ormrod observed that a fledgling profession must seek from Parliament statutory powers to inflict sanctions on its errant members.

There have been two recent examples of what Page calls the 'adjustment' of self-regulatory regimes. These illustrate the interdependence of self-regulation and government regulation, and contain interesting lessons for any sector aspiring to professional self-regulation. The first was the establishment by government of a self-regulatory framework in the field of investment business. Effective regulation of the sale of investment products to the public was long overdue. Individuals were being sold products that were unnecessary, unsuitable or both. Many of those doing the selling had a training that was inadequate or non-existent and were bound by no code of conduct that gave primacy to the interests of the client. Most salesmen were driven by the prospect of commission that was often substantial and hardly ever revealed to the purchaser. In this environment it was all too easy for the unsophisticated client to be fleeced by the unscrupulous salesman.

The financial services industry was one that cried out for regulation. The inherent inequality between the parties to the transactions would suggest that professional self-regulation, developing in the classic manner described by Ormrod, would have been the best way forward. But the ideal world that might have given rise voluntarily to such self-regulation did not exist. There was no single profession engaged in the provision of financial services, and the market itself was extremely complex. Government established a supervisory body to operate at arm's length from itself, the Securities and Investments Board, to which it devolved the main statutory powers. It then encouraged the establishment of self-regulatory organizations to work under it. The model did not work. Like the curate's egg, it was good in parts, especially those parts that were able to draw on established regulatory machinery.

However, the abuses and mis-selling went on, and self-regulation took much of the blame. The self-regulatory elements of the model were progressively reduced, with the consumer voice being given greater prominence. Finally, the government announced that a single new regulator was to be established. The great experiment in self-regulation had failed. What went wrong? At root was the 'natural lack of enthusiasm for regulation on the part of the group to be regulated' identified by the Securities Subcommittee of the US Senate. Or in Ormrod's terms there was no spontaneity of development of codes of conduct. Commission-hungry salesmen were not about to transform into professional financial advisers. The lesson is straightforward. Self-regulation requires the active support of those affected by it.

The second example illustrates the need for a regulatory regime to be sensitive to the public policy environment in which it operates. In some of their regulatory activities, especially in the field of education, professional bodies have shown themselves to be innovative. But in matters of professional conduct they appear sometimes to subscribe to the philosophy of the late Conservative MP Captain Charles Waterhouse: 'We are against change. We resist it for as long as we can. But when it has to come we make it decent.' Such an approach does not sit happily with public policy determined by elected governments anxious to deliver change before having next to face the electorate. In 1989 the government was impatient with both the Bar and the Law Society, the former for its resistance to ending its monopoly over rights of audience in the higher courts, the latter for its reluctance to open the market in conveyancing or to permit its members to form partnerships with other professionals. It announced its intention to legislate to change the arrangements for supervising the self-regulatory powers of the legal professional bodies. Instead of the senior judges alone being required to give their approval to new rules, most would in future require also the approval of an advisory committee with a lay majority.

Eight years after the new advisory committee came into being, the government announced its impending abolition. It had failed, in particular, to make any significant headway on the vexed question of rights of audience. Its powers were to pass to the Lord Chancellor who, as a member of the Cabinet could answer directly to Parliament (albeit through the unelected House of Lords) for the implementation of public policy. The lesson is clear. Powers of self-regulation granted by Parliament can be amended or taken away by Parliament. Parliament is most likely to do that if a self-regulatory body fails to have sufficient regard for public policy.

In granting self-regulatory powers, Parliament sometimes sets out its expectations with great clarity. For example, the Solicitors Act 1974 (as amended) states in s.32 that the Law Society 'shall' make rules concerning the keeping by solicitors of accounts for clients' money. Whether to safeguard funds entrusted by a client to a professional person is not a matter Parliament wished to leave to the discretion of the professional body. The power to make more general rules of professional conduct is permissive; s.31 says that the Law Society 'may, if they think fit, make rules'. However, if such a power is used, it must be used in the public interest. As Diplock said in the Swain case, the interests of that section of the public that may be in need of the professional services in question are paramount:

> In exercising its statutory functions the duty of the Council (of the Law Society) is to act in what it believes to be the best interests of that section of the public, even in the event (unlikely though this may be on any long term view) that those public interests should conflict with the special interests of members of the Law Society or of members of the solicitors' profession as a whole.

It cannot be put more plainly than that. Self-regulatory powers to make professional rules of conduct are to be exercised in the public interest. Furthermore, it is not just sins of commission that will be found out. They are matters to be corrected by the courts. Sins of omission, in particular a failure to have due regard for public policy, will also be found out. The government feared that the legal professional bodies and the senior judiciary would not use their powers to act on public policy on extended rights of audience in the courts. It visited upon them a lay-dominated advisory committee. That committee then failed to progress the matter satisfactorily, and was itself abolished. The power of professional self-regulation is not unfettered; it is there to be used in the public interest, and its exercise must have regard to public policy.

Thirty years ago Ormrod foresaw this public policy dimension, and considered that it would emerge in its sharpest form where the state was the paymaster. He noted that ethical codes tend to deal with the relations between the professional and the individual. State funding of professional services, through the legal aid scheme, or the National Health Service, introduces a third party into the relationship, namely the wider public in its role as paymaster/taxpayer, as represented by the state. Ormrod said:

> so far the concept of ethical obligations to the state has developed slowly. It is perhaps too soon for these difficult gestatory processes to have produced anything significant, or it may be that the existence of statutory rules, statutory terms of service and special statutory disciplinary bodies has inhibited the spontaneous development by the professions themselves of a code of conduct towards the state. It is nonetheless unfortunate. As the costs of litigation and the costs of medical treatment escalate there is a risk that the state, for its own protection, will be tempted to try to control professional decisions by regulation, unless codes of professional behaviour develop spontaneously that include not only duties to the individual but also duties to the state. There is a risk that the fashionable notion of cost effectiveness may be imposed on both professions.

The notions of professionalism discussed by Ormrod are based on a largely Victorian model of self-regulation, centred upon the self-employed sole practitioner offering services within a clearly defined field. Long-established examples of the model have adapted to modern circumstances to a greater or lesser extent, sometimes of their own volition, but more often under government or market pressure. Attempts to replicate the model in the late twentieth century by applying it in new fields were not successful. The government-inspired 'profession' of licensed conveyancer failed to get off the ground, and self-regulation proved an inadequate mechanism for controlling retail financial services.

Before university teachers attempt to establish themselves as a profession on the Victorian model, it is as well to consider what has changed in the field of professional regulation, and to try to identify a model that is more in tune with the times. Three important things have changed. The first and most significant is the relationship between the professional and the client. In many professional fields the relationship is no longer personal. The client deals with a corporate entity. If regulation is to be client-centred, then it must focus on whom the client deals with, often now an institution rather than an individual. The legal limit on professional partnerships to a size of twenty was abolished some years ago, and many professional partnerships are now multinational, multimillion-pound enterprises. Within these, professional standards of personal conduct continue to apply, but redress for the client when things go wrong will come more effectively from the employing institution.

The professional service required by the client, especially the business client, is often multi-disciplinary. Problems do not always come in neat boxes labelled 'legal' or 'accounting', and clients will often want their problem approached in a holistic manner defined by their needs, not by a historical division of labour between professional groups. This has given rise to the spectacular growth of the multi-service professional firm, a trend driven by the major accountancy firms. In general, clients are now better educated, and they play a part in a society that is, healthily, less deferential. There is still a gap in knowledge and understanding between the professional person and the client, but it is nowhere near as wide as it once was. There is a respect for professional abilities, but society no longer accepts the notion of a professional priesthood whose judgments must be regarded as infallible. A more equal partnership characterizes the relationship.

Second, occupational qualification is no longer a distinguishing mark of a professional. Zander observed: 'It is, of course, in the very nature of a profession that there should be at least one restrictive practice – limitation on entry to those who pass qualifying examinations.' That remains true, but an increasing number of occupations now require formal qualifications. In many cases the requirement is not that of a self-governing professional body, but of employers, or of insurers providing indemnity cover or fidelity bonding. Significantly, to spearhead the drive towards a better-qualified workforce, governments of both major parties turned not to bodies comprised, on the professional model, of individuals working in a given field. Instead they looked to bodies representative of employers to oversee the preparation of occupational standards and to set up National Training Organisations. That may be seen as a reflection of the reality that services are provided largely through corporate entities, rather than by individuals.

Third, the role of the state as a funder of professional services has grown substantially. It was always unrealistic for Ormrod to expect that notions of cost-effectiveness might not apply to professional activities. Nevertheless, he was right to conclude that professional bodies operating in fields where government is a major purchaser must have a particular regard to a wider accountability that includes a recognition that public resources are finite.

While some aspects of professional regulation have changed, there are fundamentals that remain constant. The notion of service to others, and measures of success other than the financial, remain central. Accountability to a wider public interest, both that of the collectivity of clients and that of society at large, is an abiding characteristic. Whilst unbridled, unaccountable self-regulation is a thing of the past, peer review continues to be a major feature of professional regulation. As a learned occupation, university teaching developed differently from the learned occupations that established professional bodies to regulate their activities. Nevertheless, as we enter a new century, it is possible to see a process of convergent evolution occurring that offers the potential for new models of professional regulation to apply equally to higher education and to the traditional professions.

The relationship with the primary client, the student, is at the level of the institution. It is the university, rather than any individual teacher, that contracts to offer an academic programme. Within that institutional arrangement there are then duties owed personally by individual teachers to their students. The parallel with the professional firm is clear. The service provided to the student is often multi-disciplinary, a modular programme rather than a single honours degree. The typical student is no longer a school-leaver; the mature learner will respect the professional abilities of the teacher, but in other respects will regard him as an equal. Qualifications to teach in higher education (insofar as they exist) are largely a matter for employing organizations. Attempts to establish a quasi-professional structure of qualifications (through the Institute for Learning and Teaching, recommended in the Dearing Report) are driven not by the spontaneous enthusiasm of practising university teachers, but by government agencies (the funding councils) and employer bodies (the Committee of Vice Chancellors and Principals and the Standing Conference of Principals).

The role of the state as funder is central, to the extent that the Further and Higher Education Act 1992 ties regulation (in the form of quality assessment) to funding. This model of a multi-disciplinary service, funded substantially by the state and delivered through large institutions by individuals holding qualifications specified by their employers, is one with which the established professions are having to come to terms. Is there room within it for traditional professional behaviour? Is it a model within which university teaching could establish a distinctive professional identity?

The model requires both institutional and individual behaviour to accord to professional norms. A respect for the obligations that arise from the inherent inequality of the relationship with the client, an acceptance of the supremacy of public rather than private interests, and recognition of a public accountability must be manifested both corporately and personally. The public interest that higher education must serve has changed dramatically with the shift from elite, exclusive provision to mass and inclusive provision. The higher education system is no longer one catering largely for young people with graduate parents, who progress to professional and blue-chip jobs to which they are recruited by managers who are themselves graduates. In such a system the values of higher education could safely be left implicit, as those who needed to understand them had personal experience of university life. Now there are new stakeholders to whom the values and benefits of higher education must be made explicit. They include families whose children are the first generation to go to university, employers recruiting in the graduate labour market for the first time, and mature students looking to higher education to equip them with the skills to cope with uncertain and rapidly changing job prospects.

Subject benchmark information, programme specifications that spell out the outcomes to be achieved, and a qualifications framework based on clear and explicit descriptors of level are the new means of defining standards in higher education. Together, they have a function similar to that of a code defining professional standards, in that they tell the individual client (the student) and the wider interested public (especially the employer) what they can reasonably expect from a professional service. Universities and their teachers must deliver to those standards if they are to convince the world that they are true professionals. That degree of explicitness about learning outcomes will require teaching to be directed to those outcomes, and not regarded as an adjunct to, or distraction from research. Setting and fulfilling explicit standards will demonstrate to the world outside exactly what it is that university teachers do. Defining teaching in 'can do' rather then 'can't do' terms will help overcome the prejudice that leads many outside higher education to be dismissive of its claims to professional status.

Accountability is now readily accepted by universities. In his presidential address to the 1998 Assembly of the Association of European Universities (CRE), Josep Bricall said that autonomous universities: 'need to take into account the interests of stakeholders and taxpayers – whose representatives will increase their weight in the governing bodies of our institutions.' The CRE's preliminary report on its institutional evaluation programme noted the need for universities to demonstrate that they were doing their utmost to satisfy the expectations of society in general. It said:

> credibility … can no longer be acquired solely through academic publications or the award of degrees and diplomas, or even through ad hoc services to the surrounding community. It also requires an overall strategy based on solid institutional foundations. Any such strategy clearly expresses the will and ability of an institution, and its constituent entities, to pursue specific objectives implying firm priorities which take account of the explicit or implicit needs of its environment.

The clearest commitment to the obligation for accountability came in the Glion Declaration 'The University at the Millennium', drafted for participants in the international Glion colloquium by Professor Frank Rhodes of Cornell University:

> The university must be properly accountable for its 'output'; the integrity of its scholarship, the quality of its professional standards, the impartiality of its judgements and the competence of its graduates. But,

beyond those things, it must remain sturdily independent, yielding neither to internal activist interests, nor to external pressure, but changing deliberately, selectively and responsibly, in the light of public needs and changing knowledge.

This statement captures the complexity of the multiple accountabilities that characterize professional practice. There is not a single accountability, there are several, and resolving conflicts between them is a fundamental part of the exercise of professional judgment. Duties are owed to individual clients, to a wider public interest, and to a proper standard of professional work. For the lawyer, resolving potential conflicts between the interests of an individual client and a wider duty to justice and the courts that administer it, lies at the heart of professional conduct. That universities are now engaging in open debate about equivalent issues demonstrates an acceptance and understanding of the nature of professional activity.

Higher education now operates within a statutory framework not dissimilar to those governing established professions, but operating primarily at the level of the institution rather than that of the individual. Mechanisms are provided for the grant of degree awarding powers (Further and Higher Education Act 1992, s.76) and of university title (s.77), for assessment of the quality of education provided (s.70), and for assessing arrangements for the maintenance of academic standards (s.82). The sanction of loss of funding is available if quality is found wanting. Significantly, those mechanisms are all dependent upon peer review. The Act provides for assessment of quality to be overseen by a committee of the Funding Council having a majority of persons with experience and current involvement in higher education. The Quality Assurance Agency undertakes assessment reviews, and evaluates applications for degree awarding powers and university title, using peer review procedures. The powers of s.82 have never been used, because institutions voluntarily established the academic audit procedures now operated by the QAA.

Although university teaching did not develop the professional infrastructure of other learned occupations, within higher education the key characteristics of a profession are now present or emerging. They are a codification of duties owed to the student, the collective establishment of standards of academic performance, acknowledgment of a wider responsibility to stakeholders of all types, a recognition of an accountability to the public interest, an acceptance of the need for competence-based qualifications, and the existence of sanctions granted by Parliament to deal with misconduct (through funding mechanisms). However, these characteristics are developing primarily at the institutional level. Elsewhere, a similar two-tier approach to professional regulation is becoming common. Professional behaviour needs to manifest itself, and be regulated, at the level of the institution, be that professional firm, hospital or university. Within institutions, the requirement for a personal commitment to professional standards remains, although it is as likely to be enforced through contracts of employment as through the disciplinary machinery of a professional body.

Institutions that behave professionally, and which promote professional standards amongst their staff, will be treated as having earned the right to play a part in the regulation of their own activities. Peer review of performance in relation to quality and standards will play a central part in that regulation. Models of professional regulation that assume a producer-defined service offered by a self-employed sole practitioner no longer accord with reality. The professional service entity now plays a role equal to that of the professional individual. University teaching has the opportunity to demonstrate that it is worthy of recognition as a true professional activity. It can do so by drawing upon the traditional norms of professional behaviour. But by recognizing the roles of institutions as well as individuals it can move on from nineteenth-century models and become truly a profession for the twenty-first century.

References

Brandeis, L.D. (1933) *Business or Profession?* in A. Lief (ed.) *The Social and Economic Views of Mr Justice Brandeis*, New York: Vanguard Press.

Bricall, J. (1998) 'Presidential Address to the Conference of European Rectors [CRE]', Geneva: CRE.

Conference of European Rectors (1998) *CRE as a Learning Organization*, preliminary version, Geneva: CRE.

Cornford, M. (1908) *Microcosmographica Academica,* Cambridge: Bowes and Bowes.

Dicey, A.V. (1867), *Fortnightly Review*, 1, London.

Diplock, Lord Justice (1982) *All England Law Reports*, London: HMSO.

Further and Higher Education Act 1992, London: HMSO.

Gower, L.C.B. (1982) *Review of Investor Protection*, London: HMSO.

National Committee of Inquiry into Higher Education (1997) *Higher Education in the Learning Society*, London: HMSO.

Ormrod, R. (1968) 'Medical Ethics', *British Medical Journal*, 2, London: British Medical Association.

Page, P. (1986) 'Self-regulation: the constitutional dimension', *Modern Law Review*, 3, London.

Parliamentary Select Committee on Foreign Loans (1875) *Report*, London: HMSO.

Rhodes, F. (1998) *The University at the Millennium* ['Glion declaration'], Geneva: University of Geneva.

The Solicitors Act 1974 (consolidated with amendments to 1990), London: HMSO.

United States Senate Securities Subcommittee (1973) *Report*, Washington, DC.

Waterhouse, C. (1965) Speech at election rally, September 1964, quoted in Howard and West, *The Making of the Prime Minister*, London: Quality Book Club.

Zander, M. (1968) *Lawyers and the Public Interest*, London: Weidenfeld and Nicolson.

10 The Future of Research

Jonathan Adams

Research has enjoyed an extended 'heroic' age, characterized by the individual pursuit of discovery and creation, and it has created a paradigm – particularly in the natural sciences – that has been reinforced by the growth and success of the research university. This mode of research has unquestionably been a public good, being both excellent in its product and pervasive in its social and economic impact. But the age of discovery is coming to an end, and our model for research enterprise is subject to a legitimate reconfiguration that reflects a progressive change from discovery to utility, to an emphasis on the interaction between the producers and users of research, and towards the creation of an enterprise culture. Furthermore, in a knowledge economy, universities are not the sole locus for research or knowledge.

The paradigm shift, from hero to utility, is culturally threatening to large, elite but less agile institutions wedded to a model of substantial public funding for research programmes they devise and manage. Their objections are infectious, but obstruction to change would be unfortunate. First, because it can be argued that the change enables research that is more relevant to the delivery of improvements in wealth creation and the quality of life. Second, because our evident cultural attachment to an older paradigm legitimises the attribution of problems to the public part of the research base that are actually rooted elsewhere.

Much of this chapter is about the UK's 'knowledge transfer' problem, because that is a primary influence on the reconfiguration of research. British universities produce research that is internationally excellent – and is more competitive than specialist institutions – but industry fails to exploit it. Higher education institutions (HEIs) also contribute to knowledge transfer by producing people who are trained in a research environment, and who can transfer understanding and know-how. There are many initiatives already in place to enable people-transfer. Industry in the UK, however, has a poor record of investment in capacity-building to pick up and implement technology opportunities.

The British 'knowledge problem' is both familiar and surprising. Familiar, because it has been around for so long. Surprising, because the concept of research for useful ends has an even longer history. It was in the mind of Francis Bacon when he argued that 'the real and legitimate goal of the sciences is the endowment of human life with new inventions and riches'. It was part of the foundation of my own institution, when Yorkshire industrialists returning from the Great Exhibition in Paris determined – very purposefully – to create their own College for training and for research. It is perhaps only in this century that the separation between knowledge creation and knowledge exploitation has become problematic (Varcoe, 1974; Wilkie, 1991). Wealth creation and the quality of life are now public policy, however, and the reconfiguration of research to those ends is addressed by setting priorities for research, not by peer review but through merit review and by the criterion of consensus rather than by excellence.

I shall argue that the emergent policy is unhelpful and unbalanced. There are risks that merit review suppresses the characteristics that maintain traditional research excellence. And there are risks that consensus suppresses essential diversity in research. The continuing emphasis is – wrongly – on reconfiguring the supply side. I believe that government policy should focus not on knowledge supply but on equipping those in industry who should have a demand for understanding and innovation. Initiative funding should be redirected, away from encouraging universities to work with industry and towards encouraging industry to work with universities.

Research and the Diminishing Rate of Return

Publicly funded research is in a permanent 'Red Queen' race with government research expectations. For example, the volume growth of activity in biology has been measurably greater (doubling every 10 years) than the rate of return in new discoveries (doubling every 50 years for biology *sensu lato* and every 22.5 years for genetics this century: Glass, 1979). Such statistics are a characteristic of every research field, but the consequence is that research productivity becomes a matter of public notice. The growth of evaluation and assessment raises questions about the way in which we define, set and measure effectiveness in research and about the factors now affecting the research enterprise.

I will not rehearse arguments for the public funding of basic research, but it is worth recording how widespread research appraisal has become. In the 1980s, a policy groundswell from government led the University Grants Committee (UGC) to shift from its covert approach to the assessment of research performance in UK universities to an overt and formalized Research Assessment Exercise (RAE) linked to a more openly selective system of funding. Since then, international interest in research assessment has grown and is now very active among the UK's European neighbours.

In 1997, the German federal government introduced a draft framework law for higher education to link funding and research performance. Max

Planck President Hubert Markl has announced plans to put all Max Planck institutes through a thorough evaluation every six years. In France, Catherine Bréchignac, Director-General of the Centre National de la Recherche Scientifique (CNRS) has also said that she wants to direct funds through rigorous scientific evaluation. In July 1998, Research Minister Claude Allègre announced a (hotly contested) system of peer-reviewed grants to replace formulaic research funds and said that research evaluation, driven by external review panels, would be applied not only to CNRS but also to the Institut National de la Santé et de la Recherche Médicale (INSERM). He also announced a specific target: doubling the impact of French research papers over four years, primarily by publishing fewer papers of higher quality.

Where is Research Going?

We have been brought up in an age where research has been conducted by geniuses and heroes (Schaffer, 1998). We know far more about the natural world, about the nature of society, and about its origins and our own than could be imagined a hundred years ago, let alone a thousand. The milestones along this pathway were people: individuals whose singular contribution was to discover and create. The enterprise seemed limitless. Now we are at the end of this heroic period: research is marked by limits to the resources available for its prosecution and the revelatory paper is replaced by a new production of knowledge.

Horgan (1997) has predicted the end of science. That prediction needs interpretation, and it is not that scientific enquiry is at an end. There are, as Maddox (1998) has described, many fascinating lines of investigation still to be pursued. We have a great deal to discover about the human and other genomes. We need to understand the vagaries of global climate. We need major longitudinal studies in the social sciences, and more work on the origins and components of social exclusion. But few of these investigations are characterized by the likelihood that we shall be fundamentally surprised by the outcome. In a Kuhnian sense, the research will solve puzzles rather than lead to paradigm revolutions. And, as the efforts of research yield diminishing returns, so researchers will become more self-conscious, introspective and subjective. There are only two areas where we may still expect to see research achieve a heroic scale, and these are the realms of the very big and the very small: the realms of astronomy and particle physics. Very big problems, very expensive answers, and both addressed by PPARC – the UK Research Council with the smallest budget increase in the 1998 allocations round.

The heroic model has had a wide social impact. It has, for example, both conditioned and been further reified by the structure of the Nobel awards (Crawford, 1998). No more than three individuals can receive a share in any award, and organizations cannot share at all except for the Peace prize. Although Nobel stated that rewards should go to work of discovery, invention or improvement of benefit to mankind, in practice the Royal Swedish Academy exalted discovery above invention and improvement. It was also much disposed against theoreticians, preferring to recognize the genius of discovery rather than thought. Now, if most of the big discoveries have been made and if the resources required to tackle the remaining ones – and perhaps even to tackle major inventions and innovations – are on a vastly greater scale, then the lone and heroic genius cannot survive. In the natural sciences, in the social sciences and in the humanities research is shifting towards collaborative and collective effort. This is a consensus reflected both in strategy statements from the Economic and Social Research Council and, reportedly, in consultations about the strategy of the new Arts and Humanities Research Board.

The transition in the research enterprise stems from two principal factors. First, the way in which research outputs are now employed has changed (Gibbons et al., 1994). Knowledge is increasingly produced in the context of application, often through the coordination of disparate disciplines and outside traditional organizational structures. Curiosity as a justification is replaced by a new social context in which researchers must respond to agendas set by stakeholders outside their own peer groups. The key conclusion that emerges is that those who use and not those who generate its outputs will set the objectives of research. Second, research in universities is faced by a paucity of resources and a plethora of opportunity. While the frontier remains endless (Bush, 1945) and the capacity to extend it has broadened with successive generations, there is now a recognizable limit to resources in the United Kingdom (Ziman, 1987, 1994) and in the United States (Council on Competitiveness, 1996). The key conclusion that emerges is that we must now decide not only what we are going to do but what we are not going to do.

Where is the Organization of Research Going?

The purpose of the organization of research is that 'individual researchers, provided with the necessary infrastructure, should be released to display their critically important gifts of spontaneity and originality' (Bernal, 1939). We need to make management a more evident feature of research in higher education in the future, because it has been weak or absent in the past. That does not mean that management becomes a replacement for resources, but nothing has given better cause for suspicion about the competency of the research base than past lack of accountability for resource management (Hague, 1991). Until recently, most universities had no way of estimating the real costs of research, despite many attempts to rectify this (eg. Clayton, 1987). Over-prescriptive and top-down management can indeed stifle creative research, but the idea that research and management do not mix is mistaken: competent researchers succeed because they are necessarily also good managers.

We need to improve the career development of researchers, but we have not yet agreed what that development should be (Scott, 1997). UK universities have been *laissez-faire* in their attitudes towards the development of human resources, although that is one of the system's key functions. The former polytechnics were rather more conscious of this role and have much good practice to offer. Graduate training uses research activity as a mode of learning and has in some institutions evolved and formalized in the 'graduate school' concept (Becher et al., 1994; Clark, 1993). There are, however, arguments for a greater concentration of research training, both into fewer institutions and into more selective programmes. In a system of mass higher education, should research training – as an advanced tier at a high level in a very long and narrowing learning trail – necessarily be uniformly dispersed?

We need to manage multi-disciplinary approaches, because the application of knowledge requires disparate, individualistic strands to be pulled together, and we need better collaborative mechanisms. One of the ways in which dispersed, rather than concentrated, research can be maintained is by using the Internet to create virtual colleges within disciplines. Bibliometric studies show that collaboration in publication is one of the strengths of the UK research base. More than half the papers published in the UK have authors from at least two higher education institutions, and the UK also publishes in international collaborations at twice the rate of the USA. This contributes significantly to impact: domestic and, even more so, international collaboration both have the effect of increasing citation rates (Katz and Hicks, 1997).

We need to manage larger teams using more complex facilities to tackle bigger problems. The growing need for sophisticated instrumentation applies to the social as well as natural sciences and is appearing in the humanities. There are three components that characterize the present state of the research infrastructure. First, research is subject to a long-recognized 'sophistication' factor. That is to say, the cost of doing any 'unit' of research tends to advance faster than the rate of inflation in the economy as a whole. Second, the replacement rate of basic equipment has fallen behind that needed to maintain parity. The latest of a series of equipment surveys has shown that some £474 million is needed over the next five years to restore the status quo (Georghiou et al., 1996). Third, the accelerating pace of technological advance has created opportunities that require resources well beyond most universities, because of either cost or scale.

Broers (1998) suggests that the solution to the infrastructure shortfall is for universities to carry out research alongside industry so that the joint enterprise can keep up with technological development. This would also provide for the exchange of people between the research, development and manufacturing organizations to ensure the rapid and effective transfer of the insight that he argues contributes to key technological advances. Insight he defines as an in-depth understanding of the fundamentals of technology and its relationship to competing technologies. Broers sets out case studies of 20 key innovations that demonstrate the importance of insight and problem-solving rather than conceptual leaps. He shows that they increasingly depend on large organizations, on teamwork and on multi-disciplinary collaboration.

We need to consider the broader societal context in which research is supported fully to capture the way in which the research enterprise is changing. For a well-reasoned discourse, I would refer the reader to, particularly, the Carnegie Commission Report (1992) and Gibbons (1997). He re, I would simply note that there have been arguments from researchers themselves that there has been a disregard – particularly from scientists – for the social and environmental consequences of research. The balance of evidence is, however, that research is increasingly sensitive to and influenced by what society deems acceptable and appropriate. For example, public opinion is shaping the development of genome work, particularly that of genetically modified organisms. This component of agenda-setting will inevitably, and rightly, grow. Together, these 'need' factors set constraints to the future organization of research. None provides any particular justification for continuing research in universities. Perhaps all add some weight to the view that research could be delivered just as well in other environments.

Research Universities: Do We 'Need' Them?

The subjective characteristics of higher education research include open enquiry, critical thinking, excitement, spontaneity, originality and serendipity. No management indicators measure these, however, nor link them to wealth creation because 'pure enquiry long precedes measurable technological development' (Dainton, 1991). The apparent success of the research university, with both teacher and student in search of knowledge, has led to an assumption in the UK and the USA that there will be a continuing social and economic requirement for universities and research to remain intimately linked. Derek Bok, President of Harvard University, commented that 'our future depends to an ever increasing extent on new discoveries, expert knowledge and highly trained people. Like it or not, universities are our principal source of each of these ingredients' (quoted in Lindsey, 1991).

Does the changing direction of the research enterprise make the characteristics of university research less important – or their value less easy to assert – in the present than hitherto? And are assumptions such as Bok's still valid? Three pieces of evidence provide room for doubt.

First, teaching and research map uneasily together. They can be organized within a single framework only under specific circumstances. In the UK, the structures for their assessment and their funding are distinct.

Second, in many countries with successful and competitive research profiles the higher education system is not the principal locus for public research. In France, for example, a large part of the function is performed by the CNRS, which employs 25,000 research scientists and engineers in Paris and the regions. Its 1,500 units are active in every research field. In Germany, the Max Planck institutes have an outstanding record in their contribution to the generation and application of knowledge. The 80 institutes, research centres, laboratories and project groups cover basic research in science and the arts and humanities and employ some 10,000 scientists, scholars and post-doctoral fellows.

Third, we need to recall that there is in the UK an extensive system of successful research establishments attached to the Research Councils, including some units on university sites. There are also industrial research and training organizations and other quasi-independent laboratories.

In gross financial terms, the research and development (R&D) capacity of the higher education system is relatively small, being only some 20 per cent of about £15 billion per year spent in the UK. It is true that expenditure in universities accounts for the bulk, but not by any means all, of the UK's basic research capacity. Industry spends much of its 70 per cent share on product development. But in some sectors, such as pharmaceuticals and biotechnology, that balance is more even and the industrial sector makes perhaps the major contribution to Britain's research competitiveness (Hicks and Katz, 1997; Adams et al., 1998).

Clearly, then, we should be wary in asserting that a nation depends on research in higher education institutions (HEIs). For arguments in favour, we could refer to the Dearing Committee's conclusions (National Committee of Inquiry into Higher Education [NCIHE], 1997):

Within the aims and purposes of higher education, there [are] four main roles for research and reasons for supporting it in higher education institutions:

• to add to the sum of human knowledge and understanding;
• to inform and enhance teaching;
• to generate useful knowledge and inventions in support of wealth creation and an improved quality of life;
• to create an environment in which researchers can be encouraged and given a high level of training.

This is a little thin. It is far from clear that any of these roles *requires* research to be supported in HEIs. Scholarship provides a capability for gathering knowledge and using it to 'inform and enhance teaching' at a level appropriate to higher education without active engagement in research. If this were not true, then large swathes of the UK HEI system, unfunded for research after the last RAE, should no longer be permitted to function. Others can 'generate knowledge' and, although patented technology increasingly cites publicly funded science (Breitzmann et al., 1998), most 'inventions' (using patents as a proxy for invention) are generated outside the publicly funded research base.

Only Dearing's last point has a strong base, but there is a counter argument, that too long a period spent in an undirected research environment actually disables the brightest minds of their potential for application to any subsequent career. Industry suspects, to quote Bacon again, that 'universities incline wits to sophistry and affectation'.

Research Universities: Are They a Good Investment?

Historically, investing in university research has been an act of faith. Up until 1970 'successive [British] governments believed that there was a necessary connection between science and growing national wealth' (Wilkie, 1991). Allan Bromley, the former US Presidential Science Adviser, commented that 'since the war years, both Congress and the different administrations have shared the conviction that support of research in the nation's universities ... represented an investment in the national future' (Clinton and Gore, 1994). Governments now expect the return on their investment to take some tangible form.

Would we gain some greater economic return if we remodelled the UK research system? We could look for comparison to Germany, where there is a concentration of resources in research institutes with well-defined missions and often co-located with relevant industry. Our recent comparative study of international research performance (Adams et al., 1998) allows us to make just such a comparison. We first assessed the relative productivity of those countries which are the major contributors to global research volume, by major research sector (physical sciences, social sciences, etc.) and specific research area (physics, physiology, politics, etc.). We then analysed their research performance for the period 1988–1996, aggregating data across 47 subject areas corresponding to units of assessment (UOAs) used in the UK Research Assessment Exercise and 13 research sectors corresponding to clusters of cognate UOAs (Table 10.1).

Two key impressions emerge from this overview. First, competitiveness in research tends to be a package: some nations perform well (USA, England – note, not the UK in this study) at both specific and general levels, while others perform less well. The second impression is that some countries perform relatively evenly across areas, while others have more evident and characteristic core strengths. For example, while there is a widely recognized correlation between publications and citations, it is weaker for England than it is for other

Table 10.1 *A comparison between the research performance of major research nations and their industrial R&D expenditure compared with the volume of sales*

	USA	*Japan*	*England*	*Germany*	*France*	*Canada*	*Australia*
Total publication output							
000s papers	2,509	546	501	487	368	326	162
000s cites	23,450	3,007	3,877	3,099	2,331	2,269	984
Performance by UOAs							
impact	1.32	0.70	1.07	0.82	0.86	1.02	0.89
rank	1.38	6.17	2.96	5.06	4.53	3.19	4.70
Performance by categories							
impact	1.32	0.74	1.05	0.85	0.86	1.02	0.74
rank	1.08	6.00	3.15	4.77	4.62	3.15	5.23
R&D investment[a]							
R&D/sales	4.3	4.9	2.3	4.7	4.0	10.8	1.0
rank[b]	9	7	12	8	10	2	15

Notes:
[a]*Data relate to UK total, not England.*
[b]*There were fifteen countries in this analysis. Denmark, Sweden and Switzerland (which were not covered by our major analysis for HEFCE) also have higher citation impact than the UK (see OST, 1997) and higher R&D ratios.*

countries (correlation coefficient across 47 UOAs: England=0.78, Germany=0.93, USA=0.94). In other words, England has a higher impact than expected in areas of low output relative to the rest of the world.

We can illustrate this difference in research configuration. Figure 10.1 shows the relationship between relative output (as a proxy for investment) and impact for three countries whose research systems are essentially higher education based. The correlation between output and impact is negative for these countries. Figure 10.2 makes the same comparison for three countries whose publicly funded research systems are strongly resourced outside higher education. The correlation between output and impact is strongly positive for these countries.

These graphs suggest that there is a pattern of association between research competitiveness and research organization. Those research economies that are typically more directed, through mission-led institutes such as the CNRS, tend to have positive associations between the output and impact of research. There is also a link with applied research areas, and some general relationship might also be inferred between historical traditions and well-founded industrial sectors. On the other hand, research performance in those economies in which research activity is HEI-led is good across the broad sweep of disciplines. Performance may even be high despite relatively low world share: for example, Canada ranks third in the world ahead of France and Germany (Table 10.1).

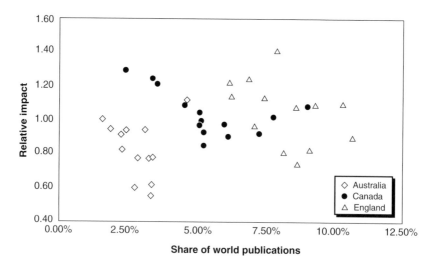

Figure 10.1   *Relative output (share of world publications) and impact across major research fields for three countries characterized by a university-based research system*

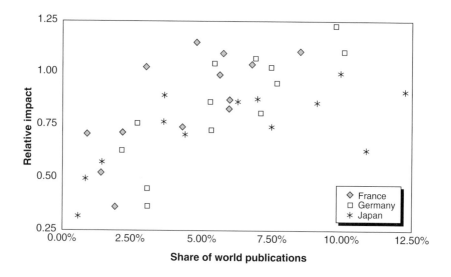

Figure 10.2   *Relative output (share of world publications) and impact across major research fields for three countries characterized by an institute-based research system*

The outcomes of our study closely accord with two studies carried out by May (1997, 1998), and there is a similar pattern of relative research effectiveness in relation to population and to total and civil research expenditure (Office of Science and Technology [OST], 1997). The bibliometric evidence does not, therefore, support the idea that the UK research system should be reconfigured. May argues that the significant differences in performance are a consequence of differences in institutional settings. Higher education, the normal host for basic research in the USA, England, Canada and Australia, appears to provide a better return on investment than does a dedicated research institute system. Managed research regimes can produce peaks of performance, but not the breadth of excellence (Figure 10.1).

Knowledge Transfer: How Do We Mobilize the Return on Investment?

The underlying outputs of research in HEIs are packets of knowledge, carried by publications and people that enable the knowledge (or technology) to be transferred to users. These users may be other researchers or they may be public or private sector customers who apply the knowledge to improved or novel products and processes. The impact and utility of publications is measured by their influence on subsequent work, reflected in citation counts (Adams et al., 1998). Such bibliometric indices are only a proxy for 'real' information and reflect only one aspect of the utility of research. Citation counts are less informative for applied research and meaningless in the arts, and the shift in the production of knowledge means that this measure has even less utility as more publications circulate in forms that are not amenable to primary impact measures. One of the reasons why there is a shift to this different, or 'Mode 2' (Gibbons et al., 1994), knowledge production is that traditional academic publications are a very inefficient way of transferring information.

Knowledge produced in isolation from its utilization and application is a bit like kicking a ball against a garage door. You might develop your skills, up to a point, but it's not terribly productive. If the ball goes over a fence, it's difficult to know from the reaction what you did right or wrong. What you actually want is someone to test your skills by kicking it back. This is the difference between the linear model of innovation and more interesting and explanatory models that have emerged since the early 1990s. Kicking ideas and problems backwards and forwards raises the level of Broers' 'insight' on both sides.

People make a more efficient channel for knowledge and technology transfer than pieces of paper. For much of UK industry, the individuals trained under the Research Councils' Masters and Doctoral schemes are at least as valuable as any combination of publications, because people carry with them not only knowledge but also know-how. The utility of this output is its employability: on average about one half of Research Council funded MSc graduates and about one third of PhDs go into industry. A similar number of PhDs go into academic appointments (OST, 1998).

People can transfer knowledge in other ways. Dainton (1991) commends the practice of von Humboldt in encouraging the system of dual appointments to the University of Berlin. These straddled industry and the university, forming an effective bridge for the two-way flow of ideas and the possibility of building mutual understanding. The difference in academic and industrial salaries probably makes this untenable today, but project sharing in intermediate institutes is an alternative 'island' between knowledge-producers and technology-users. The former Advisory Board for the Research Councils (ABRC) sent a group to Germany in 1991 to look at the function of the Fraunhofer Institutes with a view to developing policies for a comparable UK system (of Faraday Institutes). Of course, the problem with such institutions is, as one member of the ABRC commented, that you actually need two bridges to complete the links. The ABRC's Fraunhofer study led to the establishment of Postgraduate Training Partnerships (PTPs) where academia and industry came together in the common ground of an industrial training organization jointly to supervise a portfolio of postgraduate research projects. In Leeds, we decided that our BBSRC biotechnology PTP was so useful that we put our own money into a joint materials PTP with the Cookson Group's Centre near Oxford.

Knowledge Transfer: Does Industry Buy the Product?

Another route for knowledge transfer opens when industry chooses to out-source research contracts and consultancies to academia. While this is worth about £190 million per year in the UK, it is not evenly spread across subject areas. This problem is most obvious in the engineering sector (Department of Trade and Industry [DTI], 1998). There is low intensity of industrial R&D compared to other manufacturing nations and a low rate of skilled employment, particularly among higher technical and craft grades. There is a consequently poor understanding of what the research base can do for innovation or how its outputs might be applied.

For example, among the engineering-based sectors, the construction industry (with a £58 bn output in 1998 and employing 1.4 million people) has recently come in for particularly close scrutiny (Department of the Environment, Transport and the Regions [DETR], 1998). The chair of the Construction Task Force, Sir John Egan, has noted that the sector investment in R&D has fallen by 80 per cent over 15 years and training has halved over 25 years. The construction industry lacks the capacity for innovation in processes and technology and fails to satisfy clients. On the academic side, civil engineering is one of the weaker areas in the UK research base (Adams et al., 1998), perhaps because of the lack of any 'intelligent customers' to develop an insightful dialogue.

There is a long-standing UK concern about the strength of the manufacturing sector. This is where output and R&D intensity is weakest compared to the rest of the G7, and the pattern is often assumed to be general to all sectors. It is sometimes said to be a reflection of the hypothetical British 'knowledge problem', the trait that makes us bad at translating research ideas and outputs into practical innovation and technology. Fortunately, the pharmaceutical sector provides an important contrast to manufacturing. The sector is characterized by a vibrant industrial research culture mirrored by a high-performing part of the UK research base (Adams, 1998). There is extraordinary growth in the European life science industry, significantly outstripping the USA, and the greatest number of companies and most large enterprises are in the UK (Ernst and Young, 1998). There is significant investment of industrial R&D in higher education based research and training through contracts and studentships, and thus extensive dialogue between knowledge and technology. The pharmaceutical sector is also marked by a significant level of industrial research publication (Hicks and Katz, 1997) which is actually more highly cited than UK academic publications in the same disciplinary area (Adams et al., 1998).

There are parallels elsewhere. The shift in strength from Germany to the USA in chemical engineering post-1945 has been attributed partly to a resource shift from coal to oil, but mainly to the capability of specialist engineering firms to design and develop new processes. Chemical engineering emerged in the USA as a recognizable profession at the same time and was supported by the growth of relevant degrees and departments in universities. Japan is usually cited as the modern epitome of technology exploitation and innovation. However, although Japanese chemical firms have taken out USA patents since 1990 at twice the rate of German companies, technology is not being translated into innovation because capability has been lost in industrial under-specialization and over-capacity (Arora et al., 1998).

The lesson here is that the effective transfer of knowledge, the utilization of research, depends on the user as much as the producer. For most industrial sectors, with the exception of pharmaceuticals, the UK continues to underperform its major competitors in R&D commitment (DTI, 1997). OECD data show that it has also recorded a lower growth in industrial R&D expenditure since 1992 than not only the USA but also most other European countries. UK industry continues to have the lowest ratio of R&D to sales of any G7 country (Table 10.1).

An effective two-way flow of ideas may be the weakest link in the dialogue between British industry and academia, but where dialogue exists, in pharmaceuticals, technology is transferred. There is no national British malaise that prevents research outputs being turned into effective applications. The problem is that most of industry fails to capture the outputs of the research enterprise because of short-term and risk-averse thinking, behaviour characterized by the construction sector (May, 1995; DETR, 1998). Table 10.1 can be interpreted as an affirmation that it is not the higher education research system that needs to be reconfigured. To realize the benefits of investment in research, attention should be paid not to output and delivery, the supply side, but to enabling the user to receive, interpret, understand and implement.

Has Government Enabled the Research User?

Research customers are given a greater sense of ownership of research outcomes if they are involved in setting objectives and priorities. Industries are not the only stakeholders, and they may actually have a shorter-term interest in the outcomes of research than, for example, government itself (either as a direct user or as a proxy for the public interest). Many sectors therefore need to contribute to the setting of long-term research goals to achieve the balance that preserves an appropriate overall mission.

Informed by carefully considered advice (ABRC, 1992), the White Paper on science, engineering and technology – 'Realising Our Potential' (HMSO, 1993) proposed that:

> steps should be taken which, on the basis of other countries' experience, will help to harness [the UK's science and technology] strength ... to the creation of wealth in the United Kingdom by bringing it into closer and more systematic contact with those responsible for industrial and commercial decisions. Such a systematic interchange between industry, scientists, engineers and science policy makers (both in the public sector and the charitable sector) would improve mutual understanding and allow each group to make its decisions against a better-informed background.
>
> (para. 1.16)

One of the initiatives used to achieve that objective was the Technology Foresight Programme. Some 15 Foresight panels consulted some 10,000 people and published reports aimed at identifying 'the likely social, economic and market trends in each sector over the next 10–20 years and the developments in science, engineering, technology and infrastructure required to best address future needs'. Championed as a way of picking winners (Irvine and Martin, 1984), Foresight had great appeal in a time of increasing selectivity but its shortcomings have also been widely recognized. For example, legitimization and ownership of the process by stakeholders is only achieved if a dialogue is established between the producers and users of research. But, as one observer remarked, instead of HEIs' scientists talking to industry's managers, it was more that 'our scientists got an opportunity to talk to their scientists'. It was also noted that the disciplinary crossover between panels was poor.

More problematically, 'Foresight' is by its nature fundamentally disposed against foresight. The late David Phillips, former Chairman of the ABRC and of the House of Lords Science and Technology Committee, remarked that if Technology Foresight had been in use in the nineteenth century we would now have one of the most efficient gas-powered street lighting systems in the world. The process of consultation and discussion is more naturally disposed towards the development of consensus: it is a process from which revelation and decision is absent; it achieves either an averaging or, worse, a lowest common denominator. The 27 high priority 'generic technologies' identified by the panels (HMSO, 1995) are striking by their ordinariness. A feeling emerges that Foresight, like most consultation exercises, is an excuse for avoiding difficult decisions and for minimizing the risks of commission.

Nonetheless, Foresight priorities have had an impact, particularly in the public sector where government departments reflect the findings in their policy development and spending decisions. Although HEFCE argues that none of its funding is predicated against Foresight criteria, the Guidance on Submissions for the 1996 Research Assessment Exercise (HEFCE RAE96 2/95) specifically asks for 'the department's response to the Government's Technology Foresight programme'. Research Councils are also expected to 'take note' of Foresight panels' reports and to use these to inform their research spending when developing new directed grant programmes and in developing criteria for awards. For example, the EPSRC Materials Programme sets aside approximately £2.5 million to fund industrially relevant projects in the area of 'Processing of Functional Materials'. EPSRC comments that: 'while much of the research supported by EPSRC is long term or "blue skies" in nature, the overall support provided for Foresight is high at approximately 70% of the current grant portfolio. This is particularly marked in the technology programmes, Materials and IT & Computer Science, where many basic research subjects have been identified as underpinning Foresight priorities.' ('Action for Foresight', May 1998, para. 3.1).

For stated areas of studentship funding and applied-strategic research programmes, an incentive to encourage collaboration between industry and higher education should bring tangible benefits. Schemes with collaboration as an objective or a requirement are therefore a significant part of the Science Budget. For example, in addition to taught Mastership courses sponsored by industry, there are over 1000 Cooperative Awards in Science and Engineering (CASE) studentships each year. The Teaching Company Schemes have produced 2000 partnerships since 1975 (77 per cent of which are with small and medium sized enterprises – SMEs), and more than 200 new programmes started in 1997. 'Realising Our Potential' Awards (ROPA) are a further and very tangible reward for those with a track record of successful and well-supported industrial links (at least £25,000 of such funding in the previous year).

In addition to these existing programmes, more than £300 million has been allocated to new initiatives which explicitly reflect Foresight priorities. For example, the LINK Collaborative Research scheme now includes 17 new programmes launched in response to Foresight. Foresight Challenge, launched at the end of 1995, supports work to address one or more Foresight priorities. Challenge Fund resources also have to be at least matched by private sector contributions, and the public sector contribution may not exceed 50 per cent of the total. The 1996 Foresight Challenge competition made a theoretical £92 million available. Of this, £62 million is provided by industry; the remaining £30 million is from OST.

The principle has been taken a step further by its application to infra-structure funding. The Joint Research Equipment Initiative (JREI) required applicants to be able to demonstrate matching industrial funding, thereby gearing significant sums for research equipment: up to £200,000 supported by the Research Councils, and over that threshold supported by the Funding Councils. Clearly, the likelihood that any sponsor would provide the matching investment was related to some expectation of return. By no means all the awards made under the JREI (£23.5 million in total in 1997) were obviously geared to industrial purpose, but the broad policy thrust was nonetheless established.

The returns from these initiatives, in terms of people trained, jobs created, turnover increased, and so on, has been measurably beneficial and often highly significant. It means that more money is invested in higher education than government alone provides. But such funding is now not only for specific research but also for the environment in which research takes place. As the dual-support system has eroded, so the heart of the well-founded laboratory has become dependent on the nature and utility of the work in which the laboratory proposes to engage. There is nothing improper about this, but it represents a shift in determining priorities for the research enterprise. Instead of choosing to take ideas to industry, the academic now must seek out an industrial partner to support core activity. The impact of this on the agenda for the supply side is clear enough. But it is very much less clear that these policies have actually done anything to enable the users to increase their capacity to acquire and exploit the outcomes of research, however much the research fits their requirements.

From Heroic to HEROIC

Research is changing. The problems now to be tackled demand greater investment; there is a generally greater scale of management, of equipment and of teamwork; individual effort from the lone scholar has diminishing impact. The shift to research that is interdisciplinary and problem-led rather than curiosity-driven (Gibbons et al., 1994) presents a model less attractive to those brought up on a heroic diet, but it is not necessarily a bad thing for research. Demonstrating the utility, even the ordinariness of the research enterprise may reaffirm its significance and reestablish its wider support (May, 1995). There is no necessary requirement that research should take place in higher education, but the evidence is that there is a better return on investment in HEIs than in an institute-based system. This is attributed to the more volatile environment of a university, the normal host for basic research in the USA, England, Canada and Australia (May, 1997).

So is there a problem? Yes, because the policy applied by government to convert the UK's primary return on research investment into tangible economic benefit is logically flawed, lop-sided and has been so for a long time. A fundamental discontinuity has existed in government policy since 1919, where the management of the accessible university research enterprise has been used as a convenient substitute for management of the less tractable industrial development enterprise (Wilkie, 1991). This is potentially damaging to any constructive reconfiguration. Two problems stem from the uncritical involvement of customers in setting research priorities for higher education, and there is a third problem in thinking that this is the solution to bridging the innovation gap.

First, the growing dialogue between agents and users is a natural part of the evolving shift in the research enterprise. There is preparedness to interact and there are incentives to keep that moving. But if the support for natural curiosity which leads the brightest and best into research is replaced by objectives set by the humdrum and the mundane, by the rule of consensus committee and short-term accountancy, by a universal shift from peer review to merit review, then the enterprise is stifled. The stimulus for research will evaporate because researcher involvement will be too much diminished. How can the research agenda be managed to preserve a balance between internal academic priorities and research opportunities, and external influences and needs? This is no new question (see, for example, the USA Government–University–Industry Round Table: National Academy of Sciences, 1989). The answer remains unclear, but the arrival in the UK of industrial matching funding in university core infrastructure might be seen as the signal of a need for care.

Second, the consensus of Foresight creates a risk that the benefits of a plurality of funding opportunities will be eroded. Disagreement and diversity is an essential part of the originality of higher education research. One recalls that Mao Zedong thought that 'letting a hundred schools of thought contend is the policy for promoting the progress of the arts and the sciences'. Unfortunately, the ascendancy of consensus over contention is international: everybody has the same priorities. We are driven to a common global agenda by our ability to exchange information about research outcomes, industrial innovation and economic opportunity. The new electronic interdependence recreates the world in the image of the global village (*pace* McLuhan, 1962), where we all seek to emulate rather than individualize. This is unfortunate. Within Europe, we have evolved an attractive complementarity with research strengths in biotechnology in the UK, in the physical sciences in Germany and in engineering in France. That diversity makes the EU a strong contender with North America and similar complementarity can do as much for the Pacific Rim (Adams, 1998). A Foresight consensus would never have allowed that to emerge.

Finally, allowing customers driven by immediate economic need to drive the higher education research agenda misses the point. The evidence is that the effective customer is an intelligent customer. That is why pharmaceuticals buck the UK trend, investing heavily in their own R&D and growing rapidly. The generic problem is the lack of R&D capacity in industry (Table 10.1). If you want to enable industry to use the products of research, then equip it to buy the process, thereby creating an effective market so that the providers can respond to specific and coherent industrial need instead of getting money to produce dubious goods at a discount.

The DTI recognizes this, but has yet to respond effectively. Peter Mandelson, former Secretary of State, speaking at a Foresight dinner on 25 November 1998 said:

> Britain's science and engineering base is quite simply world class. Many [universities] have excellent, and enviable, track records in science and technology-related subjects. But creating this knowledge is not enough. If we are really to revolutionise our industrial performance, really seize the opportunity to catch up and overtake our competitors, we need to do more than create knowledge. We need to exploit it, transfer it, manipulate it, market it and sell it. That will be the real test. Can we take this huge pool of know-how and turn it into commercial opportunity? The recent McKinsey report showed that overall British productivity lags behind our major competitors. Yet the productivity of foreign-owned operations in the UK, with few exceptions, tends to equal the world's best. The problem is that many indigenous companies do not sufficiently exploit the knowledge available to them in this country to raise their productivity through improved processes and products.

What is the solution? It must be to invest in building up the capacity for R&D, not redirecting the research enterprise in HEIs. For example, current DTI technology transfer initiatives could be consolidated to boost the research capacity of our 'indigenous companies'. This money should no longer be used to provide additional funds to HEIs to work with industry. Instead, it should fund industry to work with universities (with, of course, matching industrial funding). There is an example of such a programme already in operation. CRAFT, an initiative in the Fourth Framework Brite-Euram programme, enabled groups of SMEs with similar technical problems but insufficient research means to engage third parties, usually HEIs, to carry out research on their behalf. The HEIs were fully paid for the work, the costs of which were funded up to 50 per cent by the Commission. Most importantly, this programme worked: CRAFT increased SME participation in Brite-Euram from 25 to 50 per cent of partners.

It may be noted that this proposal is kin to a clause in Dearing, to which Sykes (1998) draws attention. The difference is that Dearing still saw this as leading to funding for academia: 'We recommend ... to the Government that an Industrial Partnership Development Fund is established immediately to attract matching funds from industry, and to contribute to regional and economic development' (Recommendation 34 – NCIHE, 1997). We should continue the internal reconfiguration of higher education research at the same time. First, some further reorganization, selectivity and concentration, long advocated through the 1980s (ABRC, 1987), might also allow us strategically to focus on a higher education research system scaled to and as effective as that of the USA. Second, we should develop better internally (not DTI) driven 'technology transfer' strategies. In fact, HEFCE has announced a £20 million per year programme with this aim, to start sometime during 1999. This should exploit higher education experience to promote business interaction and understanding, better organizational arrangements to work with industry (cf. Broers, 1998) and improved access to higher education research resources. Bizarrely, and by chance, its acronym extends the HEROIC age for research.

References

Adams, J. (1998) 'International benchmarking of research', *Nature*, 396, 615–618.

Adams, J., Bailey, T., Jackson, L., Scott, P., Pendlebury, D. and Small, H. (1998) *Benchmarking of the International Standing of Research in England: A Consultancy Study on Bibliometric Analysis*, Leeds: University of Leeds Centre for Policy Studies in Education.

Advisory Board for the Research Councils [ABRC] (1987) *A Strategy for the Science Base*, London: HMSO.

——(1992) *Science and Technology* (advice to the Chancellor of the Duchy of Lancaster), London: HMSO.

Arora, A., Landau, R. and Rosenberg, N. (eds) (1998) *Chemicals and Long-term Growth: Insights from the Chemical Industry*, New York: Wiley Interscience.

Becher, A., Henkel, M. and Kogan, M. (1994) *Graduate Education in Britain*, London: Jessica Kingsley.

Bernal, J. D. (1939) *The Social Function of Science*, London: Routledge.

Breitzmann, A., Hicks, D. and Narin, F. (1998) 'The broadening and intensification of patented technology upon public science', *Fifth International Conference on Science and Technology Indicators*, University of Sussex: Science Policy Research Unit.

Broers, A. (1998) 'Innovation and invention, or insight and investment: what is important?', *RSA Journal*, 146 (3/4), 56–61.

Bush, V. (1945) *Science – The Endless Frontier*, Washington, DC: National Science Foundation.

Carnegie Commission (1992) *Linking Science and Technology to Societal Goals*, New York: Carnegie Commission.

Clark, B. R. (1993) *The Research Foundations of Graduate Education*, Berkeley: University of California Press.

Clayton, K. M. (1987) *The Measurement of Research Expenditure in Higher Education*, Research report for the Department of Education and Science, Norwich: University of East Anglia.

Clinton, W. J. and Gore, A. (1994) *Science in the National Interest*, Washington, DC: Executive Office of the President, Office of Science and Technology Policy.

Council on Competitiveness (1996) *Endless Frontier, Limited Resources* (US R&D policy for competitiveness), Washington, DC.

Crawford, E. (1998) 'Nobel – always the winners, never the losers', *Science*, 282, 1256–1257.

Dainton, F. (1991) 'Are some science policy issues inevitable, irresolvable and permanent?', in D. C. Hague (ed.) *The Management of Science*, London: Macmillan.

Department of the Environment, Transport and the Regions [DETR](1998) *Rethinking Construction* (report of the construction Task Force on the scope for improving the quality and efficiency of UK construction, The Egan Report).

Department of Trade and Industry [DTI] (1993) *Realising Our Potential: A Strategy for Science, Engineering and Technology*, London: HMSO (Cmnd 2250).

——(1995) *Progress Through Partnership* (report from the steering group of the Foresight Programme), London: HMSO.

—— (1997) *The UK R&D Scoreboard, 1997*, Edinburgh: Company Reporting.

—— (1998) *Differences in Companies' Performance: British Industry's Underperforming Tail*, DTI: Industry Economics and Statistics Directorate.

Ernst and Young (1998) *European Life Sciences 98* (Fifth annual report on the European entrepreneurial life sciences industry), London: Ernst and Young.

Georghiou, L., Halfpenny, P., Nedeva, M., Evans, J. and Hinder, S. (1996) *Survey of Research Equipment in UK Universities*, London: Committee of Vice-Chancellors and Principals.

Gibbons, M. (1997) 'The translation of societal needs into research agendas', in R. Barre, M. Gibbons, J. Maddox, B. Martin and P. Papon (eds) *Science in Tomorrow's Europe*, Paris: Economica International.

Gibbons, M., Limoges, C., Nowotny, H., Schwartzman, S., Scott, P. and Trow, M. (1994) *The New Production of Knowledge*, London: Sage Publications.

Glass, B. (1979) 'Milestones and rates of growth in the development of biology'. *Quarterly Review of Biology*, 54, 31–53.

Hague, D. C. (1991) 'Can scientists manage science?', in D. C. Hague (ed.) *The Management of Science*, London: Macmillan.

Hicks, D. and Katz, J. S. (1997) *The Changing Shape of British Industrial Research*, STEEP Special Report no. 6, University of Sussex: Science Policy Research Unit.

Horgan, J. (1997) *The End of Science: Facing the Limits of Knowledge in the Twilight of the Scientific Age*, New York: Broadway Books.

Irvine, J. and Martin, B. (1984) *Foresight in Science: Picking the Winners*, London: Frances Pinter.

Katz, J. S. and Hicks, D. (1997) 'How much is a collaboration worth? A calibrated bibliometric model', *Scientometrics*, 40, 541–554.

Lindsey, D. (1991) 'Building a great public university: the role of funding at British and American universities', *Research in Higher Education*, 32, 217–244.

Maddox, J. (1998) *What Remains to Be Discovered*, New York: Free Press.

May, R. M. (1995) 'The force behind a dramatic century', *Financial Times*, 18 November.

——(1997) 'The scientific wealth of nations', *Science*, 275, 793–796.

——(1998) 'The scientific investments of nations', *Science*, 281, 49–51.

McLuhan, M. (1962) *The Gutenberg Galaxy: The Making of Typographic Man*, London: University of Toronto Press.

National Academy of Sciences (1989) *Science and Technology in the Academic Enterprise: Status Trends and Issues*, Washington, DC: National Academy Press.

National Committee of Inquiry into Higher Education [NCIHE] (1997) *Higher Education in the Learning Society* (report of NCIHE, the Dearing Report), London: HMSO.

Office of Science and Technology [OST] (1997) *The Quality of the UK Science Base* (a report of the Department of Trade and Industry), London: HMSO.

——(1998) *Science, Engineering and Technology Statistics, 1998* (a report of the Department of Trade and Industry), London: HMSO (Cmnd 4006).

Schaffer, S. (1998) 'The decline (and success) of science in England', *RSA Journal*, 146 (3/4), 46–53.

Scott, P. (1997) 'The next generation of scientists', in R. Barre, M. Gibbons, J. Maddox, B. Martin and P. Papon (eds) *Science in Tomorrow's Europe*, Paris: Economica International.

Sykes, R. (1998) 'Supporting the science base: ensuring the future', *Technology, Innovation and Society*, 14 (3), 11–14.

Varcoe, I. (1974) *Organizing for Science in Britain*, London: Oxford University Press.

Wilkie, T. (1991) *British Science and Politics since 1945*, Oxford: Blackwell.

Ziman, J. (1987) 'Science in a "steady state": the research system in transition', SPSG Concept Paper no. 1, London: Science Policy Support Group.

——(1994) *Prometheus Bound: Science in a Dynamic Steady State*, Cambridge: Cambridge University Press.

11 A Tale of Three Revolutions? Science, Society and the University

Peter Scott

In the domain of science, research and (more generally) knowledge production a revolution is under way. The regularities of academic disciplines are dissolving; the boundaries of scientific communities, creators and guardians of these disciplines, are being penetrated by – and extended to include – new actors; even the fundamental methodologies and epistemologies of knowledge have been challenged. This first revolution has been described as a shift from Mode 1 science – linear or, at any rate, cumulative, rooted in theory or, at any rate, fundamental descriptions of the natural and social worlds – to Mode 2 knowledge production – trangressive, intensely reflexive, rooted in applications (and, more radically still, 'implications') (Gibbons et al., 1994).

In the domain of society, economics and politics a second revolution is under way. The great – and, it seemed, fixed – categories of the modern world are also dissolving, becoming permeable, being transformed. The domains of the state and the market, culture and society, are no longer distinct. The re-engineering of welfare states, the advance (and retreat?) of privatization, the rise of new political movements, the waxing of a symbolic-goods economy (and waning of material production) – all are examples of this transgression of old categories. More fundamentally still, the collective and individual worlds are also becoming confused with, for example, the decay of class and gender hierarchy, individualization of work and commercialization of intimacy. This second revolution has been described as the emergence of a Mode 2 society (Gibbons et al., 2000).

These two revolutions are elements within a much grander transformation, but their articulation is complex. Just as Mode 1 science is being part-supplemented and part-superseded by Mode 2 knowledge production, so the social, economic and cultural forms characteristic of industrial twentieth-century society have been modified in analogous ways. Its grand demarcations, conceptual and organizational, such as 'state', 'market' and 'culture' became increasingly fuzzy; and its key institutions were transformed, hollowed-out, even abolished. There appeared to be intriguing affinities between the growing reflexivity of the knowledge production system on the one hand and on the other the transgressive quality of contemporary society. But the relationship between these two revolutions cannot be reduced to mere cause and effect; rather both reflect co-evolutionary processes such as the rise of uncertainty and the reconfiguration of time and space.

What do these changes mean for those institutions and organizations most directly implicated in the knowledge production system and therefore, it might be expected, most radically affected – in particular, the university itself? Is it useful to describe the great changes in higher education in the second half of the twentieth century as a third revolution? After all, the transition from elite to mass forms of higher education does suggest at any rate a superficial alignment with the shift from Mode 1 research to Mode 2 knowledge and also the emergence of a Mode 2 society (Scott, 1995). Certainly, it seems unlikely that there has been no connection; the university is not only among the leading 'knowledge' institutions of the modern world (even if, as Sheldon Rothblatt suggests in Chapter 1, it came to that role belatedly) but also a key social institution in terms both of spreading educational opportunities (so contributing to democratization) and of fixing, and modifying, the division of labour. And does such a conceptualization – of a third revolution – help to anticipate the likely development of higher education in the first half of the twenty-first century?

As has already been said, the university is a key knowledge-producing institution. During the course of the twentieth century the university arguably became *the* key knowledge-producing institution, at any rate in large parts of northern and western Europe and in North America. Other institutions of scientific production have been unable to match the more demanding standards of professionalization set, or more generous resourcing enjoyed, by the post-war university; the 'freelance' scientist has disappeared, and even the autonomous intellectual is a threatened species maintaining a precarious existence on the fringes of the voracious mass media. Alternatively these other institutions have been incorporated in the wider university system; once-independent research establishments have been 'captured' by it – for managerial reasons such as administrative convenience and economies-of-scale certainly, but also for scientific reasons because they could no longer compete with the cognitive prestige and socio-professional organization of the university. Or such intimate alliances have been established between university science and military, civil and corporate R&D that they have coalesced into archipelagos of like-minded knowledge-producing institutions.

It is possible to regard these changes as unambiguous evidence of the increasing domination of the university, but it is also possible to argue that they are evidence, admittedly more allusive, of the transformation of the university itself into a Mode 2 institution. The university capturing but also captured. A generation ago the first interpretation tended to be emphasized

– the university as an triumphant institution conquering all before it. This view is still deeply ingrained in the thought and policy processes of university leaders, civil servants and politicians – many of whom, of course, had direct experience of higher education at its imperial climax in the 1960s. Another reason for the pervasiveness of this interpretation is that the most influential interpreters themselves are often based in universities and so are naturally inclined to talk-up the prestige of their base institutions.

But today the second interpretation appears equally plausible. In its 'take-over' of other, more democratic and more vocational, forms of higher education on the one hand and and on the other its involvement in more contextualized forms of research, the university has acquired new and more diverse roles that certainly resist holistic integration in normative terms and are difficult to manage (and may well be incommensurable and even incompatible). The boundaries between the university and other types of post-secondary education and other parts of the R&D system have been eroded. As a result 'university', as a distinctive category of institution, has become an anachronism; at the end of the millennium the more capacious category of 'higher education' appears destined to suffer a similar fate. Although this novelty has been concealed by the nominal, rhetorical and (to a lesser extent) organizational continuities of the university, its core may have been deeply compromised. Once the metaphor would have been the 'spreading' university; now it is more likely to be the 'stretched' university. Consequently the advance of the university, far from being inconsistent with the idea of Mode 2, of contextualized and distributed knowledge production, can itself be regarded as components, and so confirmation, of that contextualization and distribution.

The University in Science and Society

The traditional view of the university's engagement with science and society emphasizes its dual roles – first, as a producer of knowledge, whether in the form of scientific results (and other knowledge products) or of scientifically trained people; second, as a producer of 'knowledgeability', in the shape of both a more highly educated, and presumably more scientifically rational and literate, population and, more generally, a more enlightened society and more sophisticated culture. The first role reflects its scientific responsibilities; the second its social responsibilities. There is an intriguing correspondence between the discourses of Mode 1 science and of elite higher education. In the former, the discourse of Mode 1 science, universities and quasi-university institutions are acknowledged to be primary producers of knowledge; their production of 'pure' research is seen as the foundation on which society's capacity of innovation, and the economy's ability to exploit technological advances, ultimately depends. Admittedly few scientists explicitly espouse a crude and naïve account of knowledge production as an uncomplicated linear process, but they still assert the key role of 'disinterested' science, which they regard as synonymous with university science. In the second discourse (of elite higher education) the university plays a leadership role in stimulating 'knowledgeability' through its formation of future elites, social and technical. Scientific literacy (and also, perhaps, cultural authority) will trickle down to, or be imposed upon, the general population with the help of university-educated school teachers, state officials, members of established professions and (more doubtfully) private-sector managers within a framework characterized by social and intellectual deference.

There are two reasons for doubting the accuracy of this traditional view. The first is that the university's hegemony in knowledge production has never been as complete as is commonly supposed and is a comparatively recent phenomenon. Although the scientific power of the university was building towards the end of the nineteenth century, its apotheosis came only after 1945, and especially after 1960. The timing is significant because by the 1960s the university was already being accused of abandoning its cognitive responsibilities as it struggled to satisfy other, essentially social, demands (Parsons and Platt, 1973). Suggestively the scientification of the university was aligned – temporally if not causally – with its massification; the growth of an expert society (and expertise was still grounded in higher education) coincided with the apparent collapse in the university's social prestige and cultural authority. This suggests strong – and, to some, surprising – affinities between scientific and democratic cultures (Gutmann, 1987; Nussbaum, 1997). Perhaps it was this 'collapse', or at any rate erosion, of old habits of intellectual deference, which enabled a more 'scientific' culture to pervade society – as well as, more obviously, the expansion of higher education (and consequently the increase in the number and proportion of graduates). Scientification and massification are connected in two further senses. The first connection is inherent; both are fundamentally critical, even radical, movements, sceptical of received truth and orthodox interpretations in the case of 'science', and in the case of 'democracy' hostile to social exclusion and traditional hierarchy. The second connection is contingent but significant; only by implementing a democratic agenda, and expanding opportunities for higher education, could universities generate the additional resources they required to fulfil their scientific ambitions.

The second reason for doubting the traditional account of the university's scientific and social significance is that there was always tension between the university's aim to reproduce a cultivated elite, often associated with anti-scientific (or, at any rate, anti-positivistic) notions of liberal education or *Bildung*, and its development as a scientific institution (Rothblatt, 1998). This tension took the form both of 'culture wars' (for example, in England during the 1880s between Arnold and Huxley or, again in the 1950s, between Leavis and Snow) and of disputes about how universities should be organized. Liberal educators emphasized the 'college'; scientific developers the department. The former stressed general education, typically at the undergraduate level, aimed to produce cultured leaders; the latter specialized study by postgraduate students, matching the reductionist rhythms of science, to produce the next generation of researchers. These 'culture wars' continue – in normative terms between disciplines with very different life-worlds, but also in an organizational context as universities face apparently difficult choices between improving their research performance and embracing new constituencies of learners.

For these reasons it is difficult to reconcile the assumed alignment of Mode 1 science, as a model of knowledge production, and the elite university, as an ideal institution, with the historical record. There are at least as many tensions between them as there are synergies. The elite university was to a significant extent an anti-scientific (or, at any rate, prescientific) institution, and the research university of the late-twentieth century has inherited many of its elite forms and mentalities, while in crucial respects the emergence of more democratic forms of higher education has stimulated the development of a more truly scientific culture. It would certainly be misleading to imagine that the tensions between the social and scientific roles of the university, casually assumed to be sharpened by the move towards mass participation in higher education, are new phenomena.

As has already been suggested, the opposite may be happening. The social system and the knowledge system, clearly demarcated so long as the latter was defined largely in terms of Mode 1 science, seem to overlap and lose their distinctiveness if a wider Mode 2 definition of knowledge is accepted. 'Society' is now suffused with 'knowledge', a phenomenon inadequately captured in the term 'Knowledge Society' which is generally used in a technicist rather than cultural sense; in the same way 'knowledge' is suffused with the 'social'. If true, this has important implications for the university. In the past its social and scientific roles were in tension – whether, as was once assumed, between the conservatism of the elite university and the dynamism of progressive science or, as it is now argued, between the open engagement of a democratic higher education and the disengagement of 'disinterested' science. Today they may also be starting to combine in ways analogous to the interpenetration of 'society' and 'knowledge'.

Few university policy-makers yet acknowledge this – happy – possibility. Instead they are oppressed by the apparent intensification of the contradiction between the university's role as a producer of scientific knowledge and incubator of new researchers on the one hand and its responsibility to satisfy democratic or market demands for mass participation on the other. This latter role they see as inevitably attenuating the university's scientific base. They argue that students, even the brightest and best, no longer receive a sufficiently rigorous preparation for future careers in science because they are taught in mass institutions (or, at any rate, elite institutions struggling to compete for resources with their populist rivals); because PhDs, instead of being an apprenticeship for research careers, have become broader training programmes; and because scientific careers are becoming fragmented and, therefore, less attractive.

Evidence to support the claim that students are under-prepared for scientific careers is, however, either anecdotal or unavailable. The social selectivity of elite institutions in the past was no guarantee of high academic standards. According to most indicators standards of achievement have risen despite (or because of?) the development of mass higher education systems. The present age is one of unprecedented scientific productivity; never have more publications (and higher-quality publications) been produced. While it is true that many PhD programmes now have broader goals, this reflects intrinsic factors such as the growth of new interdisciplinary taxonomies of knowledge and the 'pull' from a labour market in which the demand for narrowly focused PhDs has probably declined and the demand for the more generically research-skilled has grown, as well as extrinsic factors such as the 'push' from below with the pressures of credentialization which encourage the graduates of mass higher education system to undertake further courses to regain positional advantage in an overcrowded labour market, to secure enhanced status in an increasingly volatile society or even to satisfy cravings for self-realization in an anomic post-modern world. Finally, scientific careers have indeed become fragmented (Scott, 1997), as have all 'careers' defined in mid-twentieth century terms as long-term linear professional employment (although it is true that, like all public institutions, universities have been adversely affected by the decline of the public-service ethic and the decay of the welfare state and, as a result, their capacity to sustain career opportunities for researchers has diminished).

However, the attenuation of the university's scientific base is only half the story. It is also argued that, far from producing a more scientifically literate population, the expansion of higher education has gone hand-in-hand with the growth of an anti-scientific spirit, even of a culture of irrationality. Scientific controversies have apparently been aggravated rather than resolved by mass participation. As a result, the university not only has to come to terms with the erosion of its capacities, and status, as a knowledge producer, it is also failing in its wider social responsibility to spread 'knowledge-ability'. It is to combat such effects that most efforts to improve the 'public understanding' of science are directed. But, once again, there is little to support such an analysis. The development of mass higher education, inevitably and rightly, has undermined habits of scientific deference. The growing proportion of university graduates in the general population has also increased the number of people approximately qualified to take part in scientific debate. Both factors – the weakening of the forbidding awe with which science was once regarded and the proliferation of 'experts' – have contributed to the growth of a Knowledge Society.

Of course, it cannot be denied that science has become a more contested

domain – in three main ways. First, and least important, disciplinary structures and conceptual (and substantive) orthodoxies rooted in the preferences
of comparatively narrow scientific communities have tended to be undermined by the extension of the scientific 'franchise' produced by the
expansion of higher education. This effect is not dissimilar from the growth
of interdisciplinarity as traditional taxonomies of knowledge are ceaselessly
renewed. Second, the growth of relativistic thinking – or, in less grandiose
terms, the weakening of the commitment to achieving invariance in scientific results – has probably undermined notions of scientific objectivity and
reliable knowledge. Instead new notions of contextualized science and
socially robust knowledge are being constructed (Gibbons et al., 2000).
Third, the very success of science, as exemplified by unprecedented levels of
scientific productivity, has led it into arenas of more intense contextualization, and so controversy between competing 'sciences'. The expansion of the
university has certainly played an important part in transforming both the
cognitive and social contexts of science – that cannot, and should not, be
denied. Whether this transformation has been for ill is more doubtful.

Convergence or Divergence?

Despite this optimism, it is still difficult to argue that the relationship
between the scientific – or, more broadly 'knowledge' – and social roles of
the university is not a zero-sum game (the more 'scientific', the less 'social'
and vice versa). It is even more difficult to argue that these roles may be
mutually sustaining, and even coalescing, under the impact of the two revolutions, the growing reflexivity of the knowledge production system and the
transgressivity of contemporary society, described at the start of this chapter.
Higher education and research policies in many countries are still based on
the belief that it is necessary to insulate the scientific (and elite?) functions
of the university from its social (or mass?) functions. The intention has often
been to create a clearer separation between research, in which the elite
university still plays an important but no longer exclusive role, and the
higher education (or, at any rate, socialization) of mass student populations
where such a separation does not exist, and to reinforce where it does exist,
by encouraging the emergence of more differentiated systems. Of course, the
effect of such policies (if not their intention) has sometimes been covert and
'social', to maintain social-class gradations in higher education systems, and
sometimes overt and 'scientific', to create a protected and privileged research
environment. In practice, of course, the two agendas, 'social' and 'scientific',
have been confused.

Four main strategies have been pursued to protect science from the
'social' in the modern university (and/or to preserve selective access to higher
education). First, higher education systems have been formally stratified
with a small number of research-oriented universities being granted a

monopoly of PhD programmes, a rather larger number being permitted to offer Masters programmes, and the bulk of institutions being confined to 'basic' higher education. The best-known example is the California master plan first promulgated in 1962 and revised on several occasions since, which created a three-tier system consisting of the eight-campus University of California, the California State University (CSU) campuses, and the community college sector, each with its own entry standards and range of academic programmes. The second strategy has been to maintain, or establish, binary systems of higher education as has happened in much of Europe. A clear separation has been maintained between traditional universities and higher vocational education institutions, such as Fachhochschulen in Germany and Austria and HBO (higher professional training) schools in The Netherlands. The third strategy, also common in Europe, has been to maintain a different pattern of differentiation – between universities (and higher vocational institutions) on the one hand, and on the other independent (or, at any rate, semi-detached) research institutions, such as the Max Planck, Centre National de la Recherche Scientifique (CNRS) or Academy of Sciences institutes. The fourth, and final strategy, has been pursued in those countries with unified higher education systems (for example, Australia, Sweden and the United Kingdom). Here efforts have been made to encourage institutional diversity by selective funding policies, especially for research, and through market pressures.

Each of these strategies has run into difficulties. Political pressures have tended to dissolve hard demarcations within tiered systems. For example, the University of California's monopoly of PhDs has been breached, and substantial research programmes have developed on CSU campuses. Credit transfer systems to facilitate 'upward' student mobility have been emphasized, which confirm, but also subvert, these hierarchical structures. In Europe, even where binary systems have been maintained, they have become much fuzzier (Scott, 1996). Higher vocational institutions are now typically embraced within the same legal frameworks as universities, acknowledging a degree of association which previously was denied. As a result upward academic drift has not been prevented. One reason for this shift is that many binary systems had originally been designed not to produce a clearer separation between research-led and teaching-oriented institutions, but to cater for the further education of the separate streams of 'academic' and 'vocational' students within divided secondary school systems. Their function was to police the division of labour (and also sustain social distinctions?) not to protect research-led institutions from populist contamination. As such they have come under attack as being incompatible with democratic entitlements to higher education. The 'other' binary distinction between universities and free-standing research institutions has also tended to be eroded as the logistical inefficiency and academic conservatism of the latter have come to be recognized. Finally, selective funding methodologies and market differentiation have usually failed to inhibit the development of common standards and aspirations within unified higher education systems. At their strongest they have probably done little more than slow the progress towards institutional uniformity.

Some of these difficulties can be attributed to the playing-out of distinctive higher education traditions and the impact of different political environments. Generalizations are difficult to make, and systematic explanations should be treated with caution. In Germany, for example, the formal binary division is between universities and *Fachhochschulen*. But a less formal, but perhaps more significant, binary division exists within the university itself – between the mass-participation lecture, which arguably reflects the imperatives of the 'social', and the professor's seminar for advanced students, which reflects the demands of 'science' (which the Max Planck and other institutes also reinforce). In France also competing principles of differentiation are at work. First, a complex institutional pattern of *grandes écoles*, traditional university faculties and *instituts universitaires de technologie* (IUTs) has persisted in which notions of bureaucratic elitism, radical participation (and activism) and professional formation coexist and compete. Second, this complexity is increased by the continued existence of independent research institutes, of the CNRS and other agencies. The result is a fragmented environment, although in practice strong interconnections exist between its various institutional elements through shared personnel. In Britain institutional arrangements are apparently more straightforward. The formal binary distinction between universities and polytechnics was abandoned in 1992, and the so-called dual support system of research (through undifferentiated core grants from the higher education funding councils and specific programme grants from research councils) has been maintained.

But, if a systematic explanation can be justified, it is perhaps this. In the past institutional differentiation was the product of the historical contrast between two different types of higher education broadly defined as 'academic' or 'scientific' on the one hand and 'vocational' or 'professional' on the other (the precise language has varied over time and between nations). This differentiation, of course, was closely aligned with social class hierarchies. Universities typically enrolled students from more socially privileged groups than higher vocational or teacher training institutions. Today institutional differentiation is more likely to be driven by the perceived need to enhance research excellence. For example, a recent study commissioned by the Higher Education Funding Council for England suggested that in those countries where research and teaching were separately organized, whether this separation takes the form of independent research institutes on the Max Planck or CNRS model or of clearly delineated research universities, there was a stronger correlation between the number and impact (as measured by citation indices) of scientific publications than in countries where these conditions did not apply – for example, England (Adams et al., 1998). The conclusion drawn by some policy-makers was that research funding should be even more selectively targeted, perhaps by abandoning the dual-support system entirely.

This tension between the desire to preserve or enhance 'excellence', now defined in terms of scientific quality and productivity but formerly in terms of broader cultural (and social-class?) considerations, on the one hand, and on the other the need to satisfy popular pressures for increased participation seems to confirm that there is an inescapable contradiction between the university's scientific and social roles. As a result many policy responses are designed to produce segregationist solutions. That has not always been easy. As has just been argued, high-profile attempts to maintain, or promote, differentiation between research-led and access-oriented institutions have not always been successful because of the political difficulties such attempts create, although there is still room for doubt about the extent to which old-fashioned binary systems are in decline. But the segregationist campaign has been pursued on other fronts. In Britain universities traditionally received undifferentiated block grants from the state for both teaching and core research support, but there is now a pronounced trend towards earmarking separate teaching and research budgets within block grants. One reason is to promote improved value-for-money and greater accountability; another to prevent the dilution of research budgets by the demands of mass teaching (and to produce *de facto* research universities?). As a result, the core research budgets reinforce rather than complement, and even counteract, the selectivity principle embodied in the allocation of research council grants. The growth of earmarked – and competitive – research funding has also tended to reinforce the division of university staff into teachers or researchers. In effect, free-standing research institutes with independent budgets and separate staffs have been created within universities otherwise engaged in teaching mass student populations.

The Impact of Mode 2

Yet even these politically more discreet attempts to segregate higher education systems into research-led universities and access-oriented institutions have met with only limited success. This lack of success is typically explained by the difficulties any selective public policies encounter in open societies; they appear to go against the democratic grain. These political inhibitions may help to explain the tendency to seize on quasi-market, or actual market, solutions. Yet, in the case of the university (although the United States may be an exception), the market has also failed to produce the desired segmentation. In fact there has been a marked reluctance on the part of elite universities to concentrate on their scientific functions at the expense of their wider social responsibilities – a reluctance that can only be partly explained by either political expediency (the need to maintain, and mobilize, popular support) or the stubborn persistence of archaic notions of universality. At the same time it has proved difficult to contain research within the emergent elite sector; it has spread into other, newer and more open, sectors of higher education, which again cannot be wholly explained in terms of institutional ambitions. Indeed, the containment of research (outside a few very high-cost subjects) has proved to be a failure. Not only has the number of 'researchers' within higher education systems increased as a result of the expansion of these systems since 1960, but research is now undertaken in a wider range of non-university settings which extend far beyond free-standing research institutes or dedicated R&D departments into government, business, community and the media.

If Mode 1 science is the touchstone, these difficulties in sufficiently segregating the scientific and social roles of the university are secondary phenomena. They can be attributed only to political timidity, a refusal to acknowledge that the claims of 'science' must take precedence over the clamour of the 'social'. The solution, therefore, is to depoliticize higher education and research policies – by asserting or reasserting the autonomy of the university (or, at any rate, reestablishing its privileged position within the state) and by strengthening the authority of 'expert' elites, whether scientists themselves or state officials with a compatible orientation. However, in the context of Mode 2 knowledge production, this failure of containment appears in a very different light. First, it must be regarded as a fundamental not a secondary phenomenon: segregation has not worked because research and teaching, the scientific and the social, can no longer be securely demarcated. Second, this 'failure' is actually evidence of the 'success' of science not of its decline-and-fall. It was (and perhaps still is) possible to contain Mode 1 science, 'objective' and 'disinterested' science in the sense that it is (or supposes itself to be) decontextualized, within a restricted number of institutions, including elite universities, dominated by equally restricted scientific communities. But it is not possible to contain Mode 2 knowledge production in the same way. Its reflexivity, eclecticism and contextualization mean that Mode 2 knowledge is inherently transgressive.

The specific characteristics of Mode 2 knowledge production also make containment impossible. First, Mode 2 transcends disciplinary boundaries. It reaches beyond interdisciplinarity to trans-disciplinarity. As a result, the processes of cognitive institutionalization, which have typically taken place in and through elite universities, are weakened. Scientific communities become diffused and, consequently, the university structures of faculties and departments, institutes and centres, that create and sustain these communities become less relevant. Second, Mode 2 expands the number of research, or knowledge, actors. Because of the contextualization of Mode 2 knowledge, the producers of research have become a less privileged group – or, more radically still, a problematical category which cannot readily be defined. Other actors, once dismissed as mere 'disseminators', 'brokers' or 'users' of research results, are now more actively involved in their 'production' (which itself has become a more capacious, and ambiguous, category). Third, shifting the focus from Mode 2 science to Mode 2 society, the emergence of a Knowledge Society means that a much wider range of social, economic and even cultural activities now have 'research' components. Many institutions are now learning-and-researching organizations – because they trade in knowledge products and because they employ many more 'knowledgeable' workers.

For the university these changes have important consequences. Under Mode 2 conditions, the distinction between research and teaching tends to break down. This happens not only because the definition of research actors must be extended far beyond the primary producers of research, but also because the reflexivity of Mode 2 knowledge production transforms relatively closed communities of scientists into open communities of 'knowledgeable' people. It is possible to argue that these 'knowledgeable' communities comprise all the graduates of mass higher education systems, not just the minority in elite universities who have specifically trained as researchers. The new 'knowledge economy' is a mélange of many different kinds of activity – 'basic' and 'disinterested' research certainly but also acts of contextualization, dissemination and even popularization; PhD training but also continuing education and research 'activism'. If this is accepted, research-led rather than access-oriented universities training the majority of research workers no longer occupy such a central role in this new economy. This is true not only in quantitative terms, because research universities are overshadowed by mass institutions, but also qualitatively, because the activities at which they excel, the production of Mode 1 research and researchers, are no longer necessarily the leading activities in the 'knowledge games' played in contemporary societies. Indeed, it is possible to go further, and to argue that non-elite universities may be better placed to play these 'knowledge games', because they have more experience of – and less distaste for – the construction of 'knowledgeable' communities.

The impact of Mode 2, although insidious and resisted, may help to explain why elite universities are reluctant to abandon their wider social responsibilities, and why mass institutions cannot be discounted as research organizations. The scientification of society, what most people mean by the Knowledge Society, is an uncontested phenomenon. But, if the shift from Mode 1 science to Mode 2 knowledge production is accepted, it is accompanied, inevitably, by a more contentious phenomenon, the socialization of science. Therefore, to suggest that the scientific and social purposes of the university are tending to coalesce is not unreasonable. Those who work in universities are perhaps more aware of this possibility than policy-makers; the former are more closely attuned to the intellectual dimensions of these changes and observe the transgressions between teaching and research in, for example, the development of 'professional' doctorates or the growth of programmatic research (with an increasing emphasis on dissemination), while the latter concentrate on the logistical dimensions of the research–teaching and scientific–social dichotomies. The result may be a dissonance, with institutions adopting increasingly flexible policies based on holistic perspectives which are predicated on the synergies between the scientific and social missions of the university on the one hand and on the other rigid national policies adopting increasingly selective approaches predicated on their incompatibility.

A Mode 2 University

What will become of the university in the twenty-first century? A number of possible trajectories suggest themselves. The first is that the university will cease to exist, substantively if not nominally. Universities, of course, will survive – in two different senses. One is that the label, or brand, is so durable – and valuable – that institutions, even ones quite unlike the universities with which we are familiar, will appropriate it. The other is that, such is the current and projected level of participation in higher education, there will continue to be a need for some form of specialized institutions – to act as finishing schools for the elite, and as pre-employment parking lots for the masses. But the real action will be elsewhere, both in terms of high-level training and of knowledge production. The growth of so-called 'corporate universities', which Geraldine Kenney-Wallace has described in Chapter 4, suggests that this first possibility, the death of the (traditional) university, cannot be discounted. Already the best and brightest graduates eschew academic, and other conventional scientific, careers, preferring instead to work as management consultants or in think tanks.

The second possibility is that the direction set in the second half of the twentieth century, the uneasy cohabitation of unifying and segregationist tendencies that has characterized recent decades, will be confirmed or even intensified as the twenty-first century progresses. On the one hand the territory of the university – or higher education, post-secondary education or even some broader configuration labelled the Knowledge Society – will be progressively extended, its once autonomous or unrelated fragments increasingly coordinated (whether through the action of politics or the market); on the other hand there will be increasing differentiation within this expanding territory which may penetrate deeply, into sectors, institutions and even units within institutions. If this second trajectory is followed, the first tendency towards unification is likely to be more pronounced at the level of national and perhaps institutional policy making. In the United Kingdom universities, which not so long ago barely recognized that they belonged to a wider community of higher education institutions, must now compete with further education colleges for scarce public resources. But at the level of social practices, professional identity and normative constitution the segregationist tendency may be more powerful. All sense of a shared academic community, a common home, will fade away.

However, if the argument developed in this chapter is accepted, a third – and perhaps more hopeful – trajectory is possible (Scott, 1998). If knowledge production is likely to be characterized by growing reflexivity and more intense contextualization, and if future society is increasingly transgressive, the first two trajectories appear less plausible. Under such conditions the university cannot disappear, although it will need to be transformed; nor can segregation based on anachronistic assumptions about the need, or the possibility, of being able to distinguish between the university's social and scientific roles be a realistic way forward. Instead, paradoxically, the university of the twenty-first century may need to be a holistic institution – in a double sense. First, as has already been said, it will find it difficult to delineate, and so demarcate, its activities according to anachronistic divisions between research and teaching, scientific and social roles. Second, the university will have to acquiesce in a process of deinstitutionalization, because the boundaries between 'inside' and 'outside' make no better sense than the anachronistic demarcations between research and teaching in a Mode 2 society.

The first sense in which the twenty-first-century university will be a holistic institution, which can be interpreted as a commitment to being an open rather than a closed, a comprehensive rather than a niche, institution, is comparatively easy to accept – at any rate in normative terms. Not only does it reflect the interconnections between the university's current tasks in research and teaching, it also resonates with the long-standing belief in the unity, if not universality, of the life-of-the-mind which is part of the university's traditional life-world. The pre-modern and the post-modern come together to resist the rigid categorizations of the modern. In organizational terms, of course, it is a nightmare. The efficient organization and effective management of universities, as of all complex institutions, demand clear priorities – a task which is difficult to reconcile with anything-goes (and everything-goes-into-everything else!). The most difficult task facing university leaders in the twenty-first century will be how to reconcile the university's increasingly open intellectual engagement with its enveloping environment(s) and its need to retain normative focus and managerial coherence.

The second sense in which the twenty-first-century university will be holistic, in effect its deinstitutionalization, presents more formidable challenges. One, simplistic, response which has already been discussed in earlier chapters is to highlight the growth of 'virtual' universities based on the exploitation of globally available knowledge products through new communication and information technologies. But this merely raises the question of how these products are generated in the first place. Institutions are still important, even if they are private corporations rather than public universities. Or, else, 'virtual' universities are essentially parasitic institutions, feeding on the work of actual universities. Another response is to revert to a 'primitive' model of the university based on networks of scientists, scholars and teachers (again facilitated by new technologies). Although more consistent with our accounts of Mode 2 knowledge production (and of Mode 2 society), it still begs the question of how the sophisticated infrastructures now required to generate knowledge, whether Big Science or socially distributed knowledge, are to be provided. Futurism and nostalgia offer equally invalid guides.

The university, even in mass higher education systems, still fulfils two functions that depend in its being a relatively stable institution. The first is as an incubator of new researchers. This is a task that no other institution is well adapted to undertake. Arguably it is even more of a core activity than research itself, although it is difficult to envisage how researchers could be trained except in an active research environment. This role will be more important than ever in the twenty-first century. The second is as a generator of cultural norms. At the end of the twentieth century these norms were being radically modified; they are now less substantive (canons of elite ideas are incompatible with the development of democratic forms of higher education, and disciplinary orthodoxies are inconsistent with the development of a dynamic science), and more procedural – concerned, for example, with standards of intellectual conduct and, more ambitiously, the maintenance of a culture of liberal rationality. Perhaps the epistemological core, the source of reliable knowledge, is to be found in these general rules of conduct rather than detailed research (or learning) methodologies. But the university, ideally, is the promoter of both. Its role in the generation of cultural norms is not about to disappear.

The history of the university has always been shaped by a dialectic between tradition and 'movement'. Our anticipations of the Knowledge Society of the future are also dialectically opposed. If the conventional account of the future is accepted – the 'Foresight' perspective, which is cumulative, instrumental and technicist – the university is a dynamic cutting-edge institution. Not only will it be a primary provider of the scientific and technical knowledge and professional skills on which advanced economies will depend to generate future wealth and to improve the quality of social and individual life, but the university will also offer alternative, and fairer and more rational, principles for social stratification. In earlier generations nations calibrated their greatness in terms of their conquests and colonies, and their prestige in terms of the brilliance of their cultures. In the Knowledge Society universities will become key agencies (perhaps the key agencies) of national esteem and global competitiveness. And their social significance will increase proportionately. Universities will not only become large-scale redistributors of cultural capital, as they have imperfectly become in our present age, but will themselves define, validate and even generate

such capital – in the shape of credentials that substitute for the older demar-
cators of class, gender and race. In the Knowledge Society the university will
be, more than ever before in its long history, an institution of 'movement'.

But if a rival account of future society is accepted, which emphasizes
disjuncture, regression and risk, the role of the university appears in a rather
different light. In the flux of the Knowledge Society, where knowledge itself
has slipped its moorings and the constitution of society is both contested
and shapeless, that role may be to be the main institution of stabilization.
That stabilization cannot take the form of a reaffirmation of Mode 1 science
and elite culture or a regression to the university's traditional role in the
production and reproduction of social and technical elites. Mode 1 science
has been decisively overlaid by Mode 2 knowledge production; elite culture
will become part-anachronism and part-commodity; and the reproduction of
elites may also be a vain, even reactionary, endeavour – because elites, where
they continue to exist, will have become so volatile as to be insubstantial,
and because these elites will be denominated not so much in terms of graduate credentials but of ephemeral life-styles. Instead, this stabilization role
may need to take the form of the university acting as a mediator, and inter-
preter, between the expert systems that will litter the global (and,
increasingly, globalized) economy on the one hand and on the other the
intensifying individualization of life-chances and life-styles. In functional
terms, of course, these two – expert systems, and individualization – are
linked. Global images and identities shape our individualized interpretations. But, as aesthetics, they are categorically opposed. It is in this sense
that it is possible to talk of the university's future being as an institution of
stabilization.

The twenty-first-century university, therefore, will have to be an adaptable institution – in the double sense that it must be able to accommodate
within it apparently incommensurable but actually synergistic activities,
and must also be able to adapt flexibly to new configurations of knowledge
by establishing novel alliances with other 'knowledgeable' institutions
(Scott, 1998). It must also be a resilient institution, because it has to provide
a sufficiently stable environment to enable new researchers to be trained and
cultural-scientific norms to be maintained. Of course, single institutions
will not be able to discharge all these functions. One solution will be to
recreate higher education and research systems – not top-down systems
designed to reproduce a segmented division of labour but lateral associations
to promote holistic provision. Another may be to create within universities
new sub-institutional forms to supplement, and maybe supersede, traditional research and teaching structures. It is in this sense that it is possible
to write of the hollowing-out of the university.

The university is implicated in the two revolutions discussed at the
beginning of this chapter, the reflexivity and contextualization of knowledge
production and the transgressivity of society. But its implication is active

and engaged, not passive and determined. Paradoxes abound, but choices too exist. The university cannot avoid the fragmentation that inevitably accompanies Mode 2 knowledge production or the deinstitutionalization that goes with transgressivity; it powerfully, perhaps decisively, contributes to these movements. But the university is also a site of resistance, conserving intellectual cultures that oppose these movements. It is out of an inevitably unstable, and unknowable, combination of implication and resistance that the twenty-first-century university will be constructed.

References

Adams, J., Bailey, T., Jackson, L., Pendlebury, D., Scott, P. and Small, H. (1998) *Benchmarking of International Standing of Research in England*, Bristol: Higher Education Funding Council for England.

Gibbons, M., Limoges, C., Nowotny, H., Schwartman, S., Scott, P. and Trow, M. (1994) *The New Production of Knowledge: Science and Research in Contemporary Societies*, London: Sage.

Gibbons, M., Nowotny, H. and Scott, P. (2000) *Re-Thinking Science: Knowledge Production in an Age of Uncertainties*, London: Polity Press.

Gutmann, A. (1987) *Democratic Education*, Princeton: Princeton University Press.

Nussbaum, M. (1997) *Cultivating Humanity: A Classical Defense of Reform in Liberal Education*, Cambridge, MA: Harvard University Press.

Parsons, T. and Platt, G. (1973) *The American University*, Cambridge, MA: Harvard University Press.

Rothblatt, S. (1998) 'Liberal education: a noble, troubled and ironical history', in P. Baggen, A. Tellings, and W. van Haaften (eds) *The University and the Knowledge Society*, Bemmel (The Netherlands): Concorde Publishing House.

Scott, P. (1995) *The Meanings of Mass Higher Education*, Buckingham: Open University Press.

——(1996) 'Unified and binary systems of higher education in Europe', in A. Burgen, *Goals and Purposes of Higher Education in the 21st Century*, London: Jessica Kingsley.

——(1997) 'The next generation of scientists', in R. Barré, M. Gibbons, J. Maddox, B. Martin and P. Papon *Science in Tomorrow's Europe*, Paris: Economica International.

——(1998) 'Shaking the ivory tower', *Unesco Courier*, September.

Contributors

Jonathan Adams is Dean for Strategy Development at the University of Leeds. Previously he worked in the policy division of the former Advisory Board for the Research Councils.

Ronald Barnett is Professor of Higher Education and Dean of Professional Development at the Institute of Education, University of London, and author of many books on higher education.

Denis Blight is Chief Executive, IDP Education Australia, in Canberra. A chemist by profession and a diplomat by training, he worked in Europe, Asia and Africa with Australia's Department of Foreign Affairs and in the Australian Agency for International Development before he joined IDP.

Dorothy Davis is Group General Manager, External Relations, IDP Education Australia in Sydney, with responsibility for IDP's research, consultancy, publications, communication and training programmes.

Geraldine Kenney-Wallace is Chief Executive and Vice-Chancellor of the British Aerospace Virtual University. Previously she was President of MacMaster University in Ontario.

Diana Laurillard is Pro-Vice-Chancellor (Learning Technologies and Teaching) at the Open University, and was a member of the National Committee of Inquiry into the Future of Higher Education.

Alan Olsen is a researcher and consultant on international education. He has worked in international education in Hong Kong, Canberra and Sydney and directed research commissioned by IDP on international student demand and supply.

John Randall is Chief Executive of the Quality Assurance Agency for Higher Education. Previously he was Director for Professional Standards and Development at the Law Society of England and Wales and President of the National Union of Students.

Contributors

Sheldon Rothblatt is Professor of History at the University of California at Berkeley and also visiting professor at the Royal Institute of Technology in Stockholm.

David Robertson is Professor of Public Policy and Education at Liverpool John Moores University. He is author of *Choosing to Change* published by the former Higher Education Quality Council.

Peter Scott is Vice-Chancellor of Kingston University, and was previously Professor of Education and Director of the Centre for Policy Studies in Education at the University of Leeds and Editor of *The Times Higher Education Supplement*.

Roger Waterhouse is Vice-Chancellor of the University of Derby. Previously he was Deputy Director at Wolverhampton Polytechnic, now the University of Wolverhampton.

Alan Wilson is Vice-Chancellor of the University of Leeds and a Fellow of the British Academy. Previously he was Pro-Vice-Chancellor and Professor of Geography at Leeds.

Index